Workers Without Traditional Employment

Dedicated to

Dad, Mum and Ray

Workers Without Traditional Employment

An International Study of Non-standard Work

John Mangan

Professor of Economics, University of Queensland, Australia

Edward Elgar
Cheltenham, UK • Northampton, MA, USA

Published by
Edward Elgar Publishing Limited
Glensanda House
Montpellier Parade
Cheltenham
Glos GL50 1UA
UK

Edward Elgar Publishing, Inc.
136 West Street
Suite 202
Northampton
Massachusetts 01060
USA

A catalogue record for this book
is available from the British Library

Library of Congress Cataloguing in Publication Data

Mangan, John.
    Workers without traditional employment : an international study of non-standard work / John Mangan.
    Includes bibliographical references and index.
    1. Labor. 2. Work—Forecasting. 3. Employment forecasting. I. Title.

HD4903 .M36 2000
331.2—dc21

                                                    00–044258

ISBN 1 84064 267 X

Printed and bound in Great Britain by Biddles Ltd, *www.biddles.co.uk*

Contents

PART III THE ECONOMIC AND SOCIAL IMPLICATIONS OF NON-STANDARD EMPLOYMENT

List of Figures

List of Tables

Preface

My interest in non-standard employment began, formally, in November 1995 when the Department of Industrial Relations and Training commissioned me to write the report 'Contemporary Developments in Work Organization and the Structure of Employment with Special Reference to Queensland'. The Department was interested in the extent of non-standard employment in Queensland and the implications this had for their system of labour market regulation that had been primarily developed to suit standard (permanent, full-time) employees. It soon became apparent that the issues of interest to them were being raised throughout the world. In the relatively short time since the preparation of that report, the issue of non-standard or atypical employment has received increased attention world-wide. Debate over the merits of non-standard employment has moved very quickly from an economic and human resource focus to become a major political and social issue. For example, in 1997 the largest industrial action in the USA in 30 years took place when 190 000 teamsters went on strike against the replacement of permanent workers with part-time workers in the parcel and postage industry (*The Economist*, 1997a). In the same year the Canadian Ministry of Labour, sensing a deep community concern over the speed of labour market change in that country, convened a 'Collective Reflection on the Changing Workplace' (Canadian Labour Ministry, 1997). The issues raised (but not resolved) in that inquiry set the tone for the current controversies over the merits of non-standard employment. These relate to person-specific issues such as job stability and job satisfaction, economic performance issues such as productivity and growth, public policy issues such as the provision and finance of training and workplace health safety and industrial relations issues regarding the future of union coverage and union-negotiated wage agreements.

Recently, a number of books on issues relating to non-standard employment have come onto the market, including Sheehan and Tegart (1998), Felstead and Jewson (1999) and Cappelli (1999). This reflects the widespread interest in the topic. These books are aimed at audiences covering a wide range of academic disciplines including economics, sociology, politics and business management. This is as it should be. No one area of study can fully explain the rise of non-standard employment or the multiplicity of forms it has taken. Economics has much to offer in terms of analysing the changes in business practice that have underwritten and given impetus to much of the transitions that are now occurring in labour markets. However, economics alone will not explain why some forms of non-standard employment flourish in some countries and not in others. To do this properly we need to consider the impact of country-specific welfare systems, family structures, labour market legislation and gender equity issues.

It might be asked why another book is needed on the subject and, given the county-specific features of non-standard employment, why should it be an international study? In answering the first part of this question in should be stressed that this is, in some ways, an idiosyncratic book. It is not intended to cover all aspects of this complex issue or to extend equal coverage to all countries. The author is someone fortunate enough to have entered the labour market when jobs were plentiful and who is currently shielded, to some degree, from the changed employment relationships that many young graduates now face. Yet, even within the university sector, the impacts of labour market transitions are apparent. Many of my colleagues are on contract appointments and those with a 'continuing appointment' are not exactly clear of the legal status of this arrangement. The average university academic is now a portfolio worker, combining the traditional roles of teaching and research with external consulting to the private and public sector and is just as likely to be working, via email, with someone overseas as with someone on their own campus.

While it is probably too early to pass judgement on the merits of these and other more significant labour market events, there is currently a need to understand them and the implications they have for further change. This is one of the tasks set for this book; to examine in a comprehensive fashion the extent of change that has occurred in international labour markets and the factors that are driving these changes. There is of course an overlap between the dynamics of non-standard employment and the evolution of work itself. On this topic there seems to be endless speculation at both ends of the optimism scale. At one end of the scale we read of 'the end of work' while others talk about 'the boundary-less career'. The same diversity of opinion exists as to the merits of non-standard employment. Does it represent as Watson and Fothergill (1993) suggest 'the best of both worlds' or, as some social commentators claim, the inevitable marginalisation of some workers to low wages and oppressive work relations? These and other issues are investigated within the book.

There are certain difficulties in undertaking an international study of a subject that is multifaceted and often presents itself in a country-specific manner. However, while the term 'non-standard employment' covers a wide variety of job arrangements ranging from temporary workers to self-employed contractors it should be stressed that there exists some unifying factors common to most non-standard workers. The first is that they are all not traditional workers. This simple fact divides them (in most countries) from 70-75 per cent of the working population. Secondly, they share common characteristics including the lack of employer-funded benefits, varying degrees of job instability and an almost total absence from the standard forms of industrial relations arrangements such as union coverage. Finally, they face a similar set of demand- and supply-side factors that have underpinned their emergence across the world. Non-standard workers, despite their heterogeneity, are at the interesting end of the labour market. Their emergence, growth and future developments are the driving factors in current labour market transition.

In the preparation of this book thanks are due to my colleagues at the University of Queensland, the Queensland Treasury and the Department of Employment, Training and Industrial Relations, in particular Phil Bodman, Gareth Leeves, Ben Flynn and Todd Sansness. Thanks are also due to Merinda Andrews, Amy Lindley, Marie Keynes and Barbara Dempsey from the Economics Department office and to my family, Irene, Mark and Chris for their patience and help.

John Mangan
The University of Queensland
March 2000

1. Introducing the Topic

The nature and purpose of work is changing. For a large part of this century the standard form of employment has been full-time, essentially permanent employment. When Walter Oi (1962) in his famous article described labour as a 'quasi-fixed factor of production' he had in mind a system of employment in which employers provided stability of employment, training opportunities and a variety of non-wage benefits. In return, they received certainty of labour supply, staff loyalty and the cooperation of employees in developing firm-specific as well as general skills. It is not certain how Oi would incorporate into his analysis the almost bewildering array of alternative employment relationships that have taken on such prominence in recent times. When I posed this question to him several years ago during his visit to Australia, he just shrugged his shoulders. The implication was that he had provided a labour market model for the 1960s; now it was up to the present generation to do the same for the current period.

Yet, with respect, the task now faced by labour market analysts is now much more complex than it was in the 1960s. There now exists a host of alternative working arrangements ranging from the familiar categories of part-time, temporary, casual, contract and seasonal workers to more recent developments such as leased or franchised workers, out-workers, teleworkers, freelancers and portfolio workers. Those in alternative employment relations are now in such numbers that they can no longer be regarded as peripheral to the main labour market.

All of these forms of employment have been collectively referred to as 'non-standard employment', even though they lack a common set of characteristics in terms of participants, occupations or even skill level. As a result, non-standard jobs offer up a variety of working conditions and produce wide variations in income and levels of job satisfaction among the participants. Yet there is clearly a hierarchy of non-standard jobs in terms of employment conditions. At the upper end of the desirability scale are some of the self-employed, independent contractors and retention workers (permanent part-time) who enjoy attractive combinations of income, job stability and workplace autonomy. At the lower end are those in precarious or contingent employment with low wages, low job security and little in the way of workplace discretion.

Between these two extremes are a considerable group of people for whom non-standard work is as much a lifestyle decision as it is a traditional work decision (Yeandle, 1999). Some display a marginal attachment to the labour force and use non-standard jobs as an efficient means of entering and exiting the labour force in response to current needs.[1] The *arubaito* (side-job workers) in Japan are examples of these kinds of workers. *Arubaito* workers are made up almost exclusively of students or married females (Houseman and Osawa, 1995). Yet even within this group there are differences in motivation. The students are clearly transitory, using the *arubaito* jobs as a means of financing their education. However, many of the married females prefer *arubaito* status to membership in the *nenko* wage system with its implications of lifetime employment because it allows more time for family activities (Houseman and Osawa, 1995).

It is difficult to generalise from such country-specific outcomes but throughout the world there are groups of workers for whom the normal employment benefits of training, career development and long-term stability of employment have far less immediate value than in the past. As a result they are also less likely to join labour unions, take up training programmes or seek permanent jobs. Finally, there are those, particularly school leavers, who see non-standard employment as a convenient and sometimes, only, port of entry into permanent employment (Philpott, 1999).

The first wave in the growth of non-standard employment began with an expansion of part-time work and the beginnings of corporate downsizing in the 1970s and intensified through a trend to temporary and contract employment in the 1980s and 1990s (Rudolph, 1998). Alternative (non-standard) employment has now grown so rapidly that in a number of countries and for some groups, most noticeably females, it is now as common as full-time work (Mangan, 1998).

To some, the speed of change in employment relations is both revolutionary and socially undesirable, bringing with it the threat of job insecurity and social and economic dislocation (Rosenberg and Lapidus, 1999). To others, these changes in the labour market, significant as they are, represent a return to the market-determined employment relations of earlier periods. Under this view, the type of employment relations described by Oi and others such as Doreinger and Piore (1971) are themselves atypical and grew out of the changes in industrial organisation over the period 1920-80.

The history of employment relations in the US makes clear that what we think of as traditional long-term attachments, internal development, mutual obligations, likely existed for little more than a generation. (Cappelli, 1999, p. 50)

Both views have merit. It is clear that labour markets across the world are in transition. The internalisation of the labour hiring process which reached its peak in the 1970s has unravelled to such an extent that it is difficult to know where 'traditional' employment ends and non-standard employment begins (Felstead and Jewson, 1999). As well, it is not difficult to see parallels between the arguments for organisational flexibility and reduced costs that were used to support the 'putting out systems' operating in the UK and the USA in the nineteenth century and those used to support contracting and outsourcing today.[2]

However, it is difficult to fully support those that see the present labour market changes as part of an inevitable correction away from an unsustainable employment golden age that prevailed in Western societies for most of this century.[3] Employment systems are essentially socially determined, albeit with strong input from technological and economic factors. The employment systems of the pre-1920s serviced a labour force that was predominantly male, low-skilled and, by modern standards, geographically immobile. On the demand-side the rise of traditional employment in the early part of this century was, in part, a response to the labour needs of firms that had begun the process of internalisation of production. On the supply-side firms were faced with the need to accommodate the growing power of labour unions (Cappelli, 1999). Traditional employment catered to the needs of both these groups by, on the one hand, providing firms with a reliable workforce willing to acquire firm-specific skills and, on the other hand, providing organised labour with the best institutional setting for gaining benefits for their members. It is difficult to see these past systems successfully adapting to the needs of a labour market that is characterised by the large-scale participation of women and large numbers of skilled and mobile workers. Nor would they be adequate for a production system that is increasingly globalised and underwritten by a system of mass consumption that would have been inconceivable to past generations. Moreover, past employment systems were essentially demand-(employer)-driven. There is considerable evidence to show that the current changes in the labour market are, in part, supply-driven, principally through the emergence of significant sections of the population that seek non-standard forms of employment in preference to more traditional forms (Simpson et al., 1997).

While it is clear that employment relationships across the world have undergone and are undergoing significant changes it is unlikely that we will see either the disappearance of traditional employment or a return to past systems of employment. However, labour markets are in a period of flux. At present there is no majority view as to what the predominant employment systems of the future will be. Mixed signals are emerging. At the very time that newspaper headlines dwell upon job insecurity and the changed nature of work, a significant number of employees are 'overworked'. Over the decade 1988-98, the average hours worked for British males increased to 47 hours and over one-third of all male wage and salary earners in the UK work in excess of 50 hours per week (EPI, 1999). The same pattern is emerging among a number of workers across the world (Drolet and Morissette, 1997). This points to significant dichotomy in modern labour markets with simultaneous growth in both overwork and underemployment. Part of the reason for this is undoubtedly structural, with those workers in areas of short supply being required to work more hours. But at least some of the explanation lies in the changed dynamics of employment relations, with permanent workers being expected to work longer hours as an additional price for job security (Picot and Lin, 1997). The UK employment audit for 1999 provides further evidence of this labour market dichotomy with major job growth in the UK coming at opposite ends of the labour market spectrum; either through full-time permanent employment or temporary part-time employment (EPI, 1999).

Why is this happening? A commonly suggested explanation is a rerun of the core-peripheral models that came to prominence in the 1970s (Cain, 1976), with one major difference. This time the core may be much smaller than the peripheral (Gregg and Wadsworth, 1995). If this is the case, it is likely that the job security of those, highly skilled professionals and technocrats in core jobs (permanent full-time or permanent part-time) will actually be enhanced by the flexibility enshrined in the much larger groups of casual and contracted workers on the periphery.[4] Already, some of the inevitable outcomes from these kinds of divisions are appearing. The Civilian Population Survey (CPS) in the USA, highlights the fact that managers and professionals have much greater autonomy over their work times than administrative support staff in the same industries and that the extent of the differences have grown substantially in the 1990s (US Department of Labor, 1999a).

Yet a core-periphery model is too mechanistic and restrictive to fully capture the degree of transition that is occurring in modern labour markets. There is also little empirical evidence to support the view that employers are deliberately formulating their labour force requirements on the basis of required and disposable workers.[5] What is more likely is that specific jobs and tasks now have a much shorter life-span.

Planning horizons for the firms is now much shorter than can be accommodated by an individual's career. The goal of downsizing is no longer to simply get down to a more efficient size, it is to re-arrange the competencies of the organisation. (Cappelli, 1999, p. 7).

For this reason we see firms continuing to hire while undertaking the process of refocusing or downsizing. Those who are able to adapt or display flexibility in competence take on the characteristics of permanent or core employees. Those who cannot find their jobs either downgraded or out-sourced completely. Both of these explanations see the rise in non-standard employment as an integral part of fundamental shifts in industrial organisation.

Another view is that the rush to non-standard employment over the last two decades represents a short-term reaction (overreaction) to a period of intense technological and economic change. Under this view, the growth in the relative importance of non-standard employment will stabilise or even fall in the longer term. This is because the less desirable economic costs of non-standardisation, such as productivity loss associated with morale decline, shortage of specifically skilled workers and high turnover rates will start to erode the promises of reduced production costs and the benefits of increased numerical flexibility.

Fallick (1999) reports that part-time employment in the USA, as a proportion of total employment, has remained relatively constant since the 1980s and his colleagues at the Bureau of Labor Statistics show that contingent employment, as a percentage of total US wage and salary employment, declined between 1995 and 1997. Levenson (1997), also on US data, argues that there has been no significant movement from full-time to part-time work over the past two decades. In Japan, the special survey of employment (1999) indicates that non-regular employment as a percentage of the labour force fell from a peak of 27 in 1997 to 24.9 in 1999.

However, at the same time as we are seeing a possible stabilisation of non-standard employment in the USA, across the border in Canada one variant of non-standard employment, self-employment, has been the major source of job growth since 1985 (Doirion, 1997). Similarly, in Australia the trend towards casual employment shows no sign of abating (Mangan and Williams, 1999). In Norway, there has been a major expansion in temporary work and in Spain, contract and temporary work are almost exclusively accounting for net job growth (De Grip et al., 1997). Clearly, given these differing trends across the world, there are many gaps in our ability to provide a generalised theory of non-standard employment. Instead country-specific patterns are emerging both in the forms of non-standard employment and in their relative importance. However, in the midst of this diversity are common, global questions concerning future labour market developments that require attention and analysis. We know that there is considerable concern over the social and economic implications of the current labour market transitions and that much of the fear revolves around the concepts of lack of choice for workers.

A good deal of the early growth in non-standard employment was supply-driven because it was essentially voluntary and coincided with a social movement for increased female participation. The increased economic necessity for two-income families and the growth in the economy of a student population that sought to combine education and work were additional contributory reasons.[6] More recently, the quest for labour market flexibility at the institutional level, in response to competitive pressures and the inherent cost and adjustment pressure of a globalising economy, have created considerable demand-side pressure for forms of non-standard employment (Felstead and Jewson, 1999). This has introduced an involuntary nature to some employment arrangements and raised fears among social commentators concerning the economic and social implications of current employment trends. Indicative of these concerns is the decision by the Canadian Department of Labour to convene a 'Collective Reflection on the Changing Workplace' (Canadian Labour Ministry, 1997) to consider the social and economic implications for Canadian society of current employment trends. The issues raised in that inquiry are being echoed throughout most advanced economies. They include:

1. What is the relative importance of non-standard employment to the labour market as a whole?
2. Will the growth of non-standard employment lead to the creation of subgroups of marginalised and disadvantaged workers on the one hand and privileged and highly paid workers on the other?
3. Will Governments be forced to take up the burden of funding employee benefits and training programmes previously funded by employers?
4. What are the long-term economic and social implications of having a significant section of the workforce employed under non-standard arrangements?
5. What are the implications for trade unions, collective bargaining and other traditional forms of industrial relations behaviour?
6. Will the promised benefits from labour force flexibility such as productivity gains be offset by the additional costs of controlling a less committed and less loyal workforce?

The answer to the first of these questions is now well documented. Non-standard employment is very extensive. Green et al. (1993) estimated that the proportion of workers employed under non-standard conditions for the UK and Canada was 29 and 28 per cent respectively. These estimates have recently been revised upwards for Canada to over 33 per cent (Brault, 1997; Felstead et al., 1999). To further emphasise the growing importance of alternative working arrangements, the Economic Council of Canada has estimated that during the 1980s, non-standard employment accounted for 44 per cent of the total growth in employment in that country and that its relative importance has increased in the 1990s. Further research into the labour market in that country by Lin et al. (1999) show that in the first eight years of the 1990s, self-employment contributed to three out of every four new jobs. In Japan, the 1999 special survey of the labour force found that non-regular staff now make up 20 per cent of all employment and 24.9 per cent of all employees (excluding executives of corporations). In the USA, since 1972 employment in one form of non-standard employment, the temporary services industries, has grown annually at over 11 per cent from 165 000 in 1972 to over 2 000 000 by 1995 (Sullivan and Segal, 1997). This represents an annualised percentage growth rate of 11.8 compared to a rate of 2.0 for total non-farm employment for the economy as a whole.

In Australia, non-standard employment accounts for between 30 and 35 per cent of the total labour force. Between 1988-99, the rate of increase in the number of persons employed in full-time jobs actually fell while the numbers employed in non-standard employment rose substantially.

Because employment is, for many, a crucial determinant of social and economic status, the changes in the labour market conditions will have a major impact on equity, income distribution and future prospects (Buchtemann, 1996). A major current concern is the long-term impact on the quality of family life. Recent Canadian data indicates that 40 per cent of dual-earner families work non-compatible hours, principally different shifts (Human Resources Development, Canada, 1998). While the linkages between work experiences and psychological and physical health, self-esteem and social interaction are imprecise and vary between individuals, there is little doubt that employment impacts well beyond purely economic factors (Rudolph, 1998). At the heart of these issues are the underlying causes behind the growth in alternative work arrangements and whether these changes are voluntary or being imposed by economic, structural and social forces. If the later is true what is the appropriate role for public policy?

This book examines the level and causes of non-standard employment across a range of economies and seeks to determine both common and country-specific determinants. A number of empirical and policy questions are examined including:

1. How significant is non-standard employment, and what is its relative importance by gender, occupation and industry?
2. What are the similarities and differences in the international distribution of non-standard employment?
3. Have jobs become more or less secure?
4. What are the implications for wages and equity, training and workplace health and safety?
5. What are the implications for trade unions, industrial relations and labour market legislation?
6. What are the work-family and other social implications?

However, to provide international comparisons in an area where major definitional differences exist is not an easy task (OECD, 1997). Because of these definitional differences, exact comparisons can be difficult and the results often misleading if taken on face value. A major task of this book therefore is to shift through the ever-growing literature on alternative working arrangements in an attempt to highlight both similarities and differences in international employment trends. As a result, some of the data used and the examples provided are country-specific and selected by the author on the basis of availability, interest and personal preference. For all of these reasons there is an emphasis on the industrialised economies of North America, Europe and Japan. Yet, for a book on non-standard employment, it would be difficult to do otherwise. It was in these industrialised economies that the concepts of traditional (permanent) employment first came into prominence. Their subsequent retreat into non-standard employment is really part of a broader picture of structural and economic adjustment forced upon these countries by increased global competition and changes in technological base. These broader changes are not explicitly dealt with in the book but they form a major backdrop to the labour market changes that have occurred throughout the world. As well, readers will notice that the Australian economy receives more consideration than its size in the international economy might justify. Again, there are good reasons for this beyond the natural preference of the author for the data with which he is most familiar. Until the 1970s, the Australian labour market was the most traditional of all. Low unemployment, high union coverage, low female participation and very low rates of non-standard employment. The wage structure was rigidly underpinned by a system of minimum and union-negotiated award rates and local industry was protected by significant tariff barriers. In the parlance of the modern human resource manager, the Australian economy was characterised by low numerical, wage and organisational flexibility. Since the mid-1970s the Australian economy has been buffeted by a range of economic forces that have affected most countries but few so dramatically as in

Australia. Within this context, Australia has gone from having the lowest rates of non-standard employment to among the highest. Its current industrial relations system, as with its sister country New Zealand, is almost unrecognisable from the earlier decades. In short, it is the model economy within which to view the phenomena of the growth of non-standard employment.

The book also has a number of other aims including the provision of a taxonomy of non-standard employment by type and across selected countries. In the final analysis, the aim of the book is to show that labour markets across the world are in transition and to argue the current methods by which we record, analyse and designate the labour market and even define work are becoming less useful. Once this is understood, the myriad of economic, social and public policy issues that flow from the current labour market changes will be much better appreciated. The book proceeds in this way. Part I examines the incidence of non-standard employment across the world with special reference to Australia, Germany, Japan, Sweden, Spain, the UK and the USA. Part II (Chapters 3 and 4) discusses the causes behind the growth in non-standard employment and examines empirical tests of these causes. Part III (Chapters 5, 6 and 7) analyses the economic and social implications of the rise in non-standard employment. Chapter 5 looks at the impact of non-standard employment on job stability and job satisfaction. Chapter 6 considers the implications for trade unions, other labour market organisations and economic performance and Chapter 7 covers the implications of non-standard forms of work for work/family trade-offs. Chapter 8 has the summary and conclusions.

NOTES

[1] Philpott (1999) in his analysis of temporary work in the UK found that this kind of work was rarely taken up by the long-term unemployed, who are predominantly seeking full-time work, but rather by those previously outside the labour market.

[2] See Cappelli (1999) and Chandler (1977) for a discussion of the employment conditions existing in industrialised countries until the early part of the twentieth century.

[3] An example of this type of thinking was expressed by pollster Daniel Yankelovich in his survey of US workers in the 1970s where he found that employees were no longer very worried about the risk of job or income loss. He concluded that 'employment had become too secure for the good of the organisation'.

[4] See Handy (1989) and his arguments about 'Shamrock Organisations' that strenuously protects its most valuable core employees at the expense of the bulk of peripheral and temporary workers.

[5] The exception here would be the *Job Career Path Programme* (Kosubetsu Koyo Seido) implemented by Japanese Corporations following the Equal Job Rights law of 1986. This programme divides employees into two groups, general staff group (*ippanshoku*) and the

executive candidates group (*sogshoku*) and provides little in the way of upward mobility for the *sogshoku*. For a discussion of this system see Kyotani (1999).

6   Rubery (1994) has questioned the actual degree of choice exercised by some entrants into non-standard employment such as women with family responsibilities who were compelled by circumstances to take these jobs.

PART I

The Incidence of Non-standard Employment

2. Non-standard Employment: Incidence and Definitional Problems

2.0   INTRODUCTION

Anyone attempting the task of an international study of non-standard employment soon discovers the unfortunate truth that non-standard employment arrangements are often associated with non-compatible labour force definitions or country-specific interpretations of these definitions. The data in Table 2.1 depicts labour force statistics on non-standard employment, as they are normally shown, in seven selected countries: Australia, Germany, Japan, Spain, Sweden, the UK and the USA. Some of the data in these tables are essentially non-comparable beyond the basic divisions of core and non-standard employment. Even here there is some room for disagreement between non-standard employment defined in a broad way, which includes all part-time workers and the bulk of own-account (or self-employed) workers, and narrow definitions which include only those part-timers and own-account workers that could be classified as contingent (ILO, 1997b).

Table 2.1 The changing composition of employment: selected examples

Example 1   Japan

Category	Employment in Japan by Major Labour Force Category (May 1999)		
	Number (10 000s)	Change over year	Percentage of total (%)
Self-employed workers and workers at home	708	-3	11.2
Family workers	322	-12	5.1
Total employees	5 277	-61	83.7
Employees, excluding executives of corporations	-	-	77.8
• Regular staff	3 688	-105	75.1
• Non-regular staff (part-timers, *arubaito* and others)	1 225	52	24.9

Source: 1999 Special Labour Force Survey, www.stat.go.jp/155.htm.

Example 2   UK

	The changing composition of all employment in the UK 1979-97			
	1979	1984	1990	1997
Full-time employees	76.7	69.7	67.1	65.2
Full-time permanent	NA	67.4	64.8	61.7
Full-time temporary	NA	2.3	2.3	3.5
Part-time employees	16.1	18.8	19.4	22.2
Part-time permanent	NA	16.5	17.2	19.2
Part-time temporary	NA	2.3	2.2	3.0
Full-time self-employed	6.5	9.4	11.3	9.9
Part-time self-employed	0.7	1.9	2.1	2.6

Source: Labour Force Survey, Spring (1998).

Example 3   Spain

Category	Employment status of the economically active in Spain (1995)		
	All	Male	Female
Permanent core workers	37.4	40.1	32.8
Fixed-term contracts	20.0	19.9	20.0
Unemployed	22.9	18.2	30.6
Employer	3.7	5.0	1.7
Independent workers	12.2	13.9	9.6
Members of cooperatives	0.7	0.9	0.5
Family help	2.9	1.9	4.6
Other	0.2	0.2	0.2

Source: Boletin Mensuel de Estadistica (1997).

Examples 4 and 5   Germany and Sweden

	Part-time		Fixed term & temporary		Self-employment		Core employment	
	1985	1995	1985	1995	1985	1995	1985	1995
Germany								
Female	29.6	33.8	11.1	11.1	5.4	5.8	53.9	49.3
Male	2.0	3.6	9.2	9.9	11.7	11.9	77.1	74.6
Sweden								
Female	46.0	43.0	14.2	14.4	4.8	5.9	35.0	28.1
Male	6.9	10.3	9.6	10.5	13.1	16.3	70.4	39.9

Source: Eurostat (1996).

Example 6   USA

	Full-time workers	Part-time workers
Traditional arrangements	91.3	84.6
Independent contractor	6.11	9.34
On-call workers	0.92	4.38
Temp agency employee	1.02	1.07
Workers from contract firms	0.65	0.61
Total	*100*	*100*

Source: Labour statistics from the Current Population Survey (1997), amended by the Bureau of Labor Statistics (1998).

Example 7   Australia

Year	Permanent employees		Casual employees		Self-employed		Employers	
	Full-time	Part-time	Full-time	Part-time	Full-time	Part-time	Full-time	Part-time
1971	76.4	3.4	1.3	4.7	6.8	1.2	5.3	0.5
1984	65.6	5.0	3.9	9.3	8.0	2.5	4.4	0.8
1998	56.2	7.5	7.5	14.2	6.8	2.8	3.5	0.6

Source: VandenHeuval and Wooden (1999) based on 'main job held'. Note percentages in each row do not sum to 100 due to the exclusion from this table of unpaid family helpers.

In Japan (Table 2.1, Example 1) non-standard workers are collectively referred to as non-regulars. Within this broad grouping the main sub groups are part-time, *arubaito* (side-jobs), temporary, day labour and dispatched workers.[1]

Collectively this group now constitutes approximately 25 per cent of all employees and 20 per cent of the labour force. However, within the Japanese special surveys, the self-employed and family members are not included despite evidence from other economies that a considerable number of the self-employed are non-standard, in terms of hours worked, regularity of employment and the reasons for being self-employed.[2] In the UK (Example 2) using a broad definition, non-standard workers are represented in all categories except full-time (permanent) and full-time self-employed and on that basis constitute about 25 per cent of all employees. However, UK temporaries differ in composition from Japanese temporaries. The former being a combination of fixed-term contractors, agency temps, casual workers and seasonal workers while the later are exclusively short-term (less than one year) contractors (Kyotani, 1999). In Spain (Example 3) non-standard employment, under both broad and narrow definitions, exerts a very strong influence. Less than 40 per cent of the economically active are in core employment. There are no workers classified as temporary but an extraordinarily high number of fixed-term contracts. However, these data need to be interpreted in the light of particular institutional setting in Spain which offer strong inducement for employers to avoid hiring workers under traditional arrangements (Adam and Canziani, 1998; Cousins, 1999).[3] The classification of non-standard employment in Germany and Sweden (Examples 4 and 5) is directly comparable to the UK and most other European countries although difficulties arise over country-specific interpretations as to what constitutes a part-time worker.[4] For both Germany and Sweden, non-standard work is seen as particularly important to females with 70 per cent of females in Sweden and 50 per cent in Germany able to be broadly defined as non-standard. The data also show that the coverage of non-standard employment in both these countries rose significantly between 1985-95.

In the USA (Example 6), output from the CPS depicts non-standard employment as an amalgam of part-time workers and those in 'alternative working arrangements'. This later group are very similar in composition to the UK temporaries being ICs, on-call workers, temp agency staff and workers employed by contract firms (Cohany, 1998). A special survey within the CPS identifies employees (most of which come from the alternative working arrangement group) with particularly unstable expected job tenure and classifies them as contingent workers (Rothstein, 1996; Hipple, 1998). Rosenberg and Lapidus claim that no accurate definition of what constitutes non-standard workers exists in the USA because of the 'minimal federal government legislation of working time for those aged 16 and over which prevents clear determination of part-time and temporary employment' (Rosenberg and Lapidus, 1999, p. 63). However, counting the bulk of part-time workers plus those in alternative working arrangements and the 'contingent' component of full-time workers yields a broad definition estimate of approximately 26 per cent. The narrow definition shrinks this estimate to 9 per cent of which 4.4 per cent are regarded as contingent (Hipple, 1998). Estimates of non-standard employment in Australia are, in one sense, more straightforward because the labour force is classified as permanent/non-permanent as well as by labour force status. On the other hand, many of those classified as casual in Australia could well be represented as either full-time, part-time or temporary in other parts of the world (Mangan, 1998).

At the core of these problems of comparison are issues of security of tenure, the length of the normal working week and country-specific labour market legislation all of which are further complicated by national data-gathering techniques which are often irregular and based on self-perception. The collection of statistics specifically devoted to non-standard employment is both relatively new and often the result of special or irregular surveys (Blau et al., 1998). This, combined with the rapid spread of non-standard employment, the multiplicity of forms it may take and the tendency for non-standard employment to overlap with traditional forms of labour market classification have created problems of measurement which many national statistical agencies have been slow to overcome. For example, in terms of hours worked, retention workers (permanent part-time) are clearly part of the non-standard workforce. Yet, as Tilly argues, these jobs are among the most secure and sought after in the USA and should not logically be classified within the same category as casual or contingent jobs (Tilly, 1991).

Indeed, part-time work is now so prevalent, why should we regard it as non-standard at all? Some researchers reject the use of the term 'non-standard' altogether and suggest something like 'alternative working arrangements' as a preferred umbrella term for what is, after all, a loose collection of employment forms that differ widely in terms of security, desirability, income and status (Wooden, 1999). However to completely abandon a collective term such as non-standard would make a difficult task (international comparisons) almost impossible. Researchers would need to compare each form of non-standard employment separately and would still face problems of compatibility in meaning and measurement. However, by failing to consider them as a group they would lose an appreciation of the extent of interaction and synergy between the various forms of non-standard employment and, thereby, a full appreciation of the extent of labour market transition that is now occurring world-wide. Non-traditional working arrangements are replacing traditional arrangements across the world because of a combination of international and country-specific factors. They are essentially being driven by a common set of demand and supply factors but the incidence and specific form, and in some cases the measurement, are partly determined by a range of domestic institutional and cultural factors that tend to be country-specific. This is what makes comparisons difficult, but not impossible. An initial means of gaining some broad comparisons is to identify core workers and treat the residual as non-standard. This residual is similar to the broad definition of non-standard employment. More detailed dissection of the standard output of most statistical agencies will allow the narrow definition of non-standard to be also applied. Estimates of the relative importance of total non-standard workers under both definitions within the selected economies are shown in Table 2.2.

Table 2.2 Core and non-standard employment in selected countries

Country	Percentage of non-standard (broad) (%)	Percentage of non-standard (narrow) (%)
Japan	24.9	NA
UK	24.9	10.1
Spain	59.9	33.0
Germany	21.4	11
Sweden	27.3	15
USA	26.1	9.1
Australia	33.0	25.4

Source: estimated from Table 2.1 and unpublished data.

As well, by focusing upon four core components of non-standard employment, part-time, temporary, casual/contingent and self-employment it is possible to make useful comparisons across a range of countries.

2.1   PART-TIME WORK

Part-time work is the most common and transparent form of non-standard employment but, as with most forms of non-standard employment, it is not easily defined. Convention 175 of the International Labour Organisation offers the following definition: 'the term part-time worker means an employed person whose normal hours of work are less than those of comparable full-time workers' (ILO, 1997b). These hours may be calculated weekly or over a given period of employment. Statisticians have several ways of deciding whether or not to classify a worker as part-time. First, within surveys, they can do so indirectly by asking the average number of hours worked by the respondent over a period of time. Alternatively they can rely on the person's judgement by directly asking them their employment status. Both create problems.[5] The first method, by arbitrarily setting a number of hours below which a person is declared part-time, may misclassify some occupations that have less than normal at work hours. The second faces the problems of perceptions. The person working 18 hours per week for the last ten years may not consider himself or herself a part-time worker. In addition, the multiple job-holders with, for example, a permanent (full-time) job and a part-time job may be classified as either full time or part time depending upon the way in which they choose to respond. Because of multiple job-holding we know that the number of part-time jobs is almost certainly greater than the number of part-time workers (US Department of Labor, 1996). As a result the best method of measurement will depend upon whether we are trying to determine the number of part-time workers or the number of part-time jobs.

Therefore both these methods suffer from statistical measurement problems which affect all labour market indicators and which would presumably balance themselves if applied equally across countries. However, what compounds the problems of international comparisons of part-time work and other forms of non-standard employment are the different interpretations applied by countries to the ILO guidelines. For example, the phrase 'whose normal hours of work are less than a comparable full-time worker' is interpreted differently (ILO, 1997b). The information listed in Table 2.3 shows the different definitions of part-time work used across the Organisation for Economic Cooperation and Development (OECD).

It is also possible to examine the impact of national definitions on the incidence of part-time work by applying standardised rules. For example, applying a 30-hour threshold to Sweden would (for 1995) lower the proportion of part-time workers to total employment from 27 per cent to 18 per cent. This has the effect of removing the perceived differences in the incidence of part-time work between this country and another, such as Canada, where the 30-hour rule is already in place. Most affected by this standardisation are Sweden (a drop in percentage of workforce classified as part-timers by 11.2 per cent), Austria (-8.7 per cent) and Iceland (-8.2 per cent). This indicates that these countries have a substantial number of persons working average weekly hours between 30 and 35. In comparison Australia, where the 35-hour rule also applies, only drops 0.5 of a per cent if a 30-hour rule is applied. This suggests that this country has far fewer persons working in the 30-35 hour zone and in a procedural sense it indicates that the statistical agency in that country could easily revert to a 30-hour rule without the need for any serious readjustment of past time-series. Those countries where joint classification rules exist, like the UK (2 per cent difference) and Spain (0.3 per cent difference) appear to have minimised the definitional penalty.

Table 2.3 Criteria for deciding part-time status by selected country

Country	Criteria
France	Works less than 80% of normal hours
Spain*	Works less than 60% of normal hours
Finland, Canada, New Zealand, UK,* Ireland	Works 30 hours or less paid employment per week
Australia, Austria, Iceland, Sweden, USA	Works 35 hours or less paid employment per week
Hungary and Turkey	Works 36 hours or less paid employment per week
Norway	Works 37 hours or less of paid employment per week

Note:
* These countries combine both methods in their labour force surveys, for example in Spain attention is paid to both how many hours are worked and whether or not a respondent claims to be full-time or part-time.

Source: ILO (1997a); Lemaitre et al. (1997).

2.2   THE INCIDENCE OF PART-TIME WORK

The data in Table 2.4, particularly in its standardised form, may also be used to examine the incidence of part-time work. The ILO groups countries according to the incidence of part-time work. High incidence countries (standardised rates of part-time employment above 20 per cent) include

Table 2.4 Incidence of part-time employment using national and standardised definitions

Country	% using national definitions	% if less than 30 hours per week	Differences (1-2)	% if less than 35 hours per week (4)	Differences (1-4)	Part-timers working 30 hours and over as % of all workers	Full-timers working less than 35 hours as % of all workers
Netherlands	33.4	24.7	8.7	33.4	0	8.7	0.0
Iceland	30.5	22.3	8.2	28.9	1.6	8.6	0.9
Switzerland	28.5	22.7	8.2	28.9	1.6	8.6	0.9
Sweden	28.4	17.2	11.2	27.2	1.2	11.4	0.9
Norway	26.4	20.9	5.5	26.4	0	5.5	0.0
Australia*	23.4	22.9	0.5	30.1	-6.7	3.4	6.7
UK	21.9	19.9	2.0	24.0	-2.1	2.7	2.8
Denmark	19.7	14.5	5.2	21.4	-1.7	5.6	2.1
Canada	18.2	18.2	0	24.1	-5.9	0.0	5.9
USA	17.1	12.8	4.4	17.1	0	4.4	0.0
France	15.7	14.1	1.6	19.0	-3.3	4.7	4.3
Germany	15.5	13.4	2.1	16.6	-1.1	2.4	1.1
Belgium	15.5	16.5	-1.0	20.4	-.49	2.7	5.3
Austria	13.2	10.3	2.9	12.8	0.4	4.1	1.8
Ireland	12.2	15.3	-3.1	19.5	-7.3	1.3	8.0
Finland	9.1	7.4	1.7	13.1	-4.0	3.0	4.3
Poland	8.5	13.3	-4.8	17.0	-8.5	2.1	9.3
Luxembourg	7.5	11.2	-3.7	13.4	-5.9	1.3	6.3
Spain	6.5	6.2	0.3	9.3	-2.8	0.3	2.8
Italy	5.9	11.1	-5.2	13.9	-8.0	1.7	9.3
Czech Republic	5.5	4.7	0.8	6.3	-0.8	1.7	1.4
Hungary	4.3	2.6	1.7	4.3	0.0	1.7	0.0
Portugal	3.9	6.8	-2.9	9.1	-5.2	1.0	5.6
Greece	3.2	8.0	-4.8	11.5	-8.3	0.9	8.8

Source: van Bastelar, Lemaitre et al. (1997, p. 21).

Sweden, Norway, Netherlands, Denmark, Iceland, Switzerland, the UK, Australia, Japan, Mexico and Turkey. Medium incidence countries (10-20 per cent) are the USA, Canada, Germany, France, Belgium, Austria and Ireland. Low incidence countries (less than 10 per cent) include Finland, Poland, Luxembourg, Spain, Italy, Hungary, the Czech Republic, Portugal and Greece.

The OECD survey found that part-time work is often a characteristic of female employment. Two out of every three females in the Netherlands are employed part-time, half in Iceland and Switzerland and over two out of every five in Norway, the UK, Australia, Sweden, Mexico and Turkey. The survey also found that over the period 1980-93, part-time work as a proportion of total employment had:

- increased in all of the surveyed countries except Greece;
- has grown most slowly in countries that started from a low base (especially in Southern Europe);
- has increased most rapidly in France and Belgium but levelled off in North America. In the USA the relative importance of part-time work has remained constant since 1983.

2.3   PART-TIME WORK AND MULTIPLE JOB-HOLDING

In April 1996, the US Department of Labor published data on another labour market phenomena, part-time workers who were classified as full-time workers because their total work week (at all jobs) was 35 hours or more. This data originated from a redesigned CPS survey which, for the first time, made it possible, among other things, to identify full-time workers who have additional part-time jobs and to compare their characteristics to part-time workers as traditionally defined by the Bureau of Labor Statistics. In 1995 there were approximately 6.5 million workers in the USA or 5 per cent of the labour force who were multiple job-holders. Figure 2.1 shows the distribution of these workers into three categories; full-time workers with one or more part-time secondary jobs, persons with more than one part-time job and a mixed group with varying job combinations. Of these groups the former predominates with 69 per cent of multiple job-holders being workers employed full-time in a primary job and having one or more part-time secondary jobs. The 1997 CPS data show that approximately three million multiple job-holders in the USA worked from home on their part-time job (US Department of Labor, 1998a). These workers have a younger age profile than the workforce in general and are almost all drawn into multiple job-holding by economic need. While females make up 65 per cent of all multiple job-holders, married males in low paying primary jobs make up more than half of category one. Conversely, most workers in categories two and three were young, single and female. For example, most workers in category two (combining more than one part-time job into a full-time schedule) were in their teens or twenties and 65 per cent were female. The other interesting finding from this survey was the rapid rate of growth in the number of full-time workers who held part-time jobs. Between 1994-95, the absolute number increased by 380 000 representing a nine percentage point increase over the year. The existence of this additional group of workers, who would normally be classified as full-time workers, helps to understate the true incidence of part-time work in the USA. It also became possible to contrast some of the characteristics of these multiple job-holders with those traditionally defined as part-time. Details of some characteristics of both groups are shown in Table 2.5.

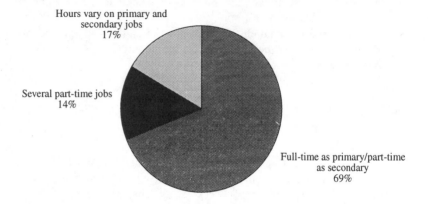

Source: calculated from data cited in US Department of Labor, April (1996).

Figure 2.1 Distribution of multiple job-holders: USA 1995

The main difference between multiple job-holders and those normally regarded as part-timers was the much higher incidence of married males in the multiple job categories. Other differences include a younger age distribution (81.4 per cent of category one multiple job-holders were 25 to 54 years compared with 48.6 per cent among part-timers) and a slightly higher incidence of whites. Home-based work featured prominently among all multiple job-holders with CPS estimates for 1997 indicating that over 60 per cent of all multiple job-holders worked from home for at least one of their jobs (US Department of Labor, 1998b).

Table 2.5 Characteristics of multiple job-holders and traditional part-time workers by per cent

Characteristic	Full-time primary/ part-time secondary	Part-time on all jobs	Various hours but total of 35+	Traditional part-timer
Age				
16 to 19 years	1.8	8.3	2.1	18.9
20 to 24 years	9.6	17.5	7.0	14.3
25 to 54 years	81.4	65.5	81.1	48.6
55 years and over	7.2	8.9	9.9	18.1
*Race**				
White	86.2	90.3	90.8	87.4
Black	10.4	7.1	6.5	8.8
Hispanic origin	6.1	6.0	4.2	7.7
Marital Status (men)				
Single	12.6	16.7	11.8	18.1
Married, spouse present	41.5	14.5	45.4	11.2
Divorced, separated, widowed	5.9	3.8	6.0	2.8
Marital Status (women)				
Single	10.9	21.2	8.8	20.3
Married (spouse present)	17.7	32.1	18.9	38.3
Divorced etc.	11.4	11.6	9.2	9.4

Note:
* because of mixed races does not add to exactly 100 per cent.

Source: Issues, US Department of Labor, April (1996).

2.4 TEMPORARY WORK

The term 'temporary worker' would seem a reasonably common and easily understood concept. The distinguishing feature of temporary workers is their lack of permanency. This lack of permanency can be explicitly acknowledged and occurs over a mutually agreed period such as within a fixed-term contract. Alternatively it can be open-ended as within some 'casual' employees in Australia; totally random and demand-driven as with on-call workers in the US or *aruabito* workers in Japan or it may mean regular but periodic working arrangements such as with seasonal workers. Finally, it can even be self-defined as in the case of workers who believe that their job is temporary, irrespective of how long they are actually employed for, as in the case of some 'contingent workers' in the USA. These differences in the meaning and interpretation of temporary workers leads to wide inter-country variations in estimates of their relative importance. In the UK, temporary workers comprise about 7 per cent of the workforce, but over half of these are fixed-term contractors. A smaller percentage are temp agency employees and about a third constitute the irregular or short-term worker of the type normally associated across the world with the name 'temporary'. In the USA, only employees of temp agencies are officially classified as temporary employees but the term overlaps with on-call workers and employees of contract firms. Overlapping still, and not distinguished in Figure 2.1, is the concept of contingent workers, that is, workers in jobs that are structured to be short-term or temporary (Cohany, 1998). Under the broadest definition there were 5.6 million contingent workers in 1997 in the US or 4.4 per cent of the employed population. In Japan, temporary workers are part of a larger, non-regular worker group. Strictly speaking only those on contracts of more than a month but less than one year are classified as temporary workers. Definitional problems again surface over the definition of temporary work. In most countries employees are classified as temporary if they are in a job which has a short and or defined duration. This definition is reasonably robust in that it caters for both contract workers, whose job duration expectancy is for the life of the contract and the irregular worker who is bought in for a short, though not necessarily specified time scale.

2.4.1   Incidence of Temporary Employment

Temporary work has been traditionally used as either a means of covering for the short-term absence of permanent staff or as a means of matching staffing levels to short-term peaks in demand. These are still major reasons for the employment of temporary staff (Atkinson et al., 1997). Table 2.6 shows the incidence of temporary employment in Europe. From this table it may be seen that temporary employment, except in Spain where institutional factors have led it to be disproportionately large, occupies on average around 10 per cent of paid employment. In every country shown in the table it is more prevalent among women.

Philpott's classification of temporary employment in the UK, which is a reasonable guide to the distribution of this type of employment throughout Europe, shows that fixed-term appointments still predominate and that casual and seasonal work are still important components.

What the data in Tables 2.6 and 2.7 do not show is the extraordinary growth in the contribution to temporary employment made by employees of temporary hire agencies (often referred to as temp agency workers). For example, according to the National Association of Temporary and Staffing Services (NATSS) the temporary help industry's receipts in the USA rose almost 13 per cent per annum over the period 1996-98. Between 1983-92 temporary employment increased almost 250 per cent - ten times faster than overall employment growth in that country. Temping is no longer limited to secretarial work. About 45 per cent of temps in 1995 were clerical but 34 per cent were industrial and 18 per cent professional. The Milwaukee-based Manpower Inc. employs over 500 000 persons a year, making it the largest employer in the USA. Its chief competitor, the Michigan-based Kelly Services, is the second largest. While countries differ over the definition and use of temporary workers, the UK provides a good example of the role and significance of temporary work within a modern labour market; still relatively small in absolute numbers but among the more dynamic and growing of sectors. The situation in the UK is discussed in some depth in case study 1.

Table 2.6 Percentage share of temporary employment in EU countries, 1995-96

Country	Men	Women
Belgium	3	7
Denmark	11	13
Germany	10	11
Greece	9	11
Spain	33	38
France	12	14
Ireland	8	13
Italy	6	9
Netherlands	8	14
Austria	6	7
Portugal	8	11
Finland	13	19
Sweden	11	14
UK	6	8
EU Average	11	13

Source: Eurostat (1996).

2.4.2   Case Study 1: Temporary Employment in the UK

In the spring of 1998, 1.7 million persons, approximately 7.4 per cent of employees in the UK, described themselves as temporary employees. As shown in Table 2.7, the share of total employment provided by temporary employees has risen in recent years from the relatively constant share of 5 per cent that they held between 1984-90. In the process of the current acceleration, temporary jobs have accounted for at least one-third of new hiring in the UK (EPI, 1999).

Table 2.7 The share of temporary employees in the UK, 1992-98

Year	Percentage of total employees (%)
1992	5.9
1993	6.2
1994	6.8
1995	7.3
1996	7.4
1997	7.7
1998	7.4
1999	7.7

Source: Employment Policy Institute (1999, p. 3).

Fixed period contractors make up the majority of all temporary workers (50.1 per cent). However, Sly and Stilwell (1997) have desegregated the data further and found that, despite the popular generalisation that temporary workers are low-skilled and concentrated in poor-quality jobs, at least one in five temporary employees are professionals and/or high-skill tradespeople. The wide spread of occupations covered by temporary workers is shown in Table 2.8. The data show that temporary workers are clearly over-represented in professional/associate professional, professional/technical and clerical categories as well as being slightly over-represented in manual occupations when compared to the workforce as a whole.

Table 2.8 Temporary workers by occupation

Occupations	% temporary	% all employees
Managerial/admin	4	15
Professional/associate	21	10
Professional/technical	10	9
Clerical	19	16
Craft and related	6	14
Personal and Protective	16	12
Selling	6	9
Plant/machine operatives	8	10
Other occupations	10	5
All	100	100
Manual	41	39
Non-manual	59	61

Source: Sly and Stilwell (1997, p. 11).

As a result of the over-representation of general and technical professionals, the hourly rate of pay for temporary workers on fixed contracts exceeds the all-employees average. This positive wage differential would also flow from the fact that some temporary workers sacrifice employer-funded benefits for higher hourly wage rates. However, this advantage does not flow on to other categories of temporary worker. All other categories of temporary worker earn substantially below the average hourly rates for all employees.

Table 2.9 Hourly rates of pay for temporary employees (UK, 1998)

Types of temporary arrangement	Median $	As (%) of all employees	Mean $	As (%) of all employees
Fixed period contract	6.74	102.4	8.30	102.2
Agency temping	4.59	70.0	5.35	66.0
Casual work	4.10	62.3	5.83	71.7
Seasonal work	3.50	53.1	4.52	55.6
Other	5.30	80.5	6.52	80.2

Source: Sly and Stilwell (1997, p. 17).

The extent of income disparity between most temporaries and the average employee would be even greater if the non-wage benefits afforded permanent employees were factored into the estimates. Indeed, even the small positive differential achieved by fixed-term contractors would seem insufficient to compensate for the loss of job stability and employer-funded benefits.

2.4.3   The Role of Hire Agencies

Increasingly, what distinguishes temporary work from other forms of non-standard employment is the central role played in their employment and employment prospects by private labour hire firms such as Adecco, Manpower and Reed. A significant proportion of temporary workers in the UK are formally attached to labour hire agencies. Current estimates place the percentage of agency temps at about 15 per cent of all temporary workers. This figure understates the role of labour hire agencies because it does not include a number of part-time temporary workers who make use of agency services but do not classify themselves as being associated with agencies[6]. Table 2.10 disaggregates temporary workers by type of temporary work.

The number of temporary workers handled by agencies in 1998 of 254 000 has increased substantially from 170 000 in 1992 (even on the basis of the normally conservative Labour Force Survey [LFS] definitions). Data provided by the Federation of Recruitment and Employment Services place the number of persons on the payroll books of employment agencies during an average week at 880 000.[7] While there is some dispute over the true number of agency workers, there is no doubt that they represent a major new dynamic in the UK labour market. Philpott (1999) argues that the rise of temporary work contracts and the central role played by labour hire agencies is the principal means by which the UK labour market is obtaining functional flexibility. The use of agency labour is now widespread across UK industries. The highest concentration is in service industries. Atkinson et al. (1996) report that 58 per cent of all UK medium- and large-sized firms used temporary workers in their year of survey (1996).

Table 2.10 Percentage breakdown of temporary employees (UK, spring 1998)

Types of temporary work	All	Men	Women
Fixed period contract	50.1	52.2	49.7
Agency temping	15.2	16.5	14.3
Casual work	18.3	17.1	19.3
Seasonal work	4.8	4.6	4.9
Other	10.6	9.6	11.8
All	100	100	100

Source: gathered from data contained in *UK Labour Force Survey*, June (1999).

However, it is important not to overstate the numerical importance of temporary workers in general and agency workers in particular. Table 2.11 shows the percentage distribution of agency workers across industries and their relative importance to total employment in those industries.

Table 2.11 Industrial distribution of temporary workers employed by agencies

Industry sectors	As (%) of all agency temps	As (%) of all employees in sector
Agriculture	1.1	0.9
Energy	2.0	2.9
Manufacturing	21.7	1.2
Construction	3.5	0.8
Distribution	8.5	0.6
Hotels/restaurants	1.0	0.2
Transport	9.4	1.6
Financial intermediation	7.6	1.7
Real estate/business	22.7	2.6
Public admin	2.3	0.4
Education	4.0	0.5
Health/social work	12.5	1.2
Other	3.6	2.1
All	100	1.1

Source: gathered from data contained in *UK Labour Force Survey*, June (1999).

In no industry do agency temps exceed 3 per cent of all employees and in most cases they make up less than 2 per cent.

As well, Cully et al. claim that for 1998 a majority of workplaces with over 25 employees did not use temporaries at all, 72 per cent did not use agency temps and 56 per cent did not use employees on fixed-term contracts. While most temporary employees are found in the private sector, the highest concentration is in the public sector, in public administration, education and health all of which rely heavily upon fixed-term employees. By contrast, the private sector tended to favour the use of agency temps over fixed-term contract because of their greater flexibility.

2.4.4   The Relative Position of the UK to the other EU Countries

The most recent comparative data on the distribution of temporary workers across the EU refers to 1995. This data (presented earlier in Table 2.6) show that the UK is still well below the EU average (both males and females) for the use of temporary workers. Spain, the Scandinavian countries and France make substantially greater use of temporaries than the UK. Additional data for Norway indicate that one possible reason for this is the tendency for European countries to classify apprentices and others on government training schemes as temporaries. For example, in 1996 these groups made up 17 per cent of all those classified as temporaries.

Recently, the need for numerical flexibility has been added as an incentive for temporary work contracts (Philpott, 1999). However, the term 'temporary' and in particular subgroups such as casuals also differ in meaning internationally and is often interpreted in line with the institutional arrangements that predominate in the country concerned. Two such examples are casual workers in Australia and contingent workers in the USA.

2.5   CASUAL AND CONTINGENT EMPLOYMENT

In Australia, temporary employment has taken a different and more pervasive form; *casual employment*. Table 2.12 shows that approximately 27 per cent of all employees in Australia are employed under casual conditions. Australia, with its tradition of strong labour unions and the presence of a union-supported Labor government for the period 1983-96, seems an unlikely setting for such large-scale changes to employment patterns. However, along with New Zealand, Australia has been affected over the last decade by government policies designed to improve international competitiveness, including the dismantling of tariffs, the floating of exchange rates, the deregulation of the financial sector and major changes to industrial relations legislation. It is thought that these changes, by inducing employers to seek greater labour market flexibility, have promoted the spread of this particular form of non-standard employment from the demand-side. On the supply-side, there are also groups of workers in the economy particularly responsive to non-standard forms of employment. Irrespective of their determinants, the changes in employment patterns have implications for labour market legislation concerning workplace health and safety, industrial relations and training, as well as for social and family life in Australia.

Table 2.12 Casual employment by Australian States as a proportion of total employees, 1988-98

States	1988	1998	% point change
New South Wales	16.8	24.8	8.0
Victoria	15.6	23.6	8.0
Queensland	24.8	31.1	6.3
Western Australia	18.2	26.3	8.1
South Australia	22.7	29.1	6.4
Tasmania	21.9	28.3	7.6
Australia	18.9	26.9	8.0

Source: ABS (1999a), '*Weekly Earnings of Employees* (*Distribution*)' Cat No. 6310.0, Canberra (unpublished data);   ABS (1999b), *'Trade Union Members'* Cat No. 6325.0, Canberra (unpublished data).

2.5.1   Defining Casual Employment in the Australian Context

The sheer size of casual employment in Australia indicates that the term 'casual workers' in Australia has a much wider currency than just the short-term contractors and irregular workers that make up temporary workers in other parts of the world. Two approaches have been used in this country to define casual employment. The Australian Bureau of Statistics (ABS) defines casual employment in terms of access to employer-funded benefits. In this context casual employees are those that are not entitled to holiday leave or sick leave in their main job.

By contrast, a common law point of view indicates that: 'Each engagement of a casual worker constitutes a separate contract of employment'. In other words, 'the common law view sees that the only distinction of significance between the casual/part-time employee and the full-time/permanent employee lies in the period of notice required properly to terminate the contract' (Brooks, 1991 p. 166). Romeyn provides a definition that summarises the legal position but recognises that the common law position has been supplemented by statutory requirements and award provisions. She stresses:

the lack of legal entitlements to benefits such as annual leave and sick leave which are associated with a continuity of employment, and the lack of legal entitlement to prior notice of retrenchment. (Romeyn, 1992, p. 1X).

Generally, casuals who are retrenched have no grounds for reinstatement or damages for arbitrary dismissal, although in some state jurisdictions re-employment (as opposed to reinstatement) may be ordered by an industrial tribunal.

An ABS survey for the South Australian Government (ABS, 1986) provides further clarification of casual work and defined the terms 'regular casuals' and 'irregular casuals'. Regular casuals usually work less than 35 hours per week, have no paid holidays, are paid for hours worked and have a steady income. Irregular casuals usually work less than 35 hours per week, have no paid holidays, are paid for hours worked and have an unstable income.

Irregular casuals would seem to have clear parallels with 'contingent workers' in the USA and casual/temps in the UK. The regular casuals appear to be a uniquely Australian creation. Most of them are part-time and are recorded as that in the official ABS statistics. However, a significant number (approximately 20 per cent) work full-time hours and are known, somewhat oddly, as permanent casuals (Mangan, 1998). What makes this group particularly interesting is that the rise in their significance has occurred at the same time as a reordering of the once rigid industrial relations system in Australia (Simpson et al., 1997). The corresponding decline in trade union membership and the observed inverse relationship between casual employment and union membership has led some to suggest that employers are driving employees into casual employment arrangements. This would be done to circumvent union agreements and labour market legislation as well as to increase numerical flexibility and increase employers' control (Burgess and Strachan, 1998). A further point of interest is that, unlike contingent work in the USA, the spread of casual work in Australia shows no sign of abating (Simpson et al. 1997; Mangan, 1999; Mangan and Williams, 1999). The data in Tables 2.13 and 2.14 provide a breakdown of employment growth by broad status in Queensland; Australia's fastest growing state between 1988–98 and a simple shift-share decomposition of that employment change.

Two facts stand out. Firstly, for both males and females, actual growth in casual employment far exceeded expected growth and, especially for males, was the major driver of employment. Secondly, percentage growth in casual employment for males far exceeded that for females and, contrary to the trend for females, appears to be at the expense of permanent jobs.

The data in Table 2.15, apart from showing the considerable below-share performance of permanent jobs for males over the ten-year period, confirm the importance of industry-mix effects in the disproportionate share of casual employment achieved in Queensland. This is particularly true for males where 80 211 (83 per cent) of the 96 249 male casual jobs created over the period were due to Queensland being over-represented in those industries that have a high propensity for casual employment. By contrast, less than half (44 per cent) of the 82 166 female casual jobs created were due to industry-mix. Most growth in female casual jobs was fuelled by competitive advantage factors within the Queensland economy. Overall, industry mix effects accounted for 66 per cent of above-expected growth in casual employment in Queensland over the period 1988-98.

Table 2.13 Employees in Queensland 1988-98 by permanent-casual status

Category	1988	1998	Absolute change	Percentage of change (%)
Male (permanent)	477 505	541 614	64 109	13.4
Male (casual)	82 967	179 216	96 249	116.0
Male (total)	560 472	720 830	160 358	28.6
Female (permanent)	232 940	370 417	137 477	59.0
Female (casual)	150 993	233 179	82 186	54.4
Female (total)	383 933	603 596	219 663	57.2
Total employment	944 404	1 324 426	380 022	40.2

Source: Mangan (1999, p. 6).

Table 2.14 Decomposition of employment change by status: Queensland 1988-98 (000s)

Employment type	Expected change (share)	Industry mix	Competitive advantage	Actual change
Male (permanent)	87 872	97 603	73 840	64 109
Male (casual)	15 268	80 211	770	96 249
Female (permanent)	42 866	10 014	84 597	137 477
Female casual	27 786	36 663	17 736	82 186

Source: Mangan (1999, p. 7).

2.6   CONTINGENT EMPLOYMENT IN THE USA

At the heart of the nature of casual employment, as it is represented in Australia, is its inherent instability. Yet it is quite likely that many of those defined as 'casual' in Australia, particularly those 'permanent' casuals are not fully aware of the limited job tenure they currently have. Many of these would be defined as contingent in the USA yet even here the term is beset by problems of definition and cross-over with other measures of labour force status. Contingent workers in the USA are defined as those who do not have an explicit or implicit contract for long-term employment (Hipple, 1998). In Figure 2.1 (Example 6), the US labour force was cross-classified by traditional and alternative arrangements and by full-time/part-time status. Contingent workers are distributed across all of these groups although they are mostly heavily represented among on-call workers, temporary agency workers and employees of contract firms. Cohany (1998) sums up the problem of classification in this way:

> Workers in alternative arrangements could be contingent as well, but were not automatically so. In fact most workers in alternative arrangements had permanent jobs and hence were not contingent. Likewise, most contingent workers had regular scheduled jobs for which they were hired directly and thus were not in an alternative arrangement. (p. 3).

Following the results of a 1997 survey, three broad definitions of contingent workers were introduced (Hipple, 1998). The narrowest relates to wage and salary earners only; the broadest includes self-employed and has no time dimension.[8] His results, using the broadest definitions, are shown in Figure 2.2. Proportionately, most workers confined as contingent in the USA are temporary help agency staff, with a contingency rate of 56.8 per cent. They are also the only group where contingency rates outweigh traditional arrangements. On-call workers also have a high rate of contingency (30.6 per cent). Another important result is the very low rate of contingency among self-employed contractors (3.5 per cent), even using the broadest definition. The distribution of contingency rates between men and women is very similar and, if anything, female rates are slightly below male rates.

There is also a relatively even spread of contingency rates across occupations and industries. The data in Table 2.15 show that professionals and those engaged in administrative support and services have the highest rates of contingency and construction, services and agriculture were the industries with the highest propensity to employ staff on a contingent basis.

The question then arises as to why contingency rates (non-permanent casuals) in Australia are so much higher than contingency rates in the USA? Differences in definitions and the country-specific interpretation of these definitions provide the bulk of the answer, but there are other reasons. As is often the case with international comparisons of non-standard employment, definitional differences and country-specific interpretations provide the bulk of the answer, but there are other reasons. Much of the contingency in Australia is by stealth. Workers whose expectations and day-to-day work

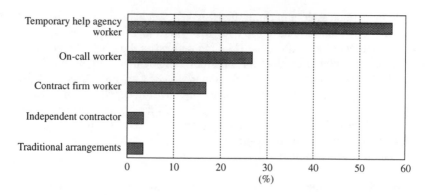

Source: compiled from data in Hipple (1998).

Figure 2.2 Contingent workers in the USA

experience appear consistent with traditional employment are actually employed, in a legal sense, under conditions of contingency (Mangan, 1998). If these workers were asked for a self-assessment of their job conditions, many would indicate that they are employed under traditional arrangements. The erosion of the Australian industrial relations system, which began in the 1980s, saw both an exodus of Australian workers from union membership and explicit industrial award cover into plant-level and individual work arrangements. In many cases, this simply meant the surrender of working conditions like employer-funded entitlements for increased hourly pay rates. However, one casualty of these arrangements that may have gone unnoticed by Australian workers was the implicit loss of job tenure (Brosnan and Thornthwaite, 1994). In contrast, job tenure in the USA has always been less well defined than in the traditional 'UK'-style labour markets that developed in Commonwealth countries such as Australia, New Zealand and South Africa. Moreover, contingency in the USA is based upon self-perceptions while in Australia it is defined by legal access to employer-funded benefits. These differences in definition produce some perverse results. In Australia, the contingency rates (as measured by casual employment) are biased upwards by including a large number of workers who are nominally contingent but who would, except in periods of recession, have secure jobs. In the USA, the contingency rate in a comparative sense is biased downwards because, under the regime of self-reporting, workers who do not have employer-funded benefits or implicit job security still consider themselves to be working under traditional arrangements. The other main difference is the current strength of the US economy. In a regime of low unemployment and high labour demand, attempts by employers to introduce increased contingency are unlikely to be successful. In contrast, until the mid- to late-

1990s the Australian economy had, by its standards, high rates of unemployment. The real concern over contingency is whether or not it is being imposed upon workers in an involuntary sense. To consider this in more detail, it is more useful to consider an economy where economic growth has not been as buoyant as in the USA and where structural changes, including changes in labour market policy have been occurring. Japan is a good example of all of these events.

Table 2.15 Per cent of US workers holding contingent jobs by occupation and industry, February 1995 and February 1997

Occupation and industry	February 1995	February 1997
Occupation		
Executive, administrative and managerial	2.7	2.2
Professional speciality	6.8	6.1
Technicians and related support	4.2	4.8
Sales occupations	2.6	2.1
Administrative support, including clerical	5.8	5.9
services	5.8	5.0
Precision production, craft and repair	4.6	4.2
Operators, fabricators and labourers	5.4	4.4
Farming, forestry and fishing	5.6	5.9
Industry		
Agriculture	5.0	5.3
Mining	2.7	3.6
Construction	8.4	7.1
Manufacturing	3.1	2.2
Transportation and public utilities	3.0	2.6
Wholesale trade	2.3	2.1
Retail trade	3.0	2.5
Financial, insurance and real estate	2.0	2.1
services	7.5	6.7
Public administration	3.6	4.2
Total US	4.9	4.4

Source: US Department of Labor, 98-5, May (1998b, p.1).

2.6.1 Case Study 2: Non-regular Work in Japan

The theme of casual and contingent jobs replacing traditional jobs is further illustrated by a closer examination of the Japanese labour market. At first glance, the behaviour of non-standard employment growth in Japan appears to follow a familiar pattern to that in Western Europe and Australia. Over the period 1992-99 the employment share of non-regular staff in Japan (defined as part-timers, *arubaito* and others) rose 80 per cent, from 11 per cent to approximately 20 per cent of all employed and 25 per cent of all employees in 1999. However, there are substantial differences between the nature and causes of non-standard employment in Japan and other advanced economies. These causes relate to the unique structure of the Japanese market and idiosyncratic labour market classifications.

Table 2.16 outlines the results of a special survey in the structure of the current Japanese labour market. It can be seen that over the year to May, the only group to experience an increase in employment was non-regular staff. In contrast, executive employees of corporations and regular (permanent) staff in general experienced a large numerical decline in numbers. This is an important observation for it is further evidence that the spread of non-standard employment in Japan is taking place almost exclusively outside the *nenko* (core) system of employment with its emphasis on lifetime employment and seniority-based wages (Houseman and Osawa, 1995). This suggests that, to a greater degree than elsewhere, non-regular employees in Japan are being used as direct substitutes for workers previously employed in the core labour market rather than as a buffer stock or as a means of screening entry level entrants (Sato, 1994; Seike, 1994). Some economists see this as a delayed reaction by Japanese companies to the rigidities of the *nenko* system which saw them unable to shed workers during the deep recessions of the late 1970s (Houseman and Osawa, 1995). If this is the case, the social implications of the spread of non-standard work in Japan may be more far-reaching than elsewhere.

Moreover, as the data in Table 2.17 indicate, the increase in non-regular work in Japan shows no sign of declining substantially. Some care needs to be taken in comparing employment status survey data (1982-92) and special labour force data (1999). However, the upward climb in the relative employment share of non-regular employment is clear from both sets of figures. In contrast to the USA, part-time work in Japan has clearly not experienced a levelling-off in the 1980s but has continued to grow into the late 1990s (Houseman and Osawa, 1995). This is most likely because non-regular work in Japan is being used, not only in the expected way of increasing workplace flexibility, but also as a means of dismantling or at least seriously reforming an overly rigid employment system. Put simply, there was more systematic need for reform of the Japanese labour market than for the US labour market. Table 2.17 also disaggregates non-regular employment by type.

Table 2.16 Definitions of non-regular employees in Japan

Part-time	Classified by employer, relates to perceived importance of job. Does not necessarily means less working hours than regular employees. Lifetime employment and *nenko* rarely apply.
Arubaito	'Side-jobs' taken by students, females or moonlighting adults
Temporary workers	Someone employed on a contract for more than one month but less than one year.
Day workers	Someone employed on a contract for less than one month
Despatched workers	Hired through labour hire companies
Sukko workers	Transferred between companies, similar to leased workers in the USA
Registered on-call workers	'Permanent' casual but normally not acting through an agency
Contract workers	Hired by special arrangement

Source: 1999 Special Labour Force Survey, www.stat.go.jp/155.htm.

Table 2.17 Non-regular workers in Japan as a percentage of paid employment (excluding self-employed and family members)

Category	1982	1987	1992	1999
Part-time	NA	10.1	11.3	12.8
Arubaito	NA	4.1	4.8	5.7
Total, part-time and *arubaito*	11	14.2	16.1	18.5
Temporary	7.9	8.9	8.4	NA
Day labourer	3.7	3.1	2.8	NA
despatched	NA	0.2	0.3	NA
Total	22.6	26.4	27.6	30.1

Source: 1982-92 estimates from Somucho Tokeikyoku Employment Status Survey (1999), estimated from Special Labour Force Survey, www.stat.go.jp/155.htm.

As may be seen from Table 2.16, part-timers in Japan are not primarily defined in terms of hours worked. Instead they are defined in terms of employer perceptions of the relative importance of the job, although it might be assumed that over an extended period they would work less than a regular employee. Employers define a job as part-time if it is outside the normal sphere of the company career path or long-term planning, irrespective of how important it may be to the company in the short run. An example in the Western labour markets would be of a temporary position or a low-skill position that is susceptible to displacement through technical change or downsizing. In this sense they come close to contingent jobs in the USA.

Arubaito jobs are best translated as side-jobs, taken by someone who is at school or has a full-time job elsewhere or is primarily responsible for home duties. These jobs are also contingent. They are defined by job status rather than time worked but there is also an implied time element. They would best be defined as part-time contingent. Initially, part-time jobs were taken by women and *arubaito* jobs by students and moonlighters. However they are becoming increasingly interchangeable both in terms of tasks performed and by the people who perform them.

Temporary workers in Japan represent fixed-term contract workers, albeit for a contract that is normally short-term (less than one year). In one sense, these workers are also contingent in that they have a brief expected stay at each employer. However, these workers are defined in terms of work duration rather than the nature of their work. There is no implicit suggestion that their work is of less intrinsic value than other forms of work. Unlike most Western 'temps', they negotiate directly with the employer rather than use labour hire agencies.

Such agencies were banned in Japan between 1947 and 1985 because they were associated with prewar worker exploitation. As a result, dispatched workers (workers managed through labour hire companies) are of far less import in Japan than elsewhere. This may be changing. Houseman and Oswara (1995) report rapid growth of this sector in the 1990s.

The other major forms of non-regular work are *sukko* workers (workers who have been transferred to a subsidiary of the company for a temporary stay), registered or on-call workers (normally registered with one or more companies) and contract workers who tend to be very specialised workers.

Overall, non-regular workers in Japan are disproportionately female. The Employment Status Survey (1992) reported that 50 per cent of *arubaito* and 90 per cent of part-time workers in Japan were female.

The industry distribution by gender for non-regular workers in 1999 are shown in Figure 2.3.

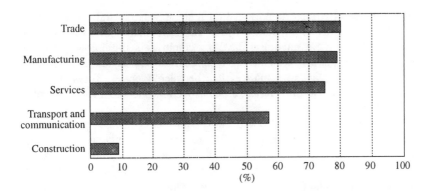

Sources: 1982-92 estimates from Employment Status Survey (1999), estimated from Special Labour Force Survey, www.stat.go.*jp/155.htm*.

Figure 2.3 Percentage of non-regular workers in Japan who are female by broad industry group

2.7   SELF-EMPLOYED

Self-employment (own-account work) is a traditional form of non-standard employment. There has always been a segment of the workforce, normally in professions or skilled trades, that worked for themselves and in many cases acted as an employer as well. Recently, new variants of self-employment, primarily centring on contracting, have emerged as a growing form of non-standard employment. Increasingly, the ranks of these have been bolstered by the 'new self-employed'. The persons involved and the motivations for their shift into self-employment are in themselves a microcosm of non-standard employment as whole. Some are 'economic refugees' unable to find permanent employment and undertaking self-employment as a measure of survival. Closely allied to these are 'dependent' contractors, workers who have had their employment status changed by employers no longer willing to accept non-wage costs, but who nonetheless work almost exclusively for the one employer or group of companies. On the supply-side, a growing number of persons are seeking self-employment for both personal flexibility and in search of tax and other economic advantages. The extent of the growth in this form of employment is impressive. However, this growth seems to be centred in North America and Australasia rather than Europe or Asia. For example, (Yeandle, 1999) has examined trends in self-employment in five European countries - Denmark, France, Germany, Italy and the UK. She found that self-employment is most important in a relative sense in Italy where it has more than a quarter of economically active males and about 13 per cent of economically active women. For the other countries, self-employment failed to rise above 10 per cent for males or 6 per cent for females and in most cases had remained constant or actually fallen between 1985-95. The situation is starkly different in North America, especially Canada and to a lesser extent in Australia and New Zealand.

In Canada, gross flows into and out of self-employment averaged nearly half a million per year between 1982-94, amounting to 42 per cent of the total self-employed population. Between 1990-97, self-employment in Canada expanded by 4.1 per cent per year, contributing to over three out of every four new jobs created (Lin et al., 1999). Self-employment now constitutes 18 per cent of all employment in Canada.

The dramatic increase in the importance of self-employment in the Canadian labour market is shown in Table 2.18.

Table 2.18 Total job creation and the contribution of self-employment in Canada, 1976-97

	Traditional employment	Part-time employment	Self-employed
1976-79			
Change (000s)	4 164.4	2 883.1	1 281.3
Per cent change	42.6	33.6	106.2
Per cent contribution		69.2	30.8
1980-89			
Change (000s)	2 003	1 657.0	346.8
Per cent change	18.1	17.2	23.7
Per cent contribution		82.7	17.3
1990-97			
Change (000s)	775.4	176.8	598.6
Per cent change	5.9	1.6	31.7
Per cent contribution		22.8	77.2

Source: Labour Force Survey (Canada) cited in Lin et al. (1999).

This rapid expansion in self-employment has coincided with a very slow increase in paid employment (0.2 per cent per year) and high unemployment, and this has led researchers to ask the question, has labour market hardship pushed people into self-employment? This question will be re-examined in the empirical section of the book. However, the pattern of self-employment that has developed in Canada offers prima-facie support for such a theory. The standard self-employed has changed for business owners to entrepreneurs working on their own. During the 1980s the large bulk (nearly two-thirds) of the growth in self-employment was accounted for by business owners who also hired labour and in so doing helped underpin the rapid expansion in paid employment over this period. In the 1990s, the large bulk of self-employees (90 per cent) were own-account entrepreneurs who, by and large, did not employ ancillary labour. This in part has also helped slow the growth in paid employment. Undoubtedly some of these more recent self-employed are either economic refugees from the loss of a paid job, while others have been forced to become 'dependent contractors' ('DCs') by firms trying to reduce the size of their core workforce. However, a number are self-motivated 'independent' contractors that have taken advantage of new technology, particularly in information technology, to gain greater work flexibility and in some cases reduce their overall tax burden, although in the specific case of Canada there should be, theoretically, no additional tax advantages to self-employment. However, for that country Schuetze (1998) has found that increases in the marginal personal income tax rates are positively correlated to the rate of increase in self-employment.[9]

The question that now arises is how many of the new breed of self-employed are demand-side-driven (economic refugees and DCs) and how many are supply-side-driven (ICs)? No data is available for the Canadian example but some attempts have been made to decompose contractors by their main source of motivation in Australia.

Researchers working on the Australian Workplace Industrial Relations Survey (AWIRS, 1991) and Dawkins and Norris (1990) were among the first to identify the important shifts towards self-employment contracts in Australia. Since then VandenHeuval and Wooden (1995) have moved much closer to obtaining a reliable estimate of the number of these workers in Australia. They argued that those calling themselves SECs extend beyond the normal boundaries of self-employment and contracting and might also be found within traditional labour market groups such as employer, employees or owner/employer. VandenHeuval and Wooden (1995), on the basis of a survey administered by the Population Survey Monitor of May 1994, found that SECs may be subdivided into four groups for Australia. These groups are shown in Table 2.19. They also found that 7.5 per cent of the non-farm workforce in Australia may be classified as SECs. This figure is more than double that found by the AWIRS (between 3.1 and 3.3 per cent) but less than half of the estimates for Canada, where as many as 15 per cent of the workforce are classified as self-employed contractors.

VandenHeuval and Wooden offered a broader framework for definition of self-employed contracting that comprised:

1. Self-employed workers whose work mainly involved the provision of services to other organisations.
2. Persons who classify themselves as wage and salary earners but do not pay income tax on pay-as-you-earn (PAYE) basis.

3. Employers who employ only family members and whose work mainly involves the provision of services to other organisations.
4. Persons who classify themselves as wage and salary earners but who are actually employed by their own company, which has no other employees or employs only family members.

Table 2.19 Self-employed contractors by type: estimates for Australia, May 1995

Status	Male	Female	Total
Self-employed	267 500	122 222	389 722
Non-PAYE	58 944	59 944	118 889
Employer	32 444	11 889	44 333
Owner/employer	7 500	1 667	9 167
Total	366 389	195 778	562 161

Source: estimates from the Population Survey Monitor, May (1994).

VandenHeuval and Wooden go on to use these definitions to make a further definitional distinction by dividing SECs into *independent* (ISEC) and *dependent* (DSEC). The distinction is essentially one of control over working conditions and methods of operation traditionally associated with contract employment. A legalistic approach to distinguishing between employees and SECs depends upon whether control is exerted over the persons performing the services. In reality many SECs have much more in common with employees than other self-employed persons. These are the DSECs.

One operational means of distinguishing between the two groups is to see whether the individual works for more than one organisation. An individual that works exclusively or mainly for one organisation is unlikely to be a fully independent contractor. This group has also been classified in other parts of the world as *de-facto* employees, fake self-employed (Bieback, 1992) or surrogate employees (Burgess, 1997). The main question here is why employees or people dependent upon one employer would choose to adopt the guise of SECs? There are several possible reasons. On the supply-side, these workers may see advantages in moving away from a PAYE tax system. While they should be subject to a prescribed payment system (PPS), at 20 to 25 per cent in Australia, there appears more scope as SECs turn to traditionally private expenses, like depreciation on a car, into work-related expenses that are tax deductible. They may also be able to charge themselves out on a higher hourly rate than previously. The long-term benefits of such actions are debatable and need to be based upon the present value of benefits received in the form of a higher hourly wage and a reduced effective tax rate against the present value of leave provisions, employer-funded superannuation and greater job security. Alternatively, the pressure may come from the demand-side with employers forcing employees into contracts to increase workplace flexibility and escape part of the fixed costs of employing standard employees. The forced signing of contracts may also be a long-term strategy by employers to undermine the union system (Underhill and Kelly, 1993; Brault, 1997).

VandenHeuval and Wooden estimate the ratio between independent and dependent contractors for Australia as a whole at 61.7 per cent to 38.3 per cent, respectively. They admit, however, that the classification of DSEC is open to error. The Population Survey Monitor estimates for August 1994 are shown in Table 2.20.

Table 2.20 Self-employed contractors in Australia by state proportions and percentage of dependent contractors

State	% of total	% DSECs
New South Wales	7.9	39.1
Victoria	6.4	35.5
Queensland	7.8	26.0
Western Australia	10.6	40.2
South Australia	6.1	NA

Source: VandenHeuval and Wooden (1995, p. 276).

2.8   DISTRIBUTION OF NON-STANDARD WORK BETWEEN PRIVATE AND PUBLIC SECTOR

In most developed countries, the public service has been in the forefront of affirmative action and gender equity programmes and has been more restrained than the private sector in the introduction of non-standard working arrangements. As a result, with the exception of some areas of part-time work, non-standard work is disproportionately contained within the private sector. Simpson (1994) estimates that at least 70 per cent of all casual workers in Australia are employed in the private sector. As well, private companies hire the majority of SECs. There are a number of reasons for this. One is the greater amount of regulation that surrounds public sector employment allied with the far greater percentage of union membership among public sector workers as opposed to private sector workers. Both these factors limit the scope of management flexibility in labour hiring. Moreover, the well-entrenched gender equity and affirmative action culture in the public service has set up barriers to the spread of labour hiring practices that might discriminate against women or minorities.

Nevertheless, the growth of corporatisation in government agencies throughout the world has created scope for the use of contract agreements. This is particularly true at the executive and senior management level where fixed or renewable contracts are seen as one way in which competitive wages required to attract high quality staff may be paid. The use of consultants to undertake what was formerly core public service business is another example of how flexibility in labour hiring practices is being introduced into the public service.

One area of non-standard employment where the public service is well represented is in part-time work, but even here there appears to be a distinction between core public service activities, within public administration, and government-supported activities such as education, health and community services. For example, in Canada, 24 per cent of the education/health and welfare sector is part-time and the corresponding figure for the UK is 37 per cent (Green et al., 1993). The figure for public administration is much lower at 7 per cent and 11 per cent, respectively. The Committee on the Changing Workplace (Canadian Labour Ministry, 1997) report that almost one in three nurses at Toronto Hospital is now employed on a casual basis. 'Permanent nurses are being laid off and replaced by casual nurses who have lower seniority and will work variable hours' (Dagg, 1997). The same Committee found that 15 per cent of all federal employees in Canada were employed on either a contract or casual basis.

2.9   OTHER FORMS OF NON-STANDARD WORK

This chapter has concentrated on four main forms of non-standard work; part-time work, temporary, casual and self-employment/contract employment. However, there exists a variety of other forms of non-standard work including seasonal work and out-workers (home-based workers), teleworkers, franchising, zero-hours contracting and flexi-time work (Felstead and Jewson, 1999). Added to this list are workers within the informal or cash-only economy. There are also considerable variations in working hours (atypical hours) resulting from non-standard employment patterns. Data on the extent of these forms of non-standard employment are often very limited. Part of the reason for this is that they often overlap with and are in effect numbered among the other forms of non-standard work. For example, out-workers and seasonal workers are often employed on both a casual and contract basis. Seasonal workers are migratory and are often working on a full-time basis, albeit, at different work sites. Moreover, in the case of some out-workers and most workers in the informal economy there are issues such as tax avoidance, criminal activity or moonlighting. In such circumstances, people are reluctant to publicise their existence. Given these data limitations, much of the information on home-working and seasonal working is anecdotal. However it is clear that the relationship between home-working and non-standard work is mixed and differs across occupation, industry and sex. This chapter considers home-based work in aggregate, using the results from the 1997 CPS survey into work at home. The non-standard aspects of home-work are covered by considering two forms which may be considered at the opposite ends of the home-working scale in terms of remuneration and desirability; teleworking and home-based pieceworking[10].

The CPS survey for 1997 provides a good indication of the scale of work at home in the USA. In May 1997, 23.3 million persons were engaged in work at home on either their primary or secondary job (US Department of Labor, 1998a). However, not all of these could be classed as non-standard. Indeed, the distribution by type of home-workers is a good example of the dichotomy that characterises modern labour markets by including both over- and under-employed workers and those that are participating in home-work in both a voluntary or involuntary sense. For example, more than half (53 per cent) of these workers were wage and salary earners operating under traditional conditions and were not expressly paid for their work.[11] Most non-standard workers came from the other 47 per cent, including 17 per cent who were wage and salary earners and who were paid for their work at home. Most of these were teleworkers. The remainder was voluntarily and involuntarily self-employed. The element of choice is again crucial to understanding what is driving these labour market changes. In some instances, the shift to home-based work is applauded as freeing up the labour market for innovative and creative people. Others see this trend as another attempt by management to shift the costs of production onto workers.[12]

2.9.1 Teleworkers

Teleworkers are among the upper echelons of non-standard workers (Luukinen, 1998). It may be defined as 'work in which an individual is for a considerable period of time physically distanced from, and in electronic communications with, the place, the customer or the organisation to which their work effort is directed' (Danish Board of Technology, 1997). The use of a definition constructed in Scandanavia is appropriate given the high incidence of and interest in teleworking in Finland and Denmark.[13] A little more than 8 per cent of all Finnish workers are teleworkers and about 10 per cent of all wage and salary earners. The data in Figure 2.3 shows that this is the second highest in Europe behind the Netherlands (18 per cent), is well above the European average of 4.5 per cent and compares favourably with the USA (12.9 per cent of all wage and salary earners). The reasons for this growth and its location are complex and are as much related to government policy and infrastructure provision as labour market trends. However, it is clear that telework, in all its forms, is increasing rapidly. Market research in the UK indicates a fivefold increase in teleworking in that country between

1992-96. UK authorities seem so enthusiastic about the benefits of teleworking that a recent British Telecom (BT) report indicated that telework via its effect on reduced physical commuting will significantly reduce both fuel consumption and peak hour road congestion. Even more dramatic are the projections for Denmark. In this country, the Ministry of Research has predicted that by 2006, the number of teleworkers in Denmark will grow from the current number of approximately 10 000 to over 250 000.[14]

Gareis (1997) describes the process by which teleworkers have become influential in German insurance companies.

Percentage of workforce
early 1999

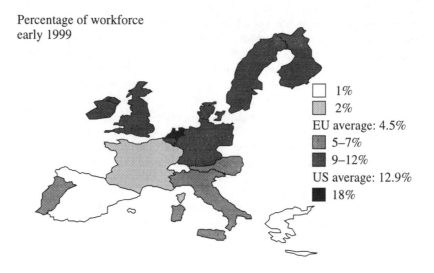

1%
2%
EU average: 4.5%
5–7%
9–12%
US average: 12.9%
18%

Source: Gareis (1997, p. 7).

Figure 2.4 Teleworkers in Europe: status 1999

Initially (phase one), there is informal telework based upon individual arrangements and involving a limited range of employees. In phase two, companies begin formalised pilot testing of teleworking solutions. This is followed in phases three and four with full-blown schemes involving a significant number of staff and accompanied by training courses for staff and information and education sessions for customers.

There is also a commonality, world-wide, among those persons and occupations attracted to teleworking. Most are men, and the bulk are white-collar workers that are either self-employed independent contractors or temporary agency employees or contractors. For example, Luukinen reports for Finland that they are '… as a rule, the more fortunate members of society. They tend to have a higher level of education and a higher level of income than others working in similar positions' (Luukinen, 1998, p. 1). Here there is an overlap with the picture of home-working in general, provided by the CPS data for teleworkers. In this survey, 90 per cent of home-workers were white-collar workers. At the other end of the teleworking spectrum are the piece-rate telephone sale operators or clerical staff who tend to be temporary and are employed under piece-rate conditions. For example, the low pay unit in the UK (1983) indicated that telephone salespersons operating from home received 19 to 29 per cent lower earnings than on-site operators did. Dagg reports that teleworking is particularly prevalent among female public sector workers in Canada where the Federal Government has been active in moving computers and telecommunication equipment into the homes of workers. For example, she estimates that 15 per cent of all federal employment is currently fixed-term or casual. Dagg argues that these practices raise complex issues such as how to balance work and family responsibilities and how to limit long hours and split shifts. In her study she estimates that federal government employees working at home on a computer are working 2.5 hours per day longer than on-site employees receiving the same income (Dagg, 1997). She concludes her study of teleworking in Canada with the observation: 'While welcomed by some, telework can be very isolating and makes workers vulnerable to abuse' (Dagg, 1997, p. 12).

2.9.2 Out-workers

Out-workers, as the name suggests, work outside of an employer-provided workplace. Many work from their own home or communally in villages. They constitute the opposite end of the home-work spectrum from teleworkers particularly in terms of work conditions, pay and job satisfaction. In some developing countries the outworking practice is associated with child labour (ILO, 1997b). For these reasons the most common perception of the out-workers is of a female working in a marginalised occupation for below award wages. This is certainly the picture painted by the 1989 Women's Research and Employment Initiatives Programme Survey of out-workers (with particular reference to out-workers engaged in clerical activity) in Australia. They estimated that there were approximately 200 000 women engaged in out-work in Australia (within a labour force of 7 million) of which 69 000 were clerical workers. A Department of Education, Employment and Training (DEET) study indicated that New South Wales seemed to be the centre of clerical outwork with 45 per cent of all out-work in the state being clerical. In a similar vein, the Illawarra Migrant Resource Centre estimated that in 1987, 60 000 textile workers worked from home. This constituted 50 per cent of all out-workers. The DEET survey also concluded that much of out-work is non-unionised and marginal. Other characteristics often associated with out-working are that of a migrant background with clear barriers to obtaining employment in the open labour market. This was confirmed by the Illawarra survey. More recent work has placed the numbers involved in out-work at closer to 330 000. The Textile, Clothing and Footwear Union of Australia (TCFUA) have provided the following state-based estimates of out-working in Australia. These are shown in Table 2.21.

The data, apart from showing the relatively large numbers involved in absolute terms of estimated out-workers, also show Victoria to have surpassed New South Wales as the main source of out-work. This may be in response to recent changes in the industrial relations laws in Victoria or it may reflect weaknesses in the federal award coverage for out-workers that has only recently been exploited. The report goes on to claim that, far from being an aberration 'outwork is not just a characteristic of the clothing industry in Australia, the industry is structured around it' (TUFCA, 1992).

Table 2.21 Out-workers in Australia by State

State	Number	% labour force
Victoria	144 000	4
New South Wales	120 000	3
Queensland	25 000	2
South Australia	25 000	2
Western Australia	15 000	1
Total	329 000	3

Note:
* no estimates for Tasmania are currently available.

Source: Marshall and Ginters (1995, p. 11).

Other evidence indicates that out-working (home-working) is on the increase across the world. To the traditional industries of clothing, textiles, carpets and footwear in Europe have been added fish processing (particularly in the Netherlands), electronics and optical industries, chemical and synthetic processing and paper and cardboard processing (especially in Germany). In Japan, small companies have arisen as agents that in turn subcontract to home-workers. These are concentrated in the coil winding and the radio and television parts industry. In India, home-workers specialise in *bedi* rolling (cigarette manufacturing), incense making, food preparation and sub-assembly of electronic parts (Marshall and Ginters, 1995).

In contrast to teleworking, out-working throughout the world is predominantly undertaken by females. Women make up over 90 per cent of out-workers in Germany, Greece, Ireland, Italy and the Netherlands and over 70 per cent in the UK, France and Spain (Marshall and Ginters, 1995).

There are some reasons why home-based workers might be expected to receive (and accept) lower pay than those at external job sites. For example, lower wages might be offset by savings on travel costs and associated costs such as child minding. However, much of the international evidence suggests that the trade-off is weighted too heavily in favour of employers, to the point of exploitation. In developing countries, the wage trade-off may be as high as 75 per cent but even in the developed economies the difference may be substantial.

The TCFUA reports cases of clothing out-workers in Australia receiving less than A$2 per hour for 14 hours per day, 7 days per week. Some caution should be used in interpreting this data, given the tendency for such reports to magnify any exploitation. For example, it is difficult to see how out-working is expanding so rapidly if such exploitative rates are being paid unless it is connected with illegal immigrants or tax evasion or other elements of the hidden economy. Nevertheless Mishel and Bernstein, in their study of marginalised workers in the USA, group home-workers with temporary help and leased workers as 'the statistically visible portion of the new marginal workforce in the US'. They provide in Table 2.22 estimates of the prevalence of these workers in the US labour force.

The Mishel and Bernstein (1995) analysis is influenced by the unique problems experienced in the USA with illegal immigration. Such immigration has created a large exploitable group of persons who seem to specialise in home-work to avoid the detection likely to occur from possessing a mainstream job. Nevertheless, the data above suggests that between 2 and 2.5 per cent of the current US labour force are at-home workers, most of which, the authors feel are marginalised. Surprisingly, this estimate is lower than the 4 per cent estimated for Australia (TCFUA), a fact that gives some concern to the accuracy of the Australian estimate.

Table 2.22 A comparison of elements of the marginal workforce in the USA

	Number of workers, 000s
Temporary help services	944
Leased workers	120
At-home workers	2 243

Source: Mishel and Bernstein (1995, p. 213).

2.10   CONCLUDING REMARKS

This chapter examined the international incidence of non-standard employment. It became immediately clear that in attempting such a study, problems of definition and data compatibility would arise. This is because in both the identification and measurement of non-standard employment across the world there is a strong country-specific element. Part-time work is a good example. This is the most common form of non-standard employment across the world but it is difficult to find a common definition that can be applied internationally. The two most commonly used definitions both define part-time workers in terms of the average number of hours worked per week. In Australia, Austria, Iceland, Sweden and the USA, part-time workers are those that regularly work less than 35 hours per week. However, in an era in which labour unions are pushing for a standard 36-hour-week for full-time workers, the distinction between part-time workers operating at the upper boundary of the 35-hour cut-off point and full-time workers in these countries will become very slight and further complicate data collection. This is the case even more so in Hungary and Turkey, where part-timers may work up to 36 hours per week and Norway where the cut-off point is 37 hours. Canada, Finland, Ireland, New Zealand and the UK operate a lower cut-off point of 30 hours. This has the advantage of making the distinction between full-time and part-time workers more distinct and would seem, in the opinion of the author, a more sensible cut-off point. Some countries do not specify a set number of hours but rather define part-time work in terms of a percentage of average full-time hours. For example, in France part-time workers are those that work a maximum of 80 per cent of average full-time hours and in Greece the level is 60 per cent. In Japan, the definition of part-time status is not even a function of hours worked but rather of the perceived importance of the job.

These differences in definition make international comparisons difficult but not impossible. The OECD has standardised estimates of part-time employment across its member states by using both 30 hours per week and 35 hours as the common base. They find that high incidence countries (those with standardised rates of part-time employment of 20 per cent or above) include Sweden, Norway, Netherlands, Denmark, Iceland, Switzerland, the UK, Australia, Japan, Mexico and Turkey. Medium incidence countries (10-20 per cent of employment) are the USA, Canada, Germany, France, Belgium, Austria and Ireland. Low incidence countries (less than 10 per cent of employment) include Finland, Poland, Luxembourg, Spain, Italy, Hungary, the Czech Republic, Portugal and Greece.

Most part-time workers (over 60 per cent) are female and there is a considerable overlap between part-time employment and other forms of non-standard employment such as temporary employment and self-employment. As well, most part-time workers have actual work-hours considerably less than the 30-35 hours which forms the upper limit of part-time work. This is a further indication that cut-off points for defining part-time workers could be lowered without seriously effecting the continuity of data collection. It was found that many full-time workers also have one or more part-time jobs. The presence of these multiple job-holders means that officially collected statistics understate the extent of part-time work because they only count employment in main job. In the USA, for example, of the estimated 6.5 million multiple job-holders in 1996, 70 per cent had a full-time primary job as well as at least one part-time job.

Along with part-time work, temporary work and self-employment are the three main building blocks of non-standard employment. Temporary employment covers a range of short-term working arrangements. Some are formalised within fixed contracts while others tend to be open-ended and/or irregular, while seasonal workers may be defined as periodic but regular temporary workers. In Europe, temporary workers comprise, on average, about 11 per cent of the male workforce and 13 per cent of the female workforce. Spain is a notable exception to these averages with 33 per cent of males and 38 per cent of females classified as temporary workers. These abnormally high levels reflect particular institutional arrangements in Spain that make dismissal of a permanent employee prohibitively expensive for employers and leads them to be very careful before offering permanent employment. Belgium has the lowest rates of temporary employment with 3 per cent of working males and 7 per cent of working females employed as temporaries. A case study of temporary employment in the UK provided a description of the break up of temporary workers by type and sex, which is believed to be typical of the rest of Europe. This showed that about half of all temporary workers were fixed period contract workers, 18 per cent were irregular temporaries (casuals), 15 per cent are employees of temp agencies and approximately 5 per cent were seasonal workers. The remaining 12 per cent were undefined. It was found that temporary employment, as a percentage of the workforce, had grown in the 1990s but not dramatically. For example, in the UK the percentage of the workforce comprised of temporary workers had risen from 5.8 per cent in 1992 to 7.7 per cent in 1998. The exception to this small but steady growth was the growth in the relative and absolute importance of agency temps. In the UK, their numbers had more than doubled between 1992-98 and surveys conducted on UK medium- and large-sized firms found that over 58 per cent regularly used temp agency staff. However, the main reason for using these workers was because of short-term needs such as unexpected demand or to cover staff vacancies rather than as part of a general management strategy to replace permanent staff with temps.

Two other variants of temporary employment were examined in some detail; casual employment in Australia and contingent employment in the USA. Casual employment in Australia is a particularly interesting case because it is so widespread (between 25-30 per cent of employees), because it is not defined by the number of hours worked and because it arose in the wake of a substantial deregulation of Australia's once stringent workplace legislation. Casual employment in Australia is defined in terms of the lack of employer-funded benefits such as sick pay and annual leave provisions and by the common law security of tenure. In such circumstances, casual employment in Australia may be subdivided into 'permanent casuals' (workers undertaking normal full-time hours) who do not have standard workplace protection and rights and irregular casuals that are much closer to the European-style casual (temporary) worker. To some, the evolution of the Australian 'permanent' casual represents the undesirable and perhaps inevitable outcome for non-standard workers in the absence of legislative protection and where the main impetus for non-standard work is imposed from the demand-side.

Similar fears are expressed about contingent workers in the USA. These workers are defined as those that do not have an implicit or explicit contract for long-term employment. They differ from Australian casuals in a number of ways. Firstly, contingents make up a much smaller percentage of the workforce at approximately 5 per cent of the US employees. Secondly, they may not even be non-standard workers. Some contingent workers are in traditional job arrangements who simply believe that their jobs are insecure and who therefore identify themselves as contingent in the CPS surveys. However, most contingents are non-standard workers. Most would also prefer a traditional job and in this sense are involuntary contingents. As a result, they constitute the most identifiable group of demand-imposed non-standard workers in the USA. Recognition of contingent workers in the USA as a definable group and the derivation of the term itself first came into prominence as a result of management techniques introduced in the 1980s that advocated employing workers only when required and then only for the duration of a specific task. Given that the US labour market, in terms of employment legislation, is one of the more deregulated labour markets, it is perhaps surprising that this group tends to make up a much smaller percentage of the workforce in the USA than they do elsewhere. Several factors account for this. The first is the strength of the US economy over the last decade that has produced a tight labour market and allowed workers to be more discerning in their job choices. The second is the relatively ill-defined labour force status definitions in the USA which almost certainly leads to an understatement of the extent of contingent work. Allied to this is the propensity of illegal immigrants and moonlighters to take contingent jobs. This would also lead to under-reporting.

Self-employment has long been a feature of the labour market. However, to the traditional professional and skilled self-employed, many of whom were also employers, has been added economic refugees, driven into self-employment by a failure to find the appropriate job in the traditional labour market. Another group featuring in the increase in self-employment has been *de-facto* employees. These are workers who, while claiming self-employed status, are in reality in a dependent relationship to one company or group of companies. Estimates vary over the relative size of this group. Evidence from Australia suggests that about 30 per cent of all SECs are in reality *de-facto* employees. Canada provides the most dramatic example of the growth in self-employment. Between 1990-97, three out of every four new jobs in Canada came from self-employment. Given the stagnant nature of the Canadian labour market as a whole, many of these new self-employed would appear to be economic refugees. This conclusion is also supported by the large differences between the trends in self-employment in Canada and the USA. In contrast to Canada, self-employment in the USA has grown slowly in response to a booming traditional labour market in that country.

Two other forms of non-standard work were covered; teleworkers and out-workers (home-based process workers). Teleworkers make up about 4.5 per cent of the European wage and salary earners, the highest levels being in the Netherlands (18 per cent) and Finland (10 per cent). This compares with a rate of 12.5 per cent for the US. Teleworkers are one group of non-standard workers where there is a clear appeal to employees. Survey evidence from Finland, the USA and the UK suggests that they tend to be paid well above the average for non-standard workers and to be among the better qualified. In contrast to other forms of non-standard employment, males tend to be the dominant group numerically, especially in Europe. The main concern expressed over teleworking is the potential it has to isolate workers and remove them from job networks. At the other end of the spectrum in terms of working at home are the out-workers or home-based process workers. These workers make a sizeable contribution to textile production in Australia, carpets and footwear in most of Europe, fish processing (the Netherlands), electronics, optical industries, paper and cardboard processing (Germany), *bedi* (cigarette), incense and food preparation in India and electronic goods assembly in most of South East Asia. In Japan, small companies have arisen as agents that in turn subcontract to out-workers. These workers have few, if any, employer-funded benefits are paid below-average wages and have low job security. Given these drawbacks, the main reason why the practice not only continues but appears to be increasing are family considerations and cultural reasons. Technological change has also made feasible a number of activities that previously could not have been done off-site. In contrast to teleworkers, the large majority of out-workers are female. Women make up over 90 per cent of out-workers in Germany, Greece, Ireland, Italy and the Netherlands and over 70 per cent in the UK, France and Spain.

NOTES

[1] These categories are discussed in more detail in Case Study 2.

[2] See a discussion of the relationship between non-standard employment and self-employment in the USA and Canada in Manser and Picot (1999).

[3] The Italian labour market offers up an interesting contrast to the Spanish labour market. Although the Spanish and Italian economies are comparable, and have similar labour market legislation, the spread of temporary employment in Italy has been far less. See Adam and Canziani (1998).

[4] Refer to section 2.3 of this chapter for a discussion of the definition of part-time workers.

[5] Recent UK data from an Omnibus Survey indicate that the principle of self-identification is working reasonably well for most forms of non-standard employment but runs into problems with emerging forms of non-standard employment such as temp agencies. The majority of

surveyed temps saw themselves as employees despite the growing tendencies of the agencies to treat them as self-employed. Only a very small number said they were contractors or freelancers. See Burchell et al. (1999).

[6] This occurs because data on temporary workers in Britain are taken from the Quarterly Labour Force Survey and is based upon self-classification by respondents.

[7] The Department of Trade and Industry (DTI) places the estimates at something like 500 000. Even at this lower estimate it indicates that the actual numbers of temporary or agency workers far exceeds LFS estimates.

[8] For the full definitions of the three forms of classification of contingent workers see Hipple (1998, pp. 34-35).

[9] One possible explanation is the greater degree of flexibility that self-employed have to report their earning and/or spread their earnings over more than one tax period. This theme has been spread in the popular press. See, for example, Fortier (1999).

[10] Often referred to as out-working (Mangan, 1998).

[11] It is often suggested from results like these that unpaid for work done outside of working hours is becoming an implicit cost of maintaining permanent employment (ACIRT, 1999). Others see this as the natural occurrence of increased competition in the labour market (US Department of Labor, 1999d).

[12] In this article she cites results from Henley Management College (1996) expressing high levels of satisfaction from employers of home-based teleworkers. However, she also cites other studies identifying high levels of social isolation and discontent among such workers.

[13] See Jackson and van der Wielen (1998). for more in-depth international survey of the spread of telework.

[14] It should be reported that this estimate by the Ministry of Research has been met with some degree of scepticism.

PART II

Explaining Non-standard Employment

3. The Determinants of the Rise in Non-standard Employment

3.0 INTRODUCTION

Many economists and business analysts view changes in the proportion of the labour force working under non-standard arrangements as evidence of a fundamental restructuring of the employee/employer relationship (Brault, 1997). This is the point of view put by Cappelli when he wrote:

> Most observers of the corporate world would believe that the traditional relationship between employer and employee is gone but there is little understanding as to why it ended or what will replace it (Cappelli, 1999, p. 3).

To Cappelli and others the driving factor in this changed relationship has been new management practices that stress labour force flexibility and that seek to reinforce market forces within a firm. Once these market forces are established within the structure of the firm they become dominant and undermine the previous relationships of reciprocity, long-term commitment and internal promotion that characterised the traditional employment relationships (Cappelli, 1999). In this new environment, employers value labour force flexibility over staff harmony and stability, and staff replace loyalty to the organisation with increased concentration on individual careers. Non-standard employment is essential to this process. It provides employers with the quickest possible means of formally severing the ties and responsibilities of traditional employment and it provides some individuals, such as independent contractors, with the best means of gaining economic rent from the new employment relationships. The rise of non-standard employment by facilitating both the demand- and the supply-side of the employment relationship may produce as Watson and Fothergill (1993) argues 'the best of both worlds'. Many analysts are predicting further growth in non-standard employment as firms continue to replace full-time workers in the belief that this will give them a more flexible and less costly workforce (Thurman and Trah, 1990; Blank, 1991; Tilly, 1991; Brosnan and Thornthwaite, 1994; Brault, 1997).

Implicit in this process is the belief that demand-side pressures are the driving forces behind the growth in non-standard employment. This in turn is the cause of much of the apprehension concerning the growth of non-standard employment. Even the term 'non-standard employment' is not value-neutral but rather has taken on the tone of something that, according to Felstead and Jewson (1999), is 'inferior, flawed or substandard'. As a result the trend has been condemned by many as creating precarious forms of employment, promoting unequal labour force treatment and being particularly unfair to women (Buchtemann and Quack, 1990; Thurman and Trah, 1990; Tilly, 1992; Brosnan and Thornthwaite, 1994; Rosenberg and Lapidus, 1999). In contrast the same trends have been defended as a 'sound means of reconciling the needs and preferences of workers with the operational requirements of enterprises and benefiting workers with family responsibilities, workers approaching retirement, and other special groups' (Sapsford and Tzannotas, 1993; Goulet, 1997). There is also, especially for some non-standard workers such as the self-employed, the promise of higher take-home salary.

In some sense both views are correct. Non-standard employment, by its nature, is outside some or all of the protection of traditional employment (union coverage, legal protection and employer-funded benefits). Increasingly employer and employee are spatially distinct. On the other hand, non-standard employment avoids the restrictions that accompany permanent employment in a fixed place of work such as inflexible working hours, PAYE taxation coverage and restrictive legislation. Therefore a combination of factors has assisted in the spread of non-standard employment. These factors are considered in this chapter under three broad categories: demand-side factors, supply-side factors and changes in labour market institutions. Clearly it is not possible to separate out fully demand factors from supply factors and as a result the division attempted below is arbitrary. In addition, the forces of demand and supply are shaped by changes in the institutions and laws governing the operation of the labour market. Yet individual consideration of each of these factors allows a clearer discussion of their relative importance to the current process of labour market transition. Before commencing this analysis it should be noted that some see the growth in non-standard employment as a temporary phenomenon, arising from the economic recessions of the last two decades, rather than a fundamental shift in preferred labour market behaviour. The recent history of the US labour market is seen as an indication that non-standard employment is a creature of recession and economic restructuring and does not flourish in a strongly growing economy. For example, Larson and Ong (1994) point out that the proportion of part-time workers in the US labour force has declined in recent years following a growth spurt in the 1980s and is now back to a level comparable with the late 1970s. Similarly, contingency rates in the USA now seem much lower than elsewhere. In some ways this line of argument is a crude form of the demand-driven explanation of non-standard employment.

Clearly, in the USA, the strong economic growth has produced a tight labour market within which employees are able to be more selective in their job choices. The tightness of the labour market has produced a situation where, despite the low union coverage, there have been large and successful strikes against the introduction of outsourcing and casualisation.[1] However, while there is some cyclical trend to the incidence of non-standard employment, it would be wrong to assign this explanation major importance. To do so would be to downplay the widespread changes in industrial organisation, management thinking and technology that have occurred in recent decades and have shaped the demand for alternative work arrangements. It would also neglect major demographic and lifestyle factors that have produced a pool of workers who specifically seek out non-standard employment. Finally, the discussion in Chapter 2 has shown that for most countries the growth in non-standard employment has not been counter-cyclical but rather one of consistent increase across the economic cycle.

3.1 DEMAND-SIDE EXPLANATIONS

Economists of the 1960s and early 1970s had a comfortable view of the labour market and labour hiring practices. The human capital theory was predominant as an explanation of wage and employment determination. Under this theory, labour market outcomes were primarily driven by employer perceptions of an individual's long-term marginal productivity. Labour market segmentation was recognised but explained by the distinction drawn between primary and secondary labour markets. Even here there was a rational, cost-minimising, explanation for this division. The segmentation was on the basis of perceived supply-side imperfections in workers either in a legitimate sense (low human capital and outdated skills) or, in an illegitimate sense (ethnic background, language, gender or age). Moreover this segmentation was restricted to a minority of the workforce who exerted little influence in the overall labour force. Most workers were in primary (internal) or semi-primary labour markets with full-time employment which provided stability to the worker as well as a rational means for employers to capture the productivity of the worker and recoup any training and hiring expenses that the firm may have entered into.

The efficient firm had high human capital workers, defined career paths and longevity of the employment relationship. It was in this environment that Walter Oi's famous description of labour as a 'quasi fixed factor of production' was born and Okun's law stated that labour demand was less sensitive to shocks than output (Oi, 1962). While lifetime employment models came, historically, to be associated with the Japanese, large corporations in the USA and Western Europe also provided continuous employment to their staff. Up until the 1980s, IBM never had a lay-off in its 40-year history (Cappelli, 1999). What happened at IBM is typical of the structural pressures that faced many of the established industries during the late 1970s and early 1980s. As technical change produced the first wave of personal PCs, the company was faced with growing international competition, changes in levels of domestic protection, microeconomic reform of monopolies and anti-competitive practices and the need to produce higher rates of return for shareholders. Labour costs were an immediate and easy target for cost reduction aimed at boosting profits. According to Rudolph (1998), 'firing people was a good place to start'. The initial labour demand changes were pure downsizing staff cuts rather than the substitution of non-standard for traditional employees. They tended to be aimed at blue-collar workers.

The experience at AT&T provides a good example. The company had a long history of being a regulated monopoly where lifetime employment was the expectation of white-collar employees. The deregulation of the telecommunications industry provided the first major shock for the company and led to a break up of the company into a number of specialised functions. Between 1984 and 1995, 120 000 jobs were lost at the company in a series of lay-offs and restructuring. Most of these were among blue-collar and service staff and even as late as 1996 the company employed over 300 000 persons and the bulk of the white-collar workers had been employed by the company for 15 years or more. However, between 1995 and 1998 a further 50 000 jobs were either reclassified or cut. The vast bulk of these were in white-collar and sales areas. The shift from blue-collar to white-collar displacement was mirrored throughout corporate America.

The US Department of Labor's Displaced Workers Survey (1996) found that in the recession of 1981-82, 7.3 per cent of blue-collar workers with three or more years' job tenure were retrenched. For the same period a decade later (1991-92), blue-collar displacement was down to 5.2 per cent and has since fallen to 4.2 per cent in 1993-94. In contrast, the displacement of white-collar workers has consistently risen since 1981-82. The same pattern is mirrored in an examination of job displacement by industry. In the early 1980s nearly half of all displaced workers came from the manufacturing sector. By the mid-1990s this proportion dropped to roughly one in four. The bulk of displacement in the USA moved to other sectors including services, trade, finance, insurance and real estate (US Department of Labor, 1999c). Part of this shift in displacement rates is explained by the continuing decline in manufacturing as an employer of labour. In the USA, manufacturing now accounts for only half the share of employment it did in 1970. Currently, within goods producing industries, only construction is predicted to increase its share of employment whereas manufacturing itself is expected to lose 350 000 jobs between 1996 and 2006. This pattern of adjustment is being repeated throughout the world. The significance of these adjustments in labour force size and composition to the spread of non-standard work is twofold. Firstly, non-standard employment is being used as a means of allowing the firm to fulfil its output functions while at the same time continuing to downsize its core workforce. The initial wave of downsizing was to reduce the labour force in an absolute way; subsequent workforce adjustment has been designed to rearrange the core competencies of the company. For this reason, downsizing of one group now exists side by side with increased hiring among other groups, particularly non-standard workers (Cappelli, 1999).

In the last six years of the 1990s, 19 million net new jobs were added to the US economy. The bulk of these were in service and other growth industries and a significant proportion were non-standard. Fallick (1999) found that employment growth was concentrated in industries in which part-time work was fairly common. Furthermore he found a positive association between the growth rate of an industry and the proportion of its workforce that worked part-time between the early 1980s and 1990s.[2] A similar association between the employment growth rates and the propensity to hire non-standard employees has been observed in seven other countries. These data are shown in Table 3.1.

Table 3.1 Correlation between employment growth and the prevalence of part-time work in seven countries: various years from 1979-94

Country	Years	N	Unweighted (Pearson)	Weighted	Spearman rank
Australia	1981-89	10	0.74 (0.01)	0.58 (0.08)	0.82 (0.01)
Canada	1987-94	12	0.27 (0.40)	0.27 (0.39)	0.50 (0.10)
Israel	1979-92	6	0.40 (0.43)	0.36 (0.49)	0.43 (0.40)
Netherlands	1983-91	8	0.87 (0.01)	0.91 (0.01)	0.67 (0.07)
Sweden	1981-92	25	0.47 (0.02)	0.43 (0.03)	0.39 (0.05)
Taiwan	1981-91	8	-0.22 (0.60)	-0.22 (0.60)	-0.19 (0.65)
UK	1979-86	28	0.18 (0.35)	0.25 (0.20)	0.34 (0.08)

Note:
level of significance shown in parentheses.

Source: Fallick (1999, p. 24).

Although there is some variation, the results across these seven countries suggest that a positive relationship between the rate of employment growth and the propensity to employ part-time workers does exist. In those countries with similar economies to the USA like Australia, Canada, the Netherlands, Sweden and the UK the results are (in the majority of cases) either significantly positive at the 5 per cent level or are verging on being positive and have the correct sign.

3.2   FLEXIBLE FIRM THEORY

Technical change and the world-wide emergence of new economic powers, particularly in South East Asia, over the last two decades has meant that labour force skills in Western economies have dated more quickly than in previous generations. To cope with these changes many firms began to adopt, or at least explore, the concept of the flexible firm. The term is associated with the work of Piore and Sable (1985) and Atkinson and Meager (1986). Under this theory, firms consciously divide their workforce into core and non-core (peripheral groups) in a manner similar to the division between traditional and non-standard workers. Their aim is to achieve 'enhanced levels of flexibility in hiring and firing, numbers of hours worked, job demarcations and worker remuneration' (Felstead and Jewson, 1999, p. 4). One reason for this was the much more rapid dating of worker skills in an era of technological change. Long-term and specifically trained employees had became negative cost factors to their employers rather than, as previously thought, a continuing source of returns on investment. As a result, the flexible firm theory also became associated with flattened managerial structures, team working and process innovation.

Despite its superficial plausibility, in terms of the apparent changes in management action and attitudes, critics of the flexible firm idea claim that it lacks sufficient generality to be called a theory principally because it has little in the way of consistent empirical support. Pollert (1988, 1991) points out that the theory is based upon a limited sample of small firms and Hunter et al. (1993) failed to find evidence of any general plan throughout industry for management to subdivide their workforce in such a clear-cut way. A more plausible scenario is that planning horizons for firms have simply become shorter than can be easily accommodated within the span of an individual career (Cappelli, 1999). Firms now tend to think in terms of the completion of discrete tasks rather than maintenance of a consistent flow of product from any one staff member. Once the firm became task-(output)-specific the role of inputs such as labour took on a different meaning and one well suited to the increased use of non-standard workers. This, broadly, is the view of Cappelli (1999). His book, *The New Deal at Work*, lists the main parameters of the new corporate thinking on employment and labour force management. These are:

- Job security for all workers has declined and become contingent upon performance.
- Middle management, in particular has gone from the most to the least secure employees.
- Employability is the only real source of worker security.

- Companies worry less about developing skills and tend to hire services from outside.
- For general skills firms rely, in part, on temporary workers or a pool of workers that they hire on a short-term basis.
- Pay is less secure and performance based.
- Seniority plays less of a role in determining pay.
- Entire functions and departments are routinely contracted out.
- Often former employees become contractors.

Within this new framework non-standard workers are essential because they can be hired on a needs basis and therefore provide the necessary numerical flexibility. But do they represent a cheaper alternative to traditional workers?

3.3   ON-COSTS AND EMPLOYMENT LEGISLATION

It is frequently argued that costs imposed by governments through payroll and other taxes and the potential threat of litigation from employment protection legislation have led employers to move away from traditional forms of employment or to hire workers for shorter periods (Burchell et al. 1999). For example, under current legislation in the UK an employee must complete two years' continuous service with the same employer to qualify for employment protection and redundancy eligibility. The recent DTI White Paper on Fairness at Work has suggested that the qualifying period should be reduced to one year to avoid some current abuses. Unfortunately, to this point, most of the discussion on the impacts of this type of legislation is speculative. While any form of potentially punitive government legislation is unlikely to encourage traditional employment, there are at present no empirical estimates of the relative importance of this form of legislation in the employment decision or its role in encouraging the spread of non-standard employment.

More effort has been spent on quantifying labour on-costs and how these differ between standard and non-standard workers. In the USA, most emphasis has been placed on measuring the differences between the two groups in terms of their respective access to employer-funded health care cover and retirement plans. Lettau and Buchmueller (1999) argue that significant differences in on-costs between standard and non-standard workers exist only for health cover. However Hipple (1998) and Copeland et al. (1999) find that a large percentage of non-standard workers are also excluded from participating in employer-sponsored retirement plans. Some of their results are set out in Table 3.2.

Table 3.2 Per cent of workers in the USA with health insurance and pension coverage by work arrangements, 1997

Health and pension status		Type of work arrangement				
	Traditional	Contingent	On-call	Temp agency	Contract company	Independent contractor
Health insurance from any source	83	67	67	46	82	73
Employer-provided health (receiving)	61	22	20	7	50	3
Pension coverage from any source	50	16	19	4	36	37
Employer-provided pension coverage (receiving)	48	16	19	4	36	14

Source: Cited in US Department of Labor (1999b) and based upon work by Hipple (1998), Cohany (1999) and Copeland et al. (1999).

The data in Table 3.2 confirms an earlier 1996 US Department of Labor survey of 500 workers that found that the per-employee cost of wages plus benefits was considerably lower for non-traditional workers, especially on-call workers (US Department of Labor, 1999c).

The main reason for this was that these workers were largely ineligible for employer-provided retirement and health care benefits. As may be seen in Table 3.2, only 7 per cent of temp agency workers and 20 per cent of on-call workers received employer-funded health care. In addition only a small minority of non-traditional workers participated in pension schemes. Results such as these are repeated in most other countries. It will be remembered from Chapter 2 that in Australia the lack of employer-funded benefits is the major criterion in determining the legal status of a worker. In that country many non-standard workers do not receive sick or holiday pay, and are not covered by employer-sponsored health cover.[3] However, recent legislation has ensured that all workers earning over a certain weekly wage now receive employer contributions to a national superannuation irrespective of job status. A number of other demand-side factors behind the increase in non-standard work have been put forward.

3.4   TECHNICAL CHANGE

Changes in technology are often cited as a major factor in the increased use of non-standard workers. Changes in technology are seen as providing both the incentive and the means for facilitating non-traditional work, particularly when this work is located off-site. For example, technologies suitable for outsourcing have provided for the expansion of home employment for clerical workers (Brosnan and Thornthwaite, 1994). Technology has also led to a blurring of job demarcation and allowed for centralisation of administration across large geographical distances. The size of technological change in some industries may be seen from recently released Canadian data. The Board of Trade in Canada estimates that technology purchases by Canadian firms rose by 80 per cent in real value over the six-year period 1986 to 1992. Baldwin et al. (1995) found that the percentage of manufacturing establishments in Canada using advanced technologies rose from 15 per cent in 1985 to 48 per cent in 1989. Many believe that the impact of technical change on work structures was greatly exacerbated because it coincided with economic recession and unprecedented competition in the product market (Krahn, 1995). A striking example of the pace of technical change and innovation is the computer industry. By 2006 the US Bureau of Labor predicts that nearly half of all US workers will be in industries that produce or intensively use information technology (IT). However, the tasks carried out by these workers will bear little resemblance to the tasks performed at IBM, RCA, Honeywell or Univac less than 50 years before. The average life of the PC from introduction to obsolescence has decreased from four-and-a-half years in 1992 to three years in 1999 and is predicted to be two years in 2006. Moore's Law (after the founder of Intel) holds that the processing power of microchips doubles every 18 months (Atkinson and Court, 1998). This increased power is one of the driving forces behind the rapid introduction of the Internet. It has taken only seven years for regular Internet usage to be a feature of work for 30 per cent of the US working-age population. This compares with diffusion rate (for the same percentage) of 17 years for the television and 38 years for the telephone (Atkinson and Court, 1998). Considerable debate surrounds the overall jobs' impact of such rapid technical change. Less controversial is its effect in escalating the cycle of job growth, destruction and creation and the impact this has on traditional job careers. It is now estimated that the peak earnings of a recently trained IT specialist will be within six years of his or her graduation. After that they will need to retrain or face obsolescence. In this industry neither the company nor the individual are seeking long-term commitments. Certainly the IT industry is at the sharp end of technical change and it is possible to overemphasise the immediate impact rapid technical change will have in other industries by using this example. However, as predicted in the publication US Department of Labor (1999a) the new technology is flexible and this is particularly suited to the use of non-traditional workers.

3.5   NON-STANDARD WORK AS A SCREENING DEVICE

A number of recent studies have suggested that employers are regularly taking on workers under non-traditional arrangements as a precursor to offering them permanent employment (Ferber and Waldfogel, 1996; Blau et al., 1998). One reason for this caution, potentially punitive employment protection legislation, has already been discussed in the context of the UK. Similarly, Houseman and Polivka (1998) have highlighted the large number of lawsuits brought by dismissed employees in the USA and argue that these induce employers to use non-standard employment as a means of screening workers before making a final commitment. It is difficult to tell how central the screening aspect is to the decision to use non-standard employment in preference to traditional employment. In many cases the initial employment decision, for example, the employment of a temp agency worker, may be for reasons unrelated to screening. Any subsequent shift in employment status is simply the result of the individual being in the right place at the right time to take advantage of a different job offer with the same firm. However, the scenario where permanent employment follows a period of non-standard employment happens with such regularity that it is unlikely to be purely accidental. For example, UK survey data suggest that 68 per cent of those who employ temporary staff have gone on to appoint at least one temporary employee to a permanent position (Atkinson et al., 1996). In the USA, Segal and Sullivan (1997) and Houseman and Polivka (1998) found frequent transfers from non-standard to permanent employment among clerical temp agency staff. This suggests that the screening may be both ways, with employees using their temp agency placements as a means of selecting a preferred employer. Evidence on the relative importance of screening in the employment of non-standard workers is provided by the Upjohn Institute employer survey. This survey found that, among firms that used non-standard workers, 21 per cent used temp agency contracts as a means of screening potential staff and 15 per cent used part-time work for the same purpose. This suggests that screening is an important reason for the use of non-standard employment. However, it is not the major demand-side reason. The same survey reported 55 per cent of employers used direct hire temporaries primarily for seasonal needs and 69 per cent used them to fill in for absent employees. A summary of the results found by the Upjohn Institute survey outlining the reasons for the increased use of alternative work arrangements is shown in Table 3.3.

The results in Table 3.3 are interesting and open to a range of interpretations. For example while only 24.2 per cent of those using temp help agencies claimed that this was for screening purposes, a further 25.8 per cent claimed that these workers were used as part of business expansion. This raises the question as to whether these workers would remain temps or were they in effect being screened for future employment? The results also show that contracting out is almost entirely driven by competitive pressures to reduce labour costs (40 per cent), business expansion (30.5 per cent) and the inability to compete by any other means (26.3 per cent). The need for increased flexibility is the major driver in the use of part-timers (52.0 per cent) and on-call workers (50.0 per cent). Corporate restructuring or mergers does not register as a major factor in the use of non-standard workers of any kind.

Table 3.3 Reasons for increased use of flexible workers in the USA

	Per cent responding that the increase was partly due to:				
	Temps	Short-term hires	Part-time workers	On-call workers	Contract out
Screen candidates for permanent jobs	24.2	3.3	-	-	-
Fluctuations in workload	37.1	40.0	52.0	57.7	-
Competitive pressure to reduce labour costs	3.2	16.7	15.3	11.5	40.0
Corporate restructuring or merger	4.8	13.3	3.1	7.7	5.3
Increased on-costs for regular workers	1.6	6.7	12.2	3.9	-
Greater use of family medical leave by regulars	9.7	6.7	-	-	-
Difficulty finding qualified workers	37.1	-	-	-	-
Business expansion	25.8	50.0	48.0	50.0	30.5
Business contraction	4.8	13.3	6.1	3.9	5.3
Changes in hours of operation	-	-	9.2	-	-
Introduction of new machinery or equipment	-	-	-	2.0	7.7
Inability to compete on price, quality or market position	-	-	-	-	26.3
Sample size	62	30	98	26	95

Source: Adapted from an Upjohn Institute Survey cited in Houseman and Polivka (1998, table 3, p. 32).

3.6   SUPPLY FACTORS

There is strong evidence that demand-side factors have been important in the growth of non-standard employment. However, the success of this demand pressure is, in part, dependent on finding receptive pockets of the labour supply (Thurman and Tran, 1990). A number of groups currently exist in the labour market that are particularly susceptible to non-standard working arrangements. Females with family responsibilities are the most easily identified group (Romeyn, 1992). It is well known that female participation rates, particularly among married females, have risen substantially since the 1970s. However, what is less known is the high correlation between increased female participation and their propensity to work in non-standard, particularly part-time, employment. According to the International Labour Office (ILO) the two driving forces in the development of part-time employment are the increased labour market participation by women, which they predict will continue to expand in industrialised economies until at least 2006, and employers' demand for flexibility (ILO, 1997a). Another reason in countries such as Germany, Belgium, France and the UK has been direct measures, instituted by government, to subsidise part-time employment through tax relief or reduced social security contributions. This was done in France, for example, in response to rising unemployment and demands by French women for employment structures that enabled them to better combine work and family life (ILO, 1997b). Some argue that the apparent desire by women for part-time and other non-standard work in preference to traditional work may be illusory. Faced with family and other societal pressures, part-time or other forms of non-standard work may have been their only feasible option (Rubery, 1994). That notwithstanding, there is no doubt that women dominate, numerically, part-time and other forms of non-standard employment (except independent contracting) and have done so for over two decades.

The data in Table 3.4 show that in most selected countries the bulk of female employment is part-time and in countries such as the UK, Germany, Austria and Belgium, part-time work accounts for over 80 per cent of total female employment. Turkey was the only one of the selected countries where men made up a higher proportion of part-time workers than women, although the proportion of males and females who made up part-time workers in Mexico was approximately even.

Consideration of the US labour force reinforces the picture of women providing the initial supply stimulus for the growth in non-standard employment. Since 1967 the percentage of women participating in the labour force has increased by nearly 50 per cent from 41 per cent to 60 per cent. Seventy per cent of those women work for the whole of the working year. At the same time the participation rate for males has declined from 80 per cent to 75 per cent (US Department of Labor, 1999b). The initial burst in female participation was largely confined to women without children or whose children had grown up. Recent trends, however, indicate that the attraction, or necessity, for labour force participation has reached many working mothers. In the USA, the proportion of working mothers with children under six rose faster than the proportion of all women in the workforce. For example, the number of working married women with children increased by 84 per cent between 1969 and 1996 (US Department of Labor, 1999a). Naturally many of these are attracted to non-standard work. But even here there are growing social and other concerns as the more favoured forms of non-standard work dry up and are replaced by more intrusive and less predictable forms. Concern has recently been expressed over the amount of informal child care

Table 3.4 Proportion of women in part-time employment: selected years

Country	1973	1993	1996
Australia	79.4	75.3	73.4
Austria	85.8	89.7	84.2
Belgium	82.4	89.3	87.4
Canada	68.4	68.9	69.1
Czech Republic	-	70	-
Denmark	-	74.9	72.2
Finland	-	63.7	64.3
France	82.3	83.3	81.7
Germany	89	88.6	87.4
Greece	-	61.6	-
Hungary	-	-	72.3
Iceland	-	80.4	78.9
Ireland	-	71.7	73.3
Italy	58.3	70.5	69.4
Japan	70.0	67.7	68.0
Luxembourg	87.5	-	88.0
Mexico	-	45.4	51.9
Netherlands	-	75.7	73.8
New Zealand	72.3	74.2	74.3
Norway	76.4	80.5	79.3
Poland	-	-	57.2
Portugal	-	66.3	67.2
Spain	-	75.6	74.5
Sweden	-	81.3	79.5
Switzerland	-	82.5	82.8
Turkey	-	50.2	48.3
UK	90.9	84.5	81.3
USA	66.0	66.2	67.9

Source: ILO (1997a, p. 16).

that parents are required to rely on to service irregular employment (The Families and Work Institute, 1997).

While women make up the bulk of the labour supply for non-standard jobs, men are entering non-standard employment in increasing numbers. They make up, for example, the majority of independent contractors; over 65 per cent in Japan, Australia, Canada and the UK and the USA. These are the best paid and most secure of non-traditional workers and in the main prefer their current positions to traditional employment. However, several other sections of the male population, at both ends of the age spectrum, are being drawn into non-standard employment. These are retirees from traditional jobs and young males that are using non-standard employment as a means of entry into the labour market. Herz (1995) found a high proportion of male early retirees in the USA re-entered the workforce through part-time or temporary work. Some of his results are summarised in Table 3.5.

Table 3.5 Percentage of male retirees re-entering the US workforce in non-standard employment by age, 1993

Age	Percent of retirees who re-entered	Percent re-entering in non-standard jobs
50	18	42
50-54	73	12
55-61	49	26
62-64	24	41
65-69	19	51
70 years+	9	60

Source: adapted from Herz (1995, p. 15).

For all, except those aged 50-54 years, non-standard employment was a major means of re-entering the workforce, particularly for those aged 60 years and over. This trend is likely to continue as well-qualified employees leave employment or are retrenched prematurely from traditional jobs.

At the other end of the age spectrum, young men are turning to non-standard employment as a means of gaining workforce experience and entry to the traditional job ladder. Those aged 15-24 make up a disproportionate share of contingent workers in the USA and casual workers in Australia. Almost all surveys of non-standard workers have revealed a bias towards younger workers. For example, Cohany reports 'one of the more striking features of temporary help agency workers is their youth. The male temps were even younger than the female temps with nearly one third between the ages of 20 and 24' (Cohany, 1998, p. 37). By comparison less than 15 per cent of the traditional workforce are in this age group. A similar bias towards younger workers is found among employees of contract firms in the USA.

One reason for this is the attempt by younger workers to use non-traditional work as a means of gaining entry into the traditional labour market. Conspicuous among this group are recent college graduates. Wooden reports that the secondary labour market is becoming a major port of labour market entry for young graduates and that, on average, they may go through four to five non-standard jobs before finding a job of choice (Dusseldorp Skills Forum, 1998). In a similar vein, Hecker (1992) found that college graduates were being forced to lower their expectations to find work. Using occupational and demographic data from the CPS he estimated that by 1990 20 per cent of graduates in North America were either unemployed or employed in jobs requiring only high school skills. These underemployed graduates provide a ready supply of labour for non-traditional employment, particularly self-employment.[4] The other part of the youth labour market with a high preference for non-standard work is the student population. Empirical evidence recently released in Canada testifies to the special attraction this group finds for non-standard work. For example, 85 per cent of jobs held by students are part-time compared with 20 per cent for all persons in the typical student age group. This should come as no surprise as the shorter hours and greater flexibility offered by many non-standard jobs are ideal for students to combine with their studies (Canadian Labour Ministry, 1997, p. 21).

The final group for which non-standard work holds a particular attraction are marginalised workers who are prevented by lack of skill, education or for legal reasons from holding traditional jobs. This group may include:

- The long-term unemployed, who often progress from unemployment to atypical working arrangements.
- Migrants, particularly women, who prefer to work off-site for cultural reasons.
- Illegal immigrants seeking to remain anonymous.
- Multiple job-holders.
- Those seeking cash-only employment.

It might be thought that the long-term unemployed would seek to use non-standard employment as a convenient port of re-entry into the labour market. However, the available empirical evidence finds that the long-term unemployed are not a major source of labour for non-traditional employment. Most new entrants into non-traditional jobs are either new entrants to the labour market or short-term unemployed anxious to re-enter the workforce (US Department of Labor, 1996; Lin et al., 1999).

3.7 INSTITUTIONAL FACTORS

The last two decades have also seen an easing of restrictive labour laws in some countries and this has had the effect of aiding the growth of non-standard work. During this time almost all labour markets have deregulated, which in turn has come to mean an easing of employment protection legislation, watering down of minimum wage agreements and a reducing union influence in working conditions and wage outcomes (Gregory, 1996; Clinton, 1997). Not all of these factors were directly targeted to assist the spread of non-standard work but they have fostered a climate of greater labour market flexibility. The survey on Flexible and Shift Schedules (US Department of Labor, 1997) reported that in May 1997, 25 million full-time workers had flexible work schedules and this represented a 28 per cent increase on the estimate for 1991. In less market-orientated labour markets than the USA, specific legislation has been brought in to free up the market and promote non-standard employment, at least implicitly. Two good examples of this are Spain and Australia. Both of these countries have high levels of non-standard employment which in part have been encouraged by legislative change. In Australia, rulings by the Industrial Relations Commission have been cited as a major reason for increased non-standard employment. Brosnan and Thornthwaite (1994) argue that since 1987 the Industrial Relations Commission has made a series of rulings which have supported employer demands to introduce non-standard working arrangements. They highlight rulings establishing managerial control over structural efficiency in 1988 (Rimmer and Zappala, 1988) and, in particular, the amendment to Structural Efficiency Principle in 1989, which specifically required the parties (unions and employers) to introduce greater flexibility in relation to working hours (Bray, 1991). It was noted in Chapter 2 that Spain has a disproportionately high number of fixed-term contractors. Previously, during the Franco regime, while trade unions were banned, workers were granted extensive employment protection through rigid rules of entry and exit (Cousins, 1999). The legacy of this system remains with core workers protected by very high redundancy provisions. In reaction to this legislation and the entry of Spain into the mainstream European economy, employers pushed for the sanctioning of non-standard forms of employment. This has been progressively achieved through a series of amendments to the Workers' Statute Act in 1980, 1984 and 1994 (Rogowski and Schoman, 1996). The 1984 legislation, for example, allowed fixed-term contracts of six months' duration to be able to be extended for a period of three years. The net result has been a major expansion in fixed-term employment in preference to permanent employment both through choice and through fear of the prohibitive cost of dismissing unwanted core employees (Cousins, 1999). Admittedly, institutional change will normally only act to facilitate pent-up demand-side and/or supply-side pressure. However it is likely that the role of institutional change in Australia went beyond that of a background factor. In this particular case much of the impetus for change came from the Federal Government which saw labour market deregulation as an essential part of their overall strategy to deregulate the economy (Gregory, 1996).

3.8   CONCLUDING REMARKS

The chapter has argued that the rise in non-standard employment has been facilitated by a combination of demand-side and supply-side factors that have been, in the main, accompanied by complementary changes in institution arrangements in labour markets. On the demand-side, the growth in global competition and the rate of change in technology has created a climate where labour market flexibility, especially numerical flexibility, has made firms pay particular attention to their human resource policies. The US Bureau of Labor describes the current situation as 'the age of just in time production giving rise to the just-in-time worker' (US Department of Labor, 1999b, p. 7). This is an overstatement. While many firms are keen to avoid being caught with excess labour supplies during down times there is little evidence of any widespread attempt to implement the 'flexible-firm' syndrome with its rigidly defined core and disposable workers. In most of the countries at least 70-75 per cent of workers are still in traditional employment and the total percentage, although not necessarily the groups involved, has not changed dramatically in recent years. However, the days of excess workers being kept as a form of spare capacity or quasi-fixed factors of production are long gone.

The economics of employment have changed. Flexibility requirements dictate that most firms will require at least some level of non-traditional employment. For each individual firm this will vary with size, type of productive process, the nature of the product(s) sold and the competitive environment in which they operate. Cappelli (1999) has shown that, among large- and medium- sized firms, the operational planning phase has shortened to be well below the average working life of most employees. This leads firms to hedge their bets by introducing fixed-term and other non-standard work as a significant, but not dominant, part of their workforce strategy in much the same way as an investor divides his portfolio between blue-chip and speculative shares. Smaller firms are more attracted to the potential for cost savings offered up by non-traditional employment or fearful of the legal implications of hiring traditional workers. There is considerable evidence now that suggests that non-traditional employment is an important entry or re-entry point into the labour market with employers becoming increasingly aware of its value as a screening device. However, the success of much of this demand-side pressure is dependent upon having an available labour supply and a set of institutional arrangements that facilitate the growth of non-standard employment. A number of groups in the labour market either actively seek non-standard employment or gravitate towards it through circumstance or lack of choice. It is no coincidence that the initial growth of non-standard employment coincided with the rise in female participation, particularly by married women. The casual direction is not clear cut but females continue to make up the bulk of non-standard employment. Other distinct groups have been attracted to non-standard employment including students, new entrants to the labour market and early (predominantly male) retirees.

The reasons for choosing non-standard work vary across these groups. Most of these reasons relate to time-management and the need to juggle conflicting social responsibilities. The relative importance of demand- and supply-side factors in the growth of non-standard employment is a topic which is still heavily debated and is essentially an empirical question. The difficulties in untangling the prime determinants of an individual's choice of work are considerable, even within the same form of non-standard work. For example, in the area of part-time work, much would hinge upon the form of part-time work undertaken. Tilly (1991) found considerable dualism in part-time employment in the USA between 'retention' part-time jobs and secondary part-time jobs. Retention jobs are located in the primary labour market and are designed by employers to retain or attract valued workers who prefer to work part-time. Secondary part-time jobs are placed in a secondary labour market environment for the express purpose of lowering wages and increasing labour market flexibility. Tilly's view is that in secondary, part-time work which he sees as essentially demand-side-determined, predominates and that workers are either involuntary part-time workers or are voluntary only in the sense that other restrictions on their time or availability make their current style of unemployment unavoidable.

> In aggregate, critics of part-time work are substantially correct: Secondary part-time jobs greatly outnumber retention part-time jobs (Tilly, 1991, p. 331).

Similarly, Larson and Ong (1994), using US data, argue that the dominance of involuntary part-time work was constraining the overall growth in part-time employment, as workers became increasingly reluctant to accept such conditions.

In Australia the debate has been more divided. Robertson (1989) argued that while voluntary part-time work was the predominate form of part-time work in Australia, the ratio of involuntary to voluntary was increasing and that a shortage of full-time jobs was pushing people into 'bad' part-time jobs. This is disputed by Sadler and Ungles (1990) who argued that voluntary part-time work was still predominate by a ratio of three to one. Much of the debate depends upon how the labour force data concerning desired hours of work are interpreted and whether those who are reported as voluntary part-time workers are so constrained by family and other social pressures so that their current positions are tolerated rather than desired. In the following chapter, empirical evidence into the factors leading to non-standard employment is investigated.

NOTES

[1] The teamsters-led strike in the US Postal Service in 1997 is a good example of widespread opposition in the USA among blue-collar workers to changed working conditions.

[2] Fallick did inject a note of caution into these results by raising the possibility that they may be heavily dependent upon the timing of the study. For example, no such observed correlation existed before the 1980s. As a result, he was reluctant to suggest that this pattern would necessarily continue after 1993.

[3] Membership in an employer-funded health scheme is not a major issue in the Australian context as all persons are covered by a national health scheme (Medicare) funded from tax contributions.

[4] The implication of Heckers' article was that the USA was producing an over-supply of graduates. This has been challenged in a later article by Tyler et al. (1995).

4. Empirical Evidence on the Determinants of Non-standard Employment

4.0 INTRODUCTION

In Chapter 3, the main theoretical arguments concerning the increased incidence of non-standard work were outlined and grouped within the convenient terms of demand-side and supply-side and institutional factors. It was argued that all these factors, both independently, but more often in unison, have assisted in the spread of non-standard employment. This chapter continues the investigation into determinants of non-standard employment by examining the available empirical evidence behind the growth in part-time, temporary and contract employment. This is an important task. The proper identification of the main causal factors that have led to the changes in employment is relevant in a social as well as an economic sense. Many see important social issues arising from the changed working conditions, particularly where these are imposed by demand-side pressures. They fear the destruction of worker protection and union influence and a possible return to male dominance in the labour market as females are pushed into the secondary labour market component of non-standard jobs. There appears less concern when the impetus comes from supply-side factors because these are often portrayed as examples of an efficient labour market responding to different social preferences, lifestyles and family responsibilities. However, to the institutions of government, unions and employer associations and educational bodies, who have the responsibility of managing labour market change, the extent of non-standardisation in employment patterns may be just as important as its causes. This is because of the legal and economic problems associated with atypical work. Rational public policy making requires that knowledge be built up concerning the fundamental drivers of the current labour market changes.

Given the disparate nature of non-standard employment, it is likely that there is no set of explanatory factors generally applicable to all forms of non-standard employment. The factors that motivate the work choices of an SEC will differ from those that motivate or direct the work choices of a contingent part-time worker. Nevertheless, they both operate in the same broad labour market that, despite its many segmentations, is governed by the general laws of supply and demand. It is also likely that there is a commonality in causal factors across a range of different countries. It has been shown in earlier chapters that there is a considerable amount of descriptive data concerning the extent of non-standard employment. Less work has been done into the determinants of these employment changes. One reason for this is that the issues surrounding non-standard work tend to be caught up with and, in some cases, subsumed by broader discussions concerning the future of work and the economics of downsizing. Non-standard employment does play a significant role in both of these areas but it is also an important labour market factor in its own right. The decision by an individual to seek a non-standard job or by a company to offer one does not fundamentally threaten the future of work or interrupt the flow of labour services. Rather, it is a realisation by at least one of the parties concerned that their interests are best served by changing the terms and conditions of the work relationship. In this sense, every non-standard job is the result of the interaction of demand and supply factors, but it is usually not an equal interaction. Normally one side will dominate the other. This chapter will investigate under what circumstances and for which forms of non-standard employment one set of factors is dominant. The issue of the direction of causation is crucial to understanding the process of non-standard employment and for predicting its likely future path. Towards this end, the chapter reviews some of the empirical work into this area as well as introducing some original research into the determinants of casual employment.

4.1   PART-TIME WORK

A standard means of differentiating between demand-side and supply-side pressures in the growth of part-time work has been to consult labour force data on hours of work preferences and to use that data to distinguish between voluntary and involuntary part-time workers (Robertson, 1989; Sadler and Ungles, 1990; Wooden, 1995). By definition, involuntary part-time work implies that the person has been forced into that form of employment by adverse demand conditions and that they would prefer a changed working relationship either through the provision of more hours or by a switch to full-time employment. The view expressed in most countries for the period of the 1970s and 1980s is that part-time work has been mainly of a voluntary nature, although with some cyclical increases in the number of involuntary part-time workers and underemployed part-time workers as the economy moved into recession. Robertson (1989) was among the first to openly question this prevailing view. He argued that half the growth in part-time employment between 1978-84 in Australia represented underemployment and for males, almost their entire involvement in part-time work was involuntary:

> For men the increase in part-time work was almost entirely involuntary and thus appears to be a consequence of job availability. Even for married women, 26.8 per cent of the rise in part-time jobs was involuntary (Robertson, 1989, p. 391).

He concluded, somewhat controversially, by suggesting that the rising proportion of part-time jobs was 'a trend towards pushing people into bad jobs since most part-time jobs have inferior earnings and working conditions' (Robertson, 1989, p. 397). Robertson's comments are very similar in content and conclusion to those of Tilly (1991) in his analysis of part-time employment trends in the USA during the late 1980s. However, Sadler and Ungles (1990) strongly disputed these findings and instituted a debate on the nature of part-time employment in the pages of the *Australian Bulletin of Labour*. The Sadler and Ungles paper used decomposition methods to analyse the demand-side contributions to part-time employment in Australia over the period 1978-89, a longer time period than that used by Robertson. In terms of the voluntary/involuntary nature of the growth in part-time unemployment, they concluded:

> It seems very doubtful that the growth of part-time employment has been the result of a substantial shift of persons into unwanted part-time jobs. Rather, many people have quite happily taken up part-time jobs and many more would have done so if given the chance (Sadler and Ungles, 1990, p. 295).

This divergence of opinion over essentially the same data indicates not only different styles of analysis but also the limited capacity of standard labour force data to provide a complete picture of worker preferences. This is particularly true because such data fail to take into account the other factors influencing work-hours' preferences. For example, a person may be satisfied with present working arrangements only because current circumstances prevent them from undertaking any other form of work. Rubery raised this issue in her analysis of UK data on female participation and part-time work:

> There is little evidence to suggest that working time for women is voluntary in the sense of being arranged to fit with domestic constraints and women's preferences, except with the respect of total hours worked. Requirements for flexibility and for unsociable working hours suggest greater influence from the demand-side. The requirements and preferences of workers enter mainly through their choice between different jobs within the economy and not in

determining directly the hours arrangements within specific jobs (Rubery, 1994, p. 388).

Rubery's arguments suggest that the simple preferred hours question used by the ABS and other national statistical agencies should be modified to examine the real elements of choice facing the part-time worker. However, even this imperfect source of preferred hours data are indicating a growth in dissatisfaction with part-time work.

Table 4.1 Hours of work: preferences for part-time workers in Australia, 1975-95

Hours' preferences	1975	1985	1995
Voluntary part-time (%)	89.2	83.7	74
Involuntary part-time (%)	10.8	16.3	26

Source: Wooden (1995, p. 191).

The data in Table 4.1 show that those classified as involuntary part-time workers have more than doubled in relative importance since 1975 from 10.8 per cent in 1975 to 26.0 per cent in 1995. A similar trend has been identified within most OECD countries and the results for these countries are shown in Table 4.2. However, in this table the results are reported as a percentage of the economically active, rather than as a percentage of total part-time employment.

The data in Table 4.2 show that in most countries there has been a significant increase in involuntary part-time employment, particularly in Australia, New Zealand, Canada and the UK. One reason for this is the increasing use of non-standard jobs as entry-level positions. This is the argument used by Fallick (1999). He examined the relationship between employment growth rates and the ratio of involuntary part-time work to total part-time work in two-digit industries in the USA over the period 1983-93. While he found no strong overall link between the rate of growth and the proportion of involuntary workers, the opposite was the case among young workers aged 16-24 years. For these age groups the correlations indicate:

- Industries with higher accession rates have tended to employ a greater proportion of involuntary part-timers among those part-timers they hire; and
- Industries with higher growth rates in the age groups likely to be associated with entry-level career-track jobs have tended to employ a higher ratio of involuntary to voluntary part-timers.

Table 4.2 Involuntary part-time workers as a percentage of the economically active population, 1983 and 1993

Country	1983	1993
Australia	3.0	6.9
Belgium	2.4	3.8
Canada	3.9	5.5
Denmark	3.4	4.6
Finland	2.0	2.9
France	-	4.8
Germany	0.0	1.5
Greece	3.7	7.1
Ireland	2.3	3.3
Italy	2.0	2.3
Japan	2.1	1.9
Mexico	-	5.2
Netherlands	5.7	5.6
New Zealand	2.7	6.3
Portugal	1.6	1.8
Spain	2.0	1.0
Sweden	4.7	6.2
UK	1.9	3.2
USA	5.7	5.0

Source: ILO (1997a, p. 16).

Results such as this support the now widely held view that many entry-level jobs are both non-standard and being deliberately used by management as a screening device.

Another potential indicator of the trends in the causation of part-time work may be seen in the changing characteristics of part-time workers. The age and sex characteristics of some involuntary part-time workers are shown in Table 4.3. The data show that the incidence of involuntary part-time employment is more pronounced among males particularly prime-aged males (age 25-44 years), although prime-aged females are also well represented among the involuntary part-time employed. Age and marital status appear important considerations in the case of females. Among young single females, many of whom would be in full-time education, and married women over 25 years' part-time work is the preferred form of employment. For older women, single prime-aged women and young women, though most are willing to work part-time, a significant number are involuntary part-time workers.

Despite these indications of a growth in the involuntary nature of part-time work, it must be stressed that the data in Table 4.1 indicated that over 75 per cent of part-time workers were voluntary and therefore supply-side determined. However, it is clear that involuntary (demand-side determined) part-time work is on the increase, particularly among prime-aged males and entry-level workers.[1] The question then becomes why are so many persons, particularly women, apparently so willing to accept part-time jobs?

Table 4.3 Age and sex characteristics of involuntary part-time workers

Category	%
Prime-aged male	54
Prime-aged single women	37
Prime-aged married women	18
Mature-aged men	27
Mature-aged single women	35
Mature-aged married women	13
Young men	35

Source: Wooden (1995, p. 192).

The need to accommodate family responsibilities is a major reason. Traditionally, the presence of children of school age has acted to reduce female participation. This is still true of female participation in full-time employment. However, the opposite is the case for female participation in part-time employment. Hagan and Mangan (1996a) used census unit record data to examine participation decisions in Queensland and Queensland regions. A Heckman two-step procedure was used in which probit regression explained the participation decision, and ordinary least squares (OLS) analysis was used to estimate the earnings function. In the latter case, the Mills inverse ratio, obtained as an output from the probit estimation, was added as a correction factor to allow for the selectivity bias that appears because earnings are observed only for those employed. Labour force participation is presented as a binary variable Y, taking the value of one if the person is participating and zero if they are not. That is:

$$Y = 1 \text{ if } Y^* = Z'\alpha + \varepsilon > 0$$
$$Y = 0 \text{ otherwise} \tag{4.1}$$

where Y^* is an unobservable variable reflecting the gap between market wages and reservation wages. It is assumed that participation occurs if the gap is positive. In addition, it is assumed that Y^* depends linearly on a vector of Z factors that influence the participation decision. The income function takes the form:

$$\ln W = X'\beta + \delta\lambda + \mu \tag{4.2}$$

where lnW is observed if $Y^* > 0$, W stands for income, X is a vector of factors that determine income, α and β are vectors of parameters, ε and μ are error terms, and λ is the Mills inverse ratio of the standard normal density function. The explanatory variables chosen were personal income, other family income, the number of school-aged, the number of non-dependent offspring, marital status, age, place of birth, educational qualifications, proficiency in English, industry and school-leaving age. The sample was divided into two samples and the equations run on both. In one sample, the binary choice was between participating full-time or not participating, and in the other sample the binary choice was between participating part-time or not participating.

Hagan and Mangan (1996a) found that female participation in a full-time basis was inversely related to the number of school-aged children. This is the traditional result for participation models. Conversely, female part-time participation was positively and significantly related to the number of school-aged children, indicating that for females (normally married females), the presence of school age children acts as a positive incentive to work part-time. The results, contrasting the differing motivations behind female full-time and part-time participation, are shown below in Table 4.4.

Table 4.4 Partial impacts of dependent children on female participation

Region	Full-time	Part-time
Queensland	-0.033**	0.021**
Brisbane	-0.047**	0.026**
Moreton	-0.021**	0.046**
North Queensland	-0.029	0.012

Note:
** indicates significant at 95 per cent level.

Source: Hagan and Mangan (1996a, p. 31).

Miller (1993) and Doirion (1997) found similar positive relationships between part-time work and the presence of school-aged children. The study by Dorian, in particular, reinforces the general picture of female participation in part-time employment as being predominantly supply-side-determined. She compared the growth of part-time work for both sexes in Canada and Australia. Probit regressions were used to model the dependence of the part-time/full-time status on personal, household, job characteristics as well as the level of non-wage income. According to Doirion:

Given the nature of the data, it is reasonable to interpret the effects of the variables on part-time status in the context of a labour supply relationship[2] (Doirion, 1997, p. 8).

Changes in industry mix and the nature of employment have also helped the growth in part-time employment and contributed heavily to its strong sex divide as well as its division by age, marital status and level of acceptability.

On this basis it is likely that, as the proportion of males employed part-time grows, so too will the extent of involuntary part-time work. The other strong conclusion about part-time work is that it increasingly does not fit the aspirations of prime-aged workers of either sex. Many of these have clearly been forced into part-time work by demand-side factors. In this sense, the behaviour of part-time work in the USA is being interpreted by some as increasingly demand-side-determined. Larson and Ong (1994), for example, claim from their analysis of the US labour market:

> We believe that despite increasing demand for part-time workers (due to the growth of service sector employment), a shrinking supply of part-time workers effectively constrains the growth of part-time work. This produces a secular rise in the involuntary part-time employment, which is a form of involuntary unemployment that is ignored in the calculation of the standard unemployment rate (Larson and Ong, 1994, p. 189).

Taken in the context of findings by Fallick (1999) reported earlier, this secular rise in involuntary part-time work is taking place among entry-level career-path jobs and primarily affecting young males.

If this is the case, it points towards greater demand-side-induced contingency coming into the incidence of non-standard work. An ideal place to investigate whether this is happening in other forms of non-standard employment is among casual workers in Australia.

4.2   DETERMINANTS OF CASUAL EMPLOYMENT

As noted in Chapter 2, casual employment, as defined in Australia, is a unique combination of a number of other forms of non-standard employment. It is also very widespread, covering approximately one-third of employees in the country. It is a mixture of full-time (about 20 per cent), part-time and temporary workers, collectively referred to as casual because of their lack of employer-funded benefits and legally supportable job tenure. This form of non-standard employment has flourished in Australia in the wake of the decline in the once dominant trade union influence and the removal of restrictive workplace legislation. Because of its contingent nature and high incidence among the Australian workforce, it has attracted considerable research interest (Simpson et al., 1997; Hawke and Wooden, 1998). Another unusual feature of casual employment in Australia is that it is growing most rapidly among males and may represent a forerunner of future trends in non-standard employment. For all these reasons, an investigation into the determinants of casual employment will provide a useful guide to non-standard employment trends in general, particularly those with a contingent aspect. Mangan and Williams (1999) have recently re-investigated the determinants of casual employment in Australia, extending earlier work in this area by the addition of variables reflecting spatial distribution, age, occupation and gender. Their research is described in Section 4.3.

4.3 MODEL SPECIFICATION AND DESCRIPTION OF VARIABLES

The nature of the data available for analysis of casual employment in Australia, particularly the relatively short time-series available, favours the use of data-pooling techniques that allow the analysis of several years of cross-section data. A number of different models have been proposed for pooled data regression. All these derive from the general regression model but vary according to assumptions made concerning the disturbance term. In most cases, the technique used is a one-way error component model of either the fixed effects or random effects type. In their study, Mangan and Williams (1999) used fixed effects model for a number of reasons.[3]

4.3.1 Description of Variables

To achieve maximum comparison with earlier studies, the variables chosen for the analysis coincide, where possible, with those used in earlier studies (Simpson et al., 1997) and also relate back to the discussion on casual employment raised in Chapters 2 and 3. For example, there are variables reflecting the relative importance of non-wage costs to total labour costs (Non-wage Costs); the proportion of firms in the industry employing less than 20 employees (Firm Size); the relative importance of private sector workers in the industry workforce (Private Sector); the proportion of employees in the industry that are union members (Union); the proportion of workers aged 20-25 years (Young Workers); the proportion of industry employees aged 55 years and over (Older Workers); and the ratio of employed females to employed males (Sex). All of these variables have been consistently raised as possible determinants in the growth of casual employment (Simpson, 1994).

As with most studies in the area of non-standard employment, data availability was a problem. Data on casual employment in Australia are available for eight years (from 1988-95) across 12 industry groups and six States, although some variables were not available for the whole period. For example, data on the non-wage cost variable are available only for 1990, 1991, 1992 and 1994, and union membership is only available biannually. Data on the full set of variables were only available for one year, 1991. Included in the explanatory variable matrix is a set of State dummy variables to assess whether there are differences between the States with regard to the proportion of casually employed in the workforce. Industry dummies are also included to test for the presence of unobserved factors that may be industry-specific. It was recognised that there may be some endogeneity problems with two of the above listed variables: Non-wage Costs and Union. Both variables were tested for endogeneity using a Hausman specification test (Hausman 1978). No simultaneity was found between Non-wage Costs. However, there was a clear indication of a contemporaneous correlation between the Union variable and the error term in the Percentage of Casual Employees (PCE) equation.[4] To avoid the potential problem of inconsistency in the parameter estimate for the Union variable, an instrumental variable (IV) approach was used to remove this simultaneity.[5] For this reason, Mangan and Williams (1999) provided two separate sets of results. The first refers to the OLS estimation of the casual employment equation, and the second relates to the IV-estimated equations. The results are set out in Table 4.5.

Using OLS estimation on the 72 observations available for the full variable set (only available for 1991), five of the eight key variables tested were found to be significant determinants of the incidence of casual employment and all of the coefficients had the anticipated signs (Equation 1). The results from this equation indicate that the incidence of casual employment within an industry is positively related to increases in the relative importance of non-wage costs, the percentage of private sector employees, the proportion of older employees and the relative proportion of women in the workforce, but is inversely related to the proportion of employees who are members of a union. In some cases, however, the performance of some variables is equation-specific. For example, the Non-Wage Costs variable loses significance in Equation 2, while the Young Worker variable gains significance in Equations 4 and 5.

There are significant differences between the incidence of casual employment between the States, with Queensland, South Australia and Tasmania having a higher proportion of casually employed: approximately 5 to 7 per cent more casually employed in these States than in New South Wales (NSW).[6] Limited differences occur between industries, with only Agriculture having a higher incidence of casual employment after allowing for the differences in all the other variables (18 percentage points above the average level for all industries). Finance Property and Business has a much lower incidence of casual employment than other industries (22 percentage points below the average). The results are shown to be sensitive to the model specification for the key Union variable. With IV estimation (Equation 2), the coefficient on the Union variable increases to -0.631 (more than doubling from -0.254). This larger coefficient is the consistent estimate of the effect of union membership on casual employment. Most other variables are relatively unaffected by the IV estimation.

To attempt to gain the potential benefit from pooling over time (only available if some variables are excluded), a two-step approach was followed. The variables for which incomplete data are available for all the time periods are Union and Non-wage Costs, where there is only one year of overlap (1991). However, by excluding alternately the other variable from the analysis, a period of four years is possible for pooling in each instance.[7] This procedure does run the risk of inducing omitted-variable bias, as both variables are significant in the 1991 equation. However, this does not seem to occur. A comparison of Equations 1, 3 and 4 shows only minor instability in the estimated coefficients for these variables. Overall, the coefficients of most variables are quite robust under both specifications, justifying the two-stage approach followed.

First, the Union variable was excluded from the analysis.[8] In the second stage, the Union variable replaced the Non-wage Cost variable and the analysis was repeated. As before, the model was estimated twice, the second time using IV estimation for the Union variable. The coefficients of most variables are quite robust under both specifications, justifying the two-stage approach followed. Allowing for the factors that are industry-specific and represented by the industry effects columns in Table 4.5, the following conclusions can be drawn.

A number of factors appear to promote an increase in the proportion of employees that are hired as casuals. For example, an increase of 10 per cent in the proportion of employees in the private sector will lead to a 2 per cent increase in the percentage of casuals. Similarly, a 10 per cent increase in the number of firms in an industry with less than 20 employees will increase the proportion of casual employment by between 1 and 3 per cent. Finally, both a 10 per cent increase in the proportion of female employees and in the ratio of non-wage costs to total labour costs will lead to an increase in the proportion of casual employees of between 3 and 4 per cent. Conversely, an increase of 10 per cent in the proportion of employees who are members of a union would lead to a reduction of around 3 and 6 per cent in the proportion of casual workers.

The industry effects are quite stable between Equations 3 and 4 and are of greater intensity than those shown in Equation 1. This reflects the gain in efficiency from the larger data set obtained through pooling. From Equations 3 and 4, casual employment is seen to be disproportionately high in Agriculture and disproportionately low in Finance, Property and Business. The State effects are robust over the alternative specifications, with three States experiencing a higher than average incidence of casual employment. Allowing for differences in the industrial structure between the States, the proportion of employees that are casually employed is 3 to 7 per cent higher in Queensland, South Australia and Tasmania. Mangan and Williams also compared their results with earlier studies and, while finding some overlaps, they found:

Table 4.5 Determinants of casual employment in Australia, 1988-97

Key variables		Model results*			
	Equation 1	Equation 2	Equation 3	Equation 4	Equation 5
Non-wage costs	0.386 (1.88)	0.175 (0.72)	0.323 (2.51)	Excluded	Excluded
Firm size	-0.034 (-0.37)	0.025 (0.27)	0.100 (2.17)	0.138 (3.12)	0.141 (3.14)
Private sector	0.212 (2.31)	0.254 (2.54)	0.205 (4.18)	0.193 (4.02)	0.203 (4.23)
Union	-0.254(-3.28)	-0.631(-3.33)	excluded	-0.081 (-2.32)	-0.330(-4.40)
Young workers	-0.058 (-0.22)	-0.306 (-1.10)	-0.079 (-0.68)	-0.234 (1.80)	-0.252 (-1.92)
Older workers	0.634 (2.99)	1.017 (3.41)	0.134 (1.59)	0.065 (0.69)	0.083 (0.85)
Sex	0.351 (2.46)	Excluded, used in IV	0.418 (5.20)	0.306 (3.25)	Excluded, used in IV
Unemployment	0.092 (0.48)	0.286 (1.43)	-0.087 (-1.14)	0.079 (1.02)	0.094 (1.21)
State dummies					
Queensland	0.050 (3.40)	0.057 (3.59)	0.045 (5.36)	0.022 (2.88)	0.027 (3.64)
Victoria	0.002 (0.16)	-0.004 (-0.24)	-0.006 (-0.71)	-0.018 (-2.34)	-0.016 (-2.06)
Western Australia	0.003 (0.22)	0.013 (0.81)	0.005 (0.60)	-0.016 (-2.01)	-0.009 (-1.18)
South Australia	0.065 (4.77)	0.058 (3.92)	0.049 (6.14)	0.038 (5.05)	0.039 (5.13)
Tasmania	0.071 (3.98)	0.037 (2.33)	0.036 (4.22)	0.013 (1.96)	0.012 (1.75)

Industry dummies					
Agriculture	0.185 (2.06)	0.251 (3.41)	0.287 (7.72)	0.355 (7.72)	0.473 (15.19)
Mining	-0.125 (-1.04)	0.107 (3.25)	-0.242 (-4.41)	-0.112 (-1.87)	0.049 (0.80)
Manufacturing	-0.199 (-1.46)	0.009 (0.08)	-0.262 (-4.00)	-0.136 (-1.92)	0.040 (0.64)
Electricity gas and water	-0.124 (-1.28)	0.181 (1.31)	-0.235 (-5.48)	-0.075 (-1.44)	0.141 (2.24)
Construction	0.024 (0.20)	0.176 (1.35)	-0.062 (-1.10)	0.022 (0.39)	0.161 (2.79)
Trade	-0.093 (-0.59)	0.119 (0.88)	-0.148 (-1.81)	-0.012 (-0.14)	0.171 (2.54)
Transport and storage	-0.044 (-0.41)	0.191 (1.55)	-0.158 (-3.06)	-0.031 (-0.53)	0.166 (2.86)
Communication	0.008 (0.10)	0.406 (2.86)	-0.137 (-4.07)	0.011 (0.24)	0.284 (4.89)
Finance property and business	-0.220 (-1.58)	0.016 (0.14)	-0.293 (-3.99)	-0.162 (-2.06)	0.043 (0.77)
Public administration	-0.036 (-0.41)	-0.158 (-4.09)	-0.158 (-4.09)	-0.008 (-0.15)	0.263 (5.44)
Community services	-0.126 (-0.91)	-0.283 (-4.01)	-0.283 (-4.01)	-0.112 (-1.32)	0.220 (4.81)
Recreation and personal	0.052 (0.31)	-0.025 (-0.3)	-0.025 (-0.30)	0.102 (1.16)	0.322 (5.08)
R^2	0.972	0.965	0.939	0.942	0.945
F	68.2 (24, 47)	58.7 (23,48)	171.2 (24,263)	186.4 (23,264)	187.4 (22,242)

Notes:
* t-statistics in parentheses.
Equation 1: OLS using full data set for 1991.
Equation 2: Instrumental variable estimation of Union variable.
Equation 3: OLS with Union variable excluded.
Equation 4: OLS panel estimation with Non-wage Cost variable excluded.
Equation 5: Instrumental variable estimation with Non-wage Cost variable excluded.

Source: Mangan and Williams (1999, p 13).

there are also some important differences that suggest that the relationship between casual employment and commonly used explanatory variables may be sensitive to both the period of estimation and the form of the model used (Mangan and Williams, 1999, p. 14).

This suggests to Mangan and Williams that a more promising approach in the study of non-standard employment would be to move away from the aggregate time-series or pooled models and concentrate upon the use of micro data of the type provided by firm-level surveys.

4.4   SELF-EMPLOYED/CONTRACTORS

It is in the context of self-employment and the causes of its growth that the arbitrary nature behind the demand-side/supply-side division becomes apparent (Acs et al., 1991). In Chapter 2, the extraordinary growth of contract self-employment in Canada was used as an example of the incidence of this form of non-standard employment. Two reasons were offered up as to why this may be occurring. The first related to the potential gains to the individual in terms of higher earnings, reduced tax, greater flexibility, personal freedom and higher job satisfaction. Those moving into self-employment for those reasons would be seen as supply-driven. The alternative point of view is that many of the new self-employed in Canada are there because they cannot find suitable job offers (Lin et al., 1999). In a sense, these are demand-driven or more correctly, lack-of-demand-driven. However, in contrast to the contingent or casual worker, who has accepted an unsatisfactory job because that is all that is available, this group have not been willing to do that and have moved into contract work and other forms of self-employment. In this sense, their move into self-employment is supply-determined. They have established a reservation level of wages, conditions and job prospects below which they will not enter the wage and salary job market that is different from the rest of the workforce. This could be for two reasons: either they differ from the rest of the workforce only in their reservation price and/or responses to economic downturn or, alternatively, they are qualitatively different from other workers, particularly non-standard workers, by virtue of more marketable skills[9].

These two rival explanations summarise, broadly, the main current areas of empirical research into the determinants of self-employment. Despite the interest in the growth in self-employment, actual empirical studies, apart from a listing of the characteristics, of the self-employed have been limited. Economic theories into the determinants of self-employment have tended to focus on either 'recession-push' theories (Holmes and Schmitz, 1990; Aronson, 1991) or the entrepreneurial-pull model (Taylor, 1966; Blanchflower and Oswald, 1998). These two contrasting theories fall relatively neatly into the demand-side (recession-push) and supply-side (entrepreneurial-pull) division already used in this chapter, and both have considerable empirical support. For the recession-push model, Schuetze (1998) estimated probability models for being self-employed and found that it was positively correlated with the unemployment rate in both Canada and the USA. His results support earlier studies by Highfield and Smiley (1987), while in the USA, Evans and Leighton (1989) found that the unemployed have a higher likelihood of turning to self-employment than those in employment. Using data on OECD countries, Acs et al. (1991) found that the rate of growth in self-employment rose with the unemployment rate, over a number of different time periods.

However, a number of other studies have found different results that have been interpreted as supporting the entrepreneurial-pull model. Blanchflower and Oswald (1998) and Abell et al. (1995) find a negative relationship between the probability of being self-employed and unemployment rates. Whitfield and Wannell (1991) found that higher paid workers are the most likely to enter self-employment and that the highest growth rates in self-employment are found in a booming economy. Acs et al. (1991) have provided an explanation for these competing results. They argue that the relationship between economic activity and self-employment may be decomposed into two effects. By reducing the opportunity cost of entering self-employment, high unemployment may be positively related to self-employment. Alternatively, by signalling a depressed economy, increased unemployment can slow the rate of growth in self-employment by depressing the expected gains of new entrants. The net impact on the growth of self-employment effect depends upon which effect dominates.

A recent study by Lin et al. (1999) used Canadian Monthly Labour Force Survey Data, 1976 (January) to 1998 (February), pooled across the ten Canadian provinces. They estimated the following equation:

$$SERATEit = \alpha 0 + \alpha 1 \ CYCLEit + \alpha 2 \ PARTRATEit$$
$$+ \ \alpha 3 \ PROVINCEit \ + \ \alpha 4 \ TIME \ + \ \alpha 5 \ MONTH \ + \ \varepsilon it \qquad (4.3)$$

In this equation the dependent variable is the self-employment rate and the explanatory variables are the economic labour market cycle (proxied by the monthly provincial unemployment rate), the monthly provincial participation rate for all persons, and dummy variables for province, time and month. The model was estimated as a pooled fixed effects (generalised least squares model)(GLS) for both males and females and all persons. The results for all persons' equation found a statistically significant negative relationship between self-employment and the economic cycle that suggested a one percentage point increase in the unemployment rate is associated with a 0.06 percentage point decline in self-employment rate. Other equations found that men were more prone to this effect than women, having a negative self-employment/unemployment elasticity coefficient of -0.051 compared to -0.032 for women. Lin et al. also found a significant and positive relationship between the rate of growth in full-time employment and self-employment. Both these results offer up some support for the entrepreneurial-pull model by suggesting that, if anything, movements in the aggregate self-employment rate are pro-cyclical. However they are cautious in their findings arguing that a host of non-cyclical factors were driving the rapid growth in self-employment in Canada. These included:

• Demographic changes that have seen the average age of the Canadian labour force rise to the point that the per cent of youth (15-24 years) has dropped from 26 per cent in 1976 to 15 per cent in 1997. Most studies show that the propensity to enter self-employment rises with age.
• Technological change in which these changes have been most rapid in industries that are conducive to self-employment.
• Structural changes that are complementary to those industries (service) that have high self-employed components.
• Increased contracting out which Lin et al. argue is a direct result of increases in labour on-costs such as payroll tax.
• Increase in marginal personal tax rates that have induced workers to reduce tax through self-employment.

4.5   CONTRACT EMPLOYMENT

Research concerning independent contractors has largely been descriptive and concerned with the personal characteristics of those involved. One exception to this is the study by VandenHeuval and Wooden (1995) that resulted from a special survey in the August 1994 Australian Population Survey Monitor. As the necessity for this survey proved, the chief difficulty in investigating this group lies in the fact that SECs do not belong exclusively to any one of the standard labour force categories, although most belong to the self-employed. As a result, there is some doubt as to what group of workers actually constitute independent contractors. There also seems likely to be differences in motivation and employer influence between the 'independent' SEC and the DSEC. At its simplest level, SECs are far more likely to be acting on wealth-maximising criteria within a standard supply-side explanation than DSEC.

For example, independent SECs are likely to be influenced by:

• *Human capital.* Independent SECs typically have trade or vocational skills. Historically, many professionals have, in effect, been independent

SECs. This new breed of worker seems to be broadening the scope to include the vocationally rather than professionally trained workers.

- *Motivation.* The 1980s and beyond has been an era of entrepreneurship and change in social attitudes. Rightly or wrongly, many now believe that being self-employed will remove some of the restrictions on earnings imposed by permanent wage and salary and employment.

- *Tax incentives.* Self-employment offers the chance of moving some private costs (non-tax-deductible) to work-related expenditure. This may be extended if the SECs are able to incorporate or employ some family members. These avenues, under a strict interpretation of the tax and common laws, are not likely to be applicable to dependent contractors. To some extent the continued existence of 'ISECs' is linked to the emergence of an employer culture which encourages contracting-out work as part of cost and efficiency measures. However the extent to which permanent employees are induced to change status and become 'DSECs' linked to one sole or major employer is not known. There appears to be considerable scope for DSECs to be subject to demand-side pressure.[10]

The area of SEC remains one where there are considerable data shortages, particularly at regional level. The only work of recent vintage that is currently available is the work of academics from the National Institute of Labour Studies. This suggests that detailed research into the motivations, supply-side characteristics and demand-side pressure faced by the DSEC is a major research need at this time.

4.6   CONCLUDING REMARKS

The diverse nature of non-standard employment was always likely to throw up competing explanations as to its determinants. This chapter considered in some detail several major forms of non-standard employment. These were part-time, temporary (or at least its casual component), self-employment and an important subgroup of self-employment, contractors. Two broad explanations of the rise in non-standard employment were considered, demand-side and supply-side factors. While it is recognised that, in most economic systems, these factors cannot be fully decomposed from one another, there is, nonetheless, value in attempting to do so. People and society in general feel less threatened by supply-side changes if they reflect shifts in personal preference and circumstance than they do by changes to the employment relationship that they feel are imposed upon them by business, government or technology. In the remaining chapters of this book, this theme is continued with an investigation of the economic and social implications of the current changes in the employment relationship. However, in this chapter the results reported enable some generalizations to be made.

For part-time workers, the most prevalent form of non-standard worker, it is clear that supply-side factors still predominate, albeit that these supply-side factors may be a passive acceptance of family and other circumstances rather than a whole-hearted embracing of part-time work as an ideal concept. In all countries examined, the large bulk of part-time workers state that they are voluntary participants who currently prefer this form of employment. A major reason for this is that, within the evolution and expansion of part-time work, females and particularly married females have been the dominant group. The juggling of family and work which made this group seek out part-time work in the first place still predominates. Demand factors of structural and technological changes have, if anything, further expanded the opportunities for this form of work and called forth even greater supply. The labour force participation patterns of married females in the USA is a good example of the continuing preference married females have for part-time work.

However, across the world there is a growth in involuntary part-time workers both in an absolute sense and as a percentage of total part-time employment. In Australia, for example, about one-quarter of all part-time workers are demand-constrained and would prefer either more hours of work or full-time employment. Most of these are prime-aged workers (both males and females) and young males. In the USA, the involuntary part-time workers are predominantly young (under 25 years) and in entry-level career-track positions. Clearly there are demand-side factors operating here including the desire by employers to use non-standard jobs at the entry level as a screening device. Other factors leading to the growth of demand-side pressure for part-time work include the desire to avoid labour on-costs and achieve numerical flexibility in the labour force. These factors are also much in evidence in the rapid rate of growth of casual employment in Australia. Here the demand-side forces have been given a freer run than might have been expected in this country a decade ago by the rapid demise in trade union coverage. The empirical results show a strong relationship between the demise in trade union coverage of an industry and the growth of casual employment.

In general the more contingent and less desirable the form of non-standard employment, in terms of pay and conditions, the more dominant are demand-side factors. This is why independent contractors and other self-employed are generally seen as the top echelon of non-standard worker. However, the real picture is less clear cut. Canada provides a good example of some of the complexities of trying to explain the very large increases in self-employment in that and other countries in simple terms of demand and supply factors. The descriptive data over the last decade indicate that most of the new self-employed are economic refugees from a labour market that did not meet their reservation conditions. But why not? Was it because there were no jobs at all? In some cases this is true. Wage and salary job growth in Canada has been very slow in comparison to the booming US economy. However, non-standard wage and salary jobs were growing but the new self-employed were not taking them. This suggests that they were not simply economic refugees unable to find a job, but rather that they could not find the right job. To a larger extent than elsewhere, Canadians, especially young Canadians, have rejected one form of non-standard entry into the labour market, through a demand-driven secondary labour market wage and salary job, and preferred to enter through self-employment. This is not to deny that the rate of growth in self-employment would probably have been reduced if the traditional job market had been more buoyant.

One situation in which supply-side and demand-side factors become more distinct is in the area of contracting and in particular the motivations of those becoming contractors. A decomposition of the total number of contractors into those that are truly independent and those that are *de-facto* employees, working under the banner of self-employment, provides a good estimate of the relative strengths of demand-side and supply-side factors. The only available data on this, from an Australian survey, suggest that the break-down is approximately 70:30 in favour of independent contractors and the supply-side explanation. This estimate fits with the general conclusion that the more contingent or less desirable is the form of non-standard work, the more dominant are demand-side explanations.

NOTES

[1] Not everyone agrees with this view. Appelbaum (1987) after defining involuntary part-time work as workers getting their jobs due to 'slack work, plant down time or inability to find another job' argued that 40 per cent of new part-time jobs in the USA in 1992 were involuntary.

[2] She concedes however that the 'effects of job characteristics, and human capital variables can also capture effects from the demand-side of the market' (Doirion, 1997, p. 8).

[3] These include a desire to maximise comparison with the results of Simpson et al., the fact that there are a limited number of industries and the belief that casual employment patterns are expected to differ between industries. In all equations the fixed effects model was tested against both the classical regression model and the random effects model and found to be the appropriate choice.

[4] In the case of *Non-wage Costs* the t-value on its error term was 1.251, which was not statistically different from zero. For the Union variable, the t-value on the included error term was 2.031, which is significantly different from zero at the 5 per cent level.

[5] The instruments used were the proportion of women in the workforce and the 12 industry dummy variables. The use of these variables as instruments reduces the effective measurement of the (separate) impact of these variables, particularly *Sex*, on *PCE*, introducing some collinearity with the instrumented *Union* variable. However, the parameter estimates of these variables are consistent under OLS estimation.

[6] It should be noted that these differences exist after adjustment for the industry effect.

[7] No instrumental variable estimation was thus required for this section of the analysis.

[8] There seems a good deal of descriptive data to support this later proposition. See Cohany (1998).

PART III

The Economic and Social Implications of Non-standard Employment

5. Job Stability and Job Satisfaction

5.0 INTRODUCTION

A major concern expressed over the growth in non-standard employment has been its inherent instability and the economic and social effects this may have upon the workers in these job and their families. For example, it is widely held that job security and job satisfaction are closely linked. Despite this, it has been shown that considerable numbers of workers either actively seek, or at least passively accept, reductions in job security for increased hourly wage rates or greater flexibility in terms of lifestyle or family goals. This raises the possibility that the link between non-standard employment, job security and job satisfaction may not be as clearcut as it first appears. To assess the net impacts on job stability, job satisfaction and worker morale, we must again return to the fundamental observation that runs through the whole of this book; the determining factors behind the decision to enter non-standard employment. In the situation where workers deliberately seek out non-standard forms of employment for financial or personal reasons there is likely to be a reduction in job stability. However, this need not translate into decreased job satisfaction or morale, particularly where any loss in job security has been offset by wage or other work-related gains. On the other hand, workers that have had non-standard employment imposed upon them may face the double penalty of reduced job security and reduced job satisfaction. The overall impact of the increase in non-standard employment on job security and job satisfaction over the last two decades is therefore an empirical question and is crucially dependent upon the decomposition of non-standard employment into its voluntary and involuntary components. The central questions that emerge for empirical investigation are:

- Has job stability decreased significantly, and if so, what role has the increase in non-standard employment played in this decline?
- Has any consequent increase in job stability translated into reduced job satisfaction or workforce morale?

5.1   JOB STABILITY AND JOB TENURE

Canadians seem to be particularly concerned about rising job instability (Heisz, 1996a). Perhaps for this reason, they have been at the forefront of research into determining whether job insecurity has increased over the last decade. One advantage held in this area by Canadian researchers is the availability of high-quality data such as the Longitudinal Worker File (LWF) created by the Business and Labour Market Analysis (BLMA) Division of Statistics Canada. This is a 10 per cent random sample of all Canadian workers and comprises data integrated from three separate sources: the Record of Employment (ROE) files on worker separation, taxation files from Revenue Canada and the Longitudinal Employment Analysis Program (LEAP) files from the BLMA. The ROE data are particularly useful for examining job instability. All employers in Canada issue a ROE to every employee working in insurable employment who has had an interruption in earnings or a separation. The ROE allows separations to be analysed by type of separation (for example, permanent or temporary) and, when this is combined with the payroll deduction records for each employee, those workers at risk of job separations as well as those that actually separate may be accurately identified[1].

Job instability can take a number of forms. However, any significant increase in job instability might be identified by:

1.   An increase in the risk of permanent lay-off.
2.   A reduction in job tenure, with the result that workers may have to change jobs and careers more frequently than in the past or than they may wish.
3.   An increase in the proportion of persons in intermittent or non-standard jobs such as being on contract, in temporary jobs or self-employed.
4.   An increased polarisation of the workforce into core/contingent segments.

In overlapping papers, Picot and Lin (1997) and Picot et al. (1997) use the LWF to investigate separations and permanent lay-offs among Canadian Workers between 1978 and 1993. The key question they examine is whether or not there has been an upward shift in the rate of permanent lay-offs in Canada since the 1970s. They answer this question in two ways, first by examining the time trend of permanent lay-offs and then by applying logistic regression to examine changes in the probability of lay-off between the two periods. Their analysis covers all workers as well as particular subgroups such as young workers (15-24 years) and older workers (44 years and above). Table 5.1 shows the broad pattern of lay-offs, quits and hires in Canada over the period 1978-94. These data are used as the basis for their analysis.

Table 5.1 Percentage lay-offs, quits and hires in the Canadian workforce, 1978-94

Year	Permanent Lay-offs	Quits	Other	Total	Temporary Lay-offs	Other	Total	Hires Total
1978	7.4	7.3	6.3	20.9	7.0	6.5	13.5	NA
1979	6.4	8.4	6.8	21.6	6.6	6.7	13.3	23.4
1980	6.1	8.0	6.8	21.0	7.0	6.8	14.8	22.0
1981	6.8	8.9	7.0	22.6	7.6	6.7	14.3	27.3
1982	8.7	5.5	6.7	20.8	10.8	8.1	18.9	14.4
1983	7.8	5.0	6.0	18.9	9.0	6.4	15.4	21.4
1984	7.9	6.4	7.0	21.3	9.1	7.3	16.4	22.2
1985	7.5	7.4	7.1	22.0	8.4	7.2	15.6	25.6
1986	7.1	8.0	7.1	22.2	8.1	7.2	15.3	25.2
1987	6.8	9.1	7.1	22.9	7.3	6.9	14.2	26.3
1988	6.5	10.1	7.3	23.8	7.0	7.3	14.3	26.2
1989	6.2	9.9	7.1	23.3	7.1	7.2	14.3	26.0
1990	7.6	8.5	7.3	23.0	8.3	7.7	16.0	21.6
1991	7.5	6.3	7.0	21.0	9.3	7.8	17.1	18.3
1992	7.5	5.4	6.8	19.8	9.4	7.2	16.6	17.9
1993	7.3	5.2	6.7	19.2	9.1	7.0	16.1	18.5
1994	NA	NA	NA	NA	NA	NA	NA	NA

Source: Picot and Lin (1997, p. 9).

In the LWF, job separations are classified into three categories (lay-offs, quits and other) according to the reason for the separation recorded in ROA. Lay-offs are defined as separations due to shortage of work and are classified as temporary if the individual returns to work for the same employer in the same or following year; otherwise they are regarded as permanent. If a worker is observed with a firm in one year but not in the previous this is considered to be a hire. This covers replacement workers as well as expansion hiring. In Table 5.1, permanent separation rates are calculated as the number of permanent separations divided by the total employment during the year. The hiring rate is the number of hires divided by total employment in the year. By contrast, the temporary separation rate is calculated by using the number of persons with at least one temporary separation, rather than the total number of separations. From Table 5.1 it can be seen that the permanent lay-off rate fluctuates from just above 6 per cent during the business cycle peaks (1980, 1989) to between 8 and 9 per cent at the bottom of the troughs (1982, 1991). However, fluctuations in the permanent rate are much more muted than fluctuations in the temporary lay-offs and quits. For example, between 1989-91, temporary lay-offs increased by 23 per cent, quits declined by 40 per cent and hiring fell by 35 per cent.

To test the cyclical sensitivity of lay-offs more formally, Picot and Lin used the unemployment rate as a proxy for business cycle trends and regressed (using a number of different specifications) permanent lay-offs, temporary lay-offs, quits and hiring rates on the unemployment rate over the period 1978-93. All the estimated equations proved robust and yielded statistically significant results including elasticity coefficients of the movements in the business cycle and each of the dependent variables. The results suggest that a 1 percentage increase in the unemployment rate level leads to a 0.9 percentage point decline in quits, a 0.61 percentage point increase in temporary lay-offs and a 1.38 percentage point decline in hires. The same percentage point increase in the unemployment rate produced a numerically smaller 0.38 percentage point increase in permanent lay-offs. However, while permanent lay-offs, in aggregate, were clearly less sensitive than temporary labour force adjustments over the period, this result by itself, does not answer the question concerning an upward shift in the lay-off rate. A related question concerns the behaviour of permanent lay-offs across different groups in the Canadian labour market. The raw data indicate that the risk of lay-offs differs considerably across labour market groups. For example, Picot and Lin (1997) found that:

- Lay-off rates are much higher among men (with an annual average lay-off rate of 9.1 over the period) than women (4.8 per cent).
- The risk of lay-off is much higher among youths (for example, 8.3 per cent annual average lay-off for 15-24 year olds compared to 6.2 per cent for those over 45). However, the risk of lay-off has decreased for young workers since 1991.
- The risk of lay-off varies across regions. In the case of Canada, the Atlantic provinces had an average rate of 12.1 per cent compared to 5.2 per cent for Ontario.
- Two sectors of the economy where instability appears to have substantially increased are workers in the health, education and welfare sector and for workers aged over 55 years.

Picot and Lin (1997) conclude that permanent lay-offs to 1993 have shown no overall sign of an upward trend when compared to earlier periods. This holds true for unadjusted data and after controlling for changes in workplace composition by gender, age, province, industry and firm size. However, an increase in the probability of permanent lay-offs is observed among some specific groups such as older and/or more highly paid workers and those in the primary industries, health, education or welfare. The data also show that the Canadian labour market adjusts to structural changes through depressed hires rather than through increased lay-offs. Therefore, while the risk of permanently losing one's job is no higher than in earlier comparable periods, the chance of finding a new job is considerably lower, at least in aggregate. Furthermore, most job creation in the 1990s in Canada has been through self-employment, where earnings may be more unstable than among wage and salary jobs. The results from the Picot and Lin study are broadly in line with the earlier study by Picot et al. (1994) that also used Canadian labour force data. In this study, they compared permanent and temporary lay-off patterns during two recent recessions. They concluded that, although the share of permanent lay-offs rose marginally in 1989-92 compared to the 1980s recession, the level of change was insufficient to indicate a dramatic economy-wide shift towards increased losses in permanent jobs.

Another indicator of increased job instability is changes in average job tenure, because if permanent job loss increases, average job tenure should fall. Studies by Heisz (1966a, 1996b) examined job stability indicators 2, 3 and 4 by examining patterns of average job tenure in Canada over the period 1984-94. He argued that any significant increase in the incidence of short-term jobs should expose workers to more spells of unemployment, make it more difficult for them to accumulate a pension and increase the need for mid-career retraining. Hasan and de Brouker (1985) developed two ways to measure the length of job spells. These are:

- *Interrupted length of in-progress jobs.* This describes the length of an on-going job up to the point at which it was observed by a cross-section survey and is used by Statistics Canada and the US Bureau of Labor Statistics. Despite its wide acceptance, this measure has the disadvantage that the job spell is truncated or right-censored and a job sampled in this way may last for many more months. However, the measure is useful in describing the job tenure experience of the currently employed. It was first used in Canada by Hasan and de Brouker who calculated an average job tenure for Canadian workers in 1980 at 7.4 years.
- *Complete length of in-progress jobs* (Aklerof and Main, 1981; Christofides and McKenna, 1993, 1995). This measure is double the interrupted length of in-progress jobs and on this basis would have yielded an average job duration estimate of 14.8 years in 1980. Using this measure, Christofides and McKenna (1993) examined longitudinal data from 90 panels from the Canadian Labour Market Activity survey of 1987 and 1988. They found a small decline in average job duration in Canada from 14.8 years to 14.0 years.
- A third measure has been developed by Hall (1982), and extended by Ureta (1992), along lines similar to that used to generate estimates of the length of unemployment spells. Central to this technique is the calculation of the conditional probability (retention rate) that a job will continue for some specified time period after it has reached a threshold time.

$$R_{tc} = N_{t,c} / N_{t-1,c-1} \tag{5.1}$$

Where t = the amount of tenure the worker has already served, c = the additional time, R_{tc} is retention rate, and is 1 minus the hazard rate. A full set of retention rates defines a survival function. This is the number of respondents reporting tenure of t in the present survey divided by the corresponding measure from the previous survey. The computation of the retention rate is an application of the synthetic cohort method because respondents from the same cohort rather than (necessarily) the same individuals are sampled for the numerator and denominator. This measure has the advantage over the doubling method because it allows for computation over the entire distribution of job spells. However, it yielded similar, though a slightly lower, estimate of 13.6 years for Canadian workers in 1981.

Taken collectively, the main conclusions from this research were that average job tenure among Canadians had fallen marginally since the 1970s. It was also found that, pre-1990s, most of the total hours worked (work-time) were undertaken by people in long-term jobs but that most job spells were quite short. In other words, the majority of work was carried out by long-term workers which boosted the average duration figures to the point that it gave a misleading picture of the expected job spell for the workforce as a whole. Since that time, the average job spell in Canada has continued to fall. For example, Heisz (1996a), using a modified Hasan and de Brouker measure to examine the completed length of new jobs in Canada, found that the average duration of a new job spell in 1989 lasted only two years. His measure once again relied upon the retention ratio. Given a full set of retention rates the expected average complete job length for a group of individuals who begin their jobs at the same time is defined as:

$$\text{Average Length} = \Sigma^n_{t=1} \Pi^t_{1\text{-}1} R_{tc} \tag{5.2}$$

This equation is the discrete time version of the generalised result that, in continuous time, the average duration of new jobs equals the integral of the survivor function. It measures the average length of time a group of workers who just begin their jobs will remain employed, assuming they face the same economic conditions that currently prevail for the rest of their jobs. Heisz (1996a) used the amended formulae to compute the average length of a new job and the distribution of new job lengths for the period 1981-94. The tenure variable (t) is taken from the Canadian Labour Force Survey and is the number of consecutive months of uninterrupted work for the current employer. The sample includes all employees, excluding the self-employed, full-time students and unpaid family workers.[2] The results are shown in Figure 5.1.

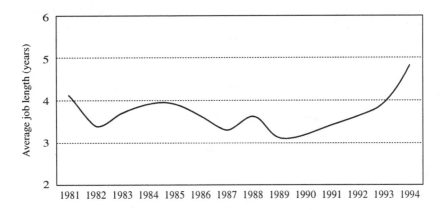

Source: Heisz (1996a, p. 7).

Figure 5.1 Average complete job length, Canada 1981-94

The length of a new job in Canada from 1981-94 for all workers in the sample was 3.7 years. Over the period, average job duration followed a cyclical period from a low of 3.5 in 1982 and 3.0 in 1991 to peaks of 4.0 in 1985 and 4.9 in 1994. No discernible upward trend was picked up with the average new jobs lasting 3.8 years from 1981-85, 3.4 years from 1986-90 and 3.8 years from 1991-94.

However, the relative stability of average new job length masked important changes in the distribution of completed job lengths. This distribution is shown in Figure 5.2, averaged at the beginning and the end of the period. There has been a substantial shift from jobs that lasted between six months and five years, to jobs lasting six months or less. For example, between 1981-85 and 1991-94, the proportion of jobs which lasted between six months and five years dropped from 34 to 26 per cent while the proportion of jobs lasting six months or less rose from 46 to 54 per cent. The proportion of jobs lasting five to twenty years and more than twenty years remained largely unchanged.

Heisz argues that the increase in the proportion of short-term jobs plus the unchanged proportion of long-term jobs indicates that a polarisation of jobs is taking place in the labour market.

How is it possible that the proportion of long-term jobs has remained unchanged while the proportion of short-term jobs has increased? The answer is that once the job has passed a six months' milestone, it has a greater chance of becoming a long job than it did in the earlier period. While the total proportion of new jobs which last beyond six months has declined, the proportion of six-month-old jobs which lasted five years and beyond increased from 37 per cent from 1981-85 to 42 per cent from 1991-94. These changes mean that workers with more than one year of job seniority now have increased job stability while at the same time the ranks of stable job-holders is becoming more difficult to join. These trends do indicate a polarisation of the labour market. This may be caused by some labour market groups benefiting at the expense of others. Alternatively, polarisation can occur within all groups. The first is a 'characteristics explanation' in that some distinctive and easily assigned features such as region, occupation, industry or human capital are setting the boundaries of the polarisation. The second explanation sees the polarisation results from factors that are economy-wide but affect individuals differently.

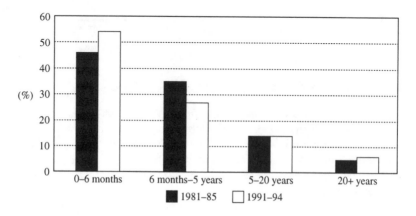

Source: Heisz (1996a, p. 8).

Figure 5.2 Distribution of complete job lengths in Canada, 1981-85 and 1991-94

When summary statistics such as the average length of new jobs, and the proportion of new jobs which exceed six months, are cross-classified by such variables as gender, age and region of employment and education, the results show that, in terms of average job tenure, there are advantages in being associated with particular demographic groups. For example:

- Average tenure is 1.7 times longer in Ontario than in Atlantic Provinces.
- Workers in community services experience average tenure twice as long as that of workers in business and personal services.
- Persons with post-secondary qualifications have job tenure twice as long as those without them.
- Older workers have shorter average lengths than younger workers.
- Few older workers pass the six months' milestone.

To further examine the pattern of job tenure, Heisz ran regressions using the data from Table 5.2 as dependent variables and the unemployment rate, monthly dummies and a linear time trend as the explanatory variables. The equations were corrected for first-order auto-regressive errors and run on 168 monthly observations. The estimating equation was therefore:

$$\log DV = a + b \text{ Monthly Dummies} + c \text{ Time} + d \log \text{Unemployment rate} \tag{5.3}$$

where *DV* is the dependent variable at the top of each column of Table 5.2. Coefficient estimates represent the average monthly change in the dependent variable by 1000 over the period.[3]

Table 5.2 Average complete job length in Canada by demographic group, 1991-94

Demographic characteristic	Average completed job length	Proportion of jobs lasting longer than		
		(a) 6 months	(b) 5 years given (a)	20 years given (a) and (b)
All	3.7	50.4	38.6	30.4
Males	3.6	48.0	39.0	31.7
Females	3.8	53.2	38.3	27.9
Age at job start				
15-24 years	3.7	45.9	37.3	39.0
25-34 years	4.3	55.7	37.3	38.5
35-44 years	4.0	53.8	44.2	23.9
45-54 years	3.2	49.1	43.7	4.1
55-64 years	1.9	41.8	31.7	1.3
Region of job				
Atlantic Canada	2.6	34.6	36.9	31.5
Quebec	3.6	46.8	40.8	31.1
Ontario	4.5	58.6	40.7	30.6
Western Canada	3.4	50.2	35.2	29.3
Industry of job				
Community Services	5.4	54.1	49.6	40.3
Manufacturing	4.0	51.4	41.4	27.9
Trade	3.8	61.2	34.6	20.9
Business and personal Services	2.7	51.6	27.2	19.6
Education				
No post-secondary	2.9	42.2	33.1	24.4
Some post-secondary	5.7	60.7	43.2	42.1

Source: Heisz (1996a, p. 9).

The results shown in Table 5.3 indicate that the probability of a new job start lasting six months declined significantly for all groups. Females, those over 55, those working in Atlantic Canada, those workers in Community Services, and workers with some post-secondary education were most affected. For females, the results indicate a year decline in the likelihood of a job lasting more than six months of 1.8 per cent or 25 per cent over the whole period. That is, 25 per cent fewer female job starters held their job for more than six months. This amounts to a drop (evaluated at the mean) of 13.5 percentage points compared with a 7.4 percentage point decline for male job starters.[4] At the same time, the number of jobs that reached five years' duration once the initial six months had been achieved rose by an average of 1.3 percentage points per time period for the workforce as a whole. The main beneficiaries of this trend were females aged 25-44 (when their jobs started), workers in Western Canada and those employed in manufacturing and community services.

Table 5.3 Changes in average job length and the distribution of completed jobs, Canada 1981-94

| | | Proportion of new jobs lasting longer than | | |
Demographic characteristic	Average job length	(a) 6 months	(b) 5 years given (a)	20 years, given (a) and (b)
All	0.055	-1.186***	1.343***	0.833
Males	0.094	-0.920***	1.121*	0.554
Females	-0.094	-1.512***	1.573**	1.300
Age at job start				
15-24 years	0.586	-0.999***	1.902***	1.166
25-34 years	-0.312	-1.249***	1.189**	-0.133
35-44 years	-0.449	-1.367***	1.101**	-1.232
45-54 years	-1.601**	-1.572***	-0.325	1.224
55-64 years	-2.920***	-4.063***	2.014	-2.728

Note:
*** significant at 1 per cent level.
** significant at 5 per cent level.
* significant at 10 per cent level.

Source: Heisz (1996a, p. 9).

Overall, despite the fact that average job tenure remained constant, some groups were badly affected. This is particularly true for older workers aged 45-54 and 55-64 years. For both groups the average tenure of a new job fell by 0.9 years over the period 1981-94. This is almost certainly the result of older job starters having reduced tenure across the economy rather than polarisation among those age 45 years and over. In this way, the job experience of older workers differs from the workforce as a whole, where there is strong evidence of polarisation. Moreover, the evidence suggests that it is in the area of new jobs where polarisation into short-term and long-term jobs has most strongly occurred in Canada over the past 15 years. The entry period into secure employment has increased. Once in the system, workers with more than one year seniority are in fact enjoying increased job security but it has become more difficult to join these ranks.[5] Green and Riddell (1996) found similar results. They point to a 'hollowing out of the middle of the job tenure distribution in Canada', with more very short jobs but a greater longevity for very stable jobs. They suggest that for young and less-educated workers there has been a rise in job instability over the past decade.

As with so much of the research into non-standard employment, the evidence for job stability and tenure in Canada is mixed. In aggregate, there has been only a small increase in aggregate job instability. This has been caused by minor increases in permanent lay-offs and reductions in average job tenure. However, there is increasing instability among particular groups of workers such as entry-level workers and those with low skill or educational requirements. This is leading to an increased polarisation of work experience within the Canadian Labour Market. Job tenure studies have also been conducted in the USA. Swinnerton and Wial (1995) conclude that there was a decline in job stability in the 1980s, while Diebold, Neumark and Polsky (1994) found that the overall job retention rates were fairly stable during the 1980s. The results by Faber (1995) are similar to those obtained by the Canadian studies. He finds that the incidence of long-term jobs in the USA did not decline over the period 1973-93 but that less-educated men are increasingly less likely to hold long-term jobs. Studies of displaced workers have also been conducted in the USA. Gardiner (1995) finds comparable job loss in the two recessions 1981-82 and 1991-92 but a significant change in industrial and occupational job loss mix. Faber (1995) finds a significant increase in job displacement over the period 1991-93 which he claims was due to job loss, from positions and shifts being abolished (downsizing), rather than plant closure.

Almost all studies cited point to the growing instability of entry-level jobs, and it is in this area of labour market entry that non-standard employment is playing a major role. Survey of Employment and Unemployment (SEUP) data in Australia provides longitudinal evidence of the entry-level jobs found by job-seekers in Australia over the period 1995-97.[6] Starting with a population of 875 000 job-seekers, the outcomes for September 1997 are shown in Figure 5.3.

The results from Figure 5.3 show that from a panel of 875 000 job-seekers in May 1995, 52 per cent of all job-seekers were working by September 1997. The breakup of these jobs were:

- 22 per cent were in a stable full-time job.
- 10 per cent were in a stable part-time job.

- 20 per cent were in an unstable job.
- A further 26 per cent of job-seekers had worked at some time since May 1995 but 23 per cent had not worked at all between May 1995 and September 1997.

The results are consistent with the Canadian and US evidence that show both the increased instability of entry-level jobs and the role played by non-standard employment in this increased instability. Part-time and unstable jobs accounted for 60 per cent of all jobs obtained by entry-level job-seekers over the period, and of those, 23 per cent who were not currently working but had worked over the period. The majority held jobs of less than six months' duration.

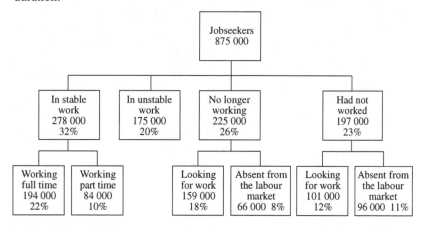

Source: Employment and Unemployment Patterns, ABS Cat. 6286.0 (1999c, p. 19).

Figure 5.3 Job-seekers at May 1995 in Australia: labour market outcomes at September 1997

5.2 JOB SECURITY: HOW MUCH IS IT WORTH?

Much of the discussion above assumes that job security is highly valued by employees. This may not be the case because some employees willingly trade security for monetary and other incentives.[7] There is little empirical evidence on trade-off rates between job security and other rewards. In the Australian Social Monitor, Kelley et al. (1998) recently asked the question, 'How much is job security worth to employees in the 1990s?' They began their analysis with a worker in a secure, public service type job (73 points on their job security scale out of 100) but a relatively low hourly wage of $10. Their survey found that such workers are moderately satisfied with their income and standard of living at 59 points (from a 100-point scale). They then try to estimate how this worker would react to a decline in job security. To do this they assume that security for this worker declines to the lower level typical of unskilled workers in the private sector, for example, to 53 points on the job satisfaction scale. How much increase in pay would be needed to maintain that worker at the same level of satisfaction? The results are shown in Table 5.4. In this particular case a $4.44 increase (44.4 per cent) is needed to maintain the level of satisfaction at 59 points.

Table 5.4 Trade-off between pay and security

High security[a]	Average security[b]	Low security[c]
10.00	12.07	14.44
20.00	22.28	24.93
30.00	32.66	35.66
40.00	43.02	46.48
50.00	53.58	57.70
60.00	64.08	69.17

Note:
a   refers to average for full-time public employees, 70 points.
b   refers to average for the Australian workforce as a whole.
c   refers to the average for part-time private sector employees at 53 points.

Source: Kelley et al. (1998, p. 5).

The results in Table 5.4 are similar to the type of results shown in an indifference map in economic theory. Both are essentially trade-off possibility statements. They assume that the participants have both the capacity to trade and the ability to make correct judgements between money and work conditions. The results clearly show an inverse relationship between expected salary and job security. For example, the worker with high-security earning $30 per hour will require hourly pay increases of $2.66 per hour and $5.66 per hour as the security of the job declines, to retain the degree of some job satisfaction.

5.3   NON-STANDARD EMPLOYMENT AND JOB SATISFACTION

Shifts in job satisfaction are often raised as one of the anticipated consequences of the spread of non-standard employment. This is not surprising because the things that tend to define the differences between standard and non-standard employment such as earnings, promotion prospects, job security, employer-funded benefits and access to training are also all influential in determining the level of job satisfaction. However, the direction of the shift in job satisfaction resulting from the spread of non-standard employment is likely to differ with the type of non-standard employment. For those who are in non-standard employment by choice, the additional flexibility they achieve may enhance job satisfaction in comparison to their previous job status. For example, a number of self-employed and skilled contractors report high levels of job satisfaction. On the other hand, the instability experienced by those in contingent and unstable jobs might be expected to lower their level of job satisfaction. A number of surveys have been conducted in Europe, North America and Australia into the aggregate levels of job satisfaction. By and large, these surveys suggest that while job satisfaction remains relatively high, the levels of satisfaction in most countries surveyed have declined significantly over the last two decades.

For example, Blanchflower and Oswald (1999) report that the proportion of Americans very satisfied with their work has fallen from 56 per cent in the 1970s to 48 per cent in the 1990s. Similarly in Europe, the number of persons highly satisfied with the terms and conditions of their employment has fallen and is lowest in those countries such as Spain where non-standard employment is most prevalent. Table 5.5 reports Eurobarometer data on job satisfaction over the period 1995-96.

Table 5.5 Percentage of job satisfaction in European countries, 1995-96

Country	Very satisfied	Change from 1989*	Moderately satisfied	Partially dissatisfied	Very dissatisfied	Number in sample
Belgium	44	NA	49	6	1	1011
Denmark	50	NA	45	3	2	997
Germany*	34	-9	51	11	4	1025
Greece	11	NA	50	29	9	1003
Italy	26	-8	56	15	4	1028
Spain	23	NA	57	16	4	996
France	22	NA	60	14	5	999
S. Ireland	57	-6	38	4	1	1004
Luxembourg	40	NA	53	5	2	494
Netherlands	46	-6	46	7	1	1064
Portugal	21	NA	62	13	3	998
UK	38	-1	49	9	5	1064
Finland	31	NA	62	6	2	1059
Sweden	39	NA	53	5	2	1055
Austria	44	NA	45	9	1	1070
All	35	-5	52	10	3	15914

Note:
* taken from *Job Satisfaction by Country, International Survey Programme* (ISSP), 1989

Source: Eurobarometers (1996).

Two points stand out immediately. The first is that, on the whole, job satisfaction for most workers appears to be remarkably high. For most European countries, the combined score for very satisfied or moderately satisfied is well over 80 per cent with Denmark (95 per cent), Belgium (93 per cent), Luxembourg (93 per cent) and Finland (93 per cent) being most satisfied. On the other hand, in all cases where a comparison can be made, levels of satisfaction have fallen between an earlier Eurobarometer survey (1989) and the latest survey (1995-96).

Given that numerous changes have been occurring at the workplace, the relevant question concerns how much of this aggregate decline in satisfaction may be attributed to increases in non-standard work. As a starting point, it is interesting to note that countries with the lowest levels of job satisfaction, such as Spain, are also those with the highest level of non-standard employment.

The data in Table 5.6 suggest that job security does have some impact on satisfaction levels. People who state that their jobs are secure are twice as likely (at 40 per cent) to have high satisfaction levels than those who feel their jobs are not secure (20 per cent). The corresponding results for the USA over the period 1977-96 show a decline in high satisfaction levels from 54 per cent to 37 per cent (General Social Surveys, 1997). Similarly, Blanchflower and Oswald report that in the USA those that expect to 'easily find another position' are the ones most likely to feel satisfied with their current jobs (Blanchflower and Oswald, 1999). Research reported earlier in this chapter has established a link between non-standard employment and decreased job stability. It is not unreasonable, therefore, to also link the spread of non-standard employment to decreased job satisfaction for a growing number of workers. However, more rigorous tests are needed before firmer conclusions may be drawn.

Table 5.6 Job security and job satisfaction in 16 European countries for the period 1995-96

Attitude	Secure	Not secure	DK secure	All	Unweighted N
Very satisfied	40	20	27	35	5559
Fairly satisfied	51	53	60	52	8291
Not very satisfied	7	19	11	10	1588
Not at all satisfied	2	8	3	3	476
All	70	22	8	100	15914
Unweighted N	11133	3451	1330	15914	

Note:
the countries used are the same as in Table 5.5, plus East Germany.

Source: Eurobarometer (1996).

The USA is the country where most research has been done into the determinants of job satisfaction with the General Social Surveys being in continuous operation from the 1970s. Blanchflower and Oswald (1999) drew upon the data from these surveys to run an ordered logit regression to examine if job satisfaction responses may be explained by a small set of variables which include personal and workplace characteristics, pay, job security and area dummies. They also tested for the presence of a statistically significant negative time trend in reported contentment in the US workplace. The results are displayed in Table 5.7.

The equations are run under different combinations of variables. These different combinations are shown in the table by numbers 1 to 7. For example, in column 2 the variables are included for union status and job security. The sign and significance of the time trend variable in equation 3 is consistent with the observed downward movements in job satisfaction identified earlier by the General Social Science Surveys. The coefficient enters the equation (column 1) at -0.013 (t of 6.37) and drops only slightly to -0.11 (4.66) in column 2, when union status and job security variables are included in the equation and rises in columns 6 and 7 when a variable for pay is added to the analysis. Given this confirmation of a downward trend in worker satisfaction over time, Blanchflower and Oswald ask two important questions:

- Is job satisfaction falling because of the decline of trade unions and worker representation?
- Is satisfaction falling because of increasing job insecurity?[8]

The results reported in column 2 cast doubt on both these possible explanations. The trade union membership variable enters the equation strongly negative (column 2), remains negative but becomes insignificant in columns 4, 5 and 6. This suggests that, if anything, union membership and job satisfaction are inversely related. This is an unlikely and unexpected result but one possibly explained by the fact that many current union members are in jobs under most threat from structural change. The security variable displays mixed results. Being 'not likely to lose your job' has a strong positive effect on worker satisfaction (columns, 2, 5, 6 and 7) but the actual job insecurity variable, though having the anticipated negative sign, was not statistically significant in any of the columns. One way of reconciling these findings with the published survey results is to suggest that the relationship between feelings of job satisfaction and job security is subject to a threshold effect and cuts in only when job security is above a certain level. Under such a scenario, as the percentage of workers in secure jobs has declined, so too would the aggregate levels of worker satisfaction.

Table 5.7 Job satisfaction in the USA, 1972–96: ordered logit (current workers only)

	1	2	3	4	5	6	7
Age	0.0267 (23.98)	0.0261 (19.78)	0.0272 (17.40)	0.0253 (12.58)	0.0261 (12.52)	0.0224 (10.11)	0.0251 (14.99)
Male	-0.0697 (2.53)	-0.0488 (1.49)	-0.0810 (2.18)	-0.0891 (1.83)	-0.0845 (1.72)	-0.1844 (3.36)	-0.1634 (3.92)
Self-employed	0.5243 (12.17)	0.5016 (9.85)	0.5714 (6.88)	0.5174 (6.88)	0.4298 (5.59)	0.4581 (5.54)	0.4352 (6.84)
Black	-0.4086 (9.63)	-0.4281 (8.38)	-0.5236 (6.49)	-0.5236 (6.29)	0.4524 (5.55)	-0.4973 (5.77)	-0.3452 (5.59)
Other non-white	-0.1732 (2.14)	-0.1963 (2.08)	-0.2522 (1.82)	-0.2522 (1.82)	-0.2295 (1.65)	-0.2290 (1.53)	-0.1793 (1.60)
Time	-0.0128 (6.37)	-0.113 (4.66)	-0.0158 (4.98)	-0.0151 (3.37)	-0.0124 (2.76)	-0.0199 (4.01)	-0.0224 (6.44)
Years of schooling	0.0417 (8.37)	0.0380 (6.45)	0.0277 (4.02)	0.0321 (3.59)	0.0217 (2.38)	-0.0049 (0.49)	0.0098 (1.28)
Union		-0.1823 (4.21)		-0.0619 (0.91)	-0.0075 (0.10)	-0.0835 (1.15)	-0.1129 (0.95)
Lose job fairly likely		-0.0841 (0.75)			-0.0630 (0.42)	-0.0823 (0.52)	-0.1129 (0.95)
Lose job not too likely		0.2016 (2.23)			0.1255 (1.04)	0.4963 (3.98)	0.1350 (1.40)
Lose job not likely at all		0.6608 (7.62)			0.6028 (5.21)	NA	0.5873 (6.33)
Lose job-go OLF		-1.5729 (2.02)			NA	0.6152 (2.30)	-1.1800 (1.31)
Lose job DK likely		0.2489 (1.42)			0.3325 (1.43)	-0.2698 (3.89)	0.3396 (1.71)
Find job somewhat easy		-0.2835 (5.60)			-0.2545 (3.85)	-0.3276 (4.77)	-0.2834 (5.33)
Find job not easy at all		-0.3084 (6.29)			-0.2805 (4.31)	-0.1869 (0.87)	-0.3549 (6.85)
Find job DK easy		-0.2569 (1.83)			-0.3599 (1.90)	-0.1869 (0.87)	-0.1731 (1.07)
Log of annual pay						0.1885 (6.31)	0.1475 (6.52)
State dummies	45	45	45	45	45	45	45
Cut-1	-2.1502	-2.2746	-2.1539	-2.5027	-2.4406	-1.5441	-1.3562
Cut-2	-0.7319	-0.9024	-0.6647	-1.1038	-1.0355	-0.1291	.13839
Cut-3	1.2803	1.0953	1.4482	0.9774	1.0818	2.0220	2.2701
Chi-squared	1139.2	817.0	934.0	393.9	542.0	515.6	879.1
Pseudo R^2	0.0266	0.0263	0.0394	0.0286	0.0394	0.0414	0.0409
N	20077	14571	11186	6573	6558	5964	10161

Source: Blanchflower and Oswald (1999, p. 21).

Moving from column 1 to 2 makes little difference to the coefficient on time. In other words, controlling for union status and job insecurity makes little difference to the conclusion that perceived well-being at work is falling. Given this, there must be other reasons why job satisfaction levels are trending downwards. In columns 6 and 7, pay enters strongly which suggests that well-paid workers are more satisfied irrespective of other factors. Education is positive but its effect disappears once income is entered as a control variable. In other words, schooling may bring income and high aspirations but does not necessarily bring happiness in the workplace.

Blanchflower and Oswald (1999) see the following points as the essence of their findings:

- Job satisfaction levels are high in Western democracies. Only a small minority say they are dissatisfied.
- Nevertheless the data show a steady decline in job satisfaction in the USA and elsewhere, especially for those aged over 30.
- The decline in job satisfaction is linked to, but not principally caused by, the decline in union power.
- Microeconomic factors (such as downsizing) which create expectations of job loss have the largest discernible impact on job satisfaction levels.
- Of the 18 countries they examined, Southern Ireland has the highest levels of job satisfaction. This is despite the fact that it is one of the poorest countries.

5.4   OTHER STUDIES OF JOB SATISFACTION

Kelley et al. (1998) modelled job satisfaction among Australian workers. They used pooled data collected from the International Social Science/Australia Surveys for the period 1989 to 1996-97 on the equation:

Satisfaction $= b_0 + b_1$ *Pay* $+ b_2$ *Pay Squared* $+ b_3$ *Security* $+ b_4$ *Part-time* $+ b_5$ *Govt* $+ b_6$ *SelfEmpl* $+ b_7$ *Complexjob* $+ b_8$ *Dirtyjob* $+ b_9$ *Age* $+ b_{10}$ *Sex* $+ b_{11}$ *Education* $+ b_{12}$ *Urban* $+ b_{13}$ *Married* $+ e$.

The variables chosen were: hourly pay (*Pay*), hourly pay squared (*Pay Squared*), security (*Security*), and job characteristics such as being employed part-time, being employed by government, self-employed, complex job, dirty or dangerous job (*Part-time, Govt, SelfEmpl, Complexjob, Dirtyjob*) and control variables such as age, sex, education, marital status and urban or rural dweller. To enable direct comparison of the effect of each variable on satisfaction and to filter out the 'noise' of partially overlapping impacts between the variables, standardised partial regression correlation coefficients were estimated. The results show that the amount of pay (a standardised regression coefficient of 0.27) is the single most important determinant of job satisfaction. Job security is the next most important variable with a standardised effect of 0.18. This variable along with marital status (standardised regression coefficient of 0.07) were the only non-wage variables that were significant. In particular, job status variables such as part-time or self-employment were not statistically significant.

5.5   CONCLUDING REMARKS

Much of the concern expressed about the spread of non-standard employment relates to its adverse impact on job stability. This decline in job stability is then put forward as a principal cause of declines in job satisfaction that have been reported in recent years. In an aggregate sense, both job security (stability) and job satisfaction have declined in most countries over the last two decades. At the same time the incidence of non-standard work has increased substantially and therefore it is not unlikely that these factors are linked. By its very nature, non-standard employment will reduce the average job tenure (an important measure of stability) of individual jobs and impact upon job satisfaction. However, many other social and economic factors effect job security and job satisfaction in addition to non-standard employment. Also, it is important, when considering this topic, to put things in perspective. Job security, as measured by average job tenure has declined in aggregate, but not by much.

For individual groups such as new entrants, the low-skilled and older workers, the decline is more pronounced. This confirms some of the conclusions reached in Chapter 4 and signifies that there is indeed some polarisation occurring in the labour market and that non-standard employment is playing an important role in this polarisation. Canadian and US studies find that, once a threshold of approximately one year is reached, those who retain their jobs actually have increased job tenure expectancy. But there is a growing number of jobs, particularly at the opposite age spectrum of the labour market, where the average job tenure has slipped below six months. In view of the discussion in Chapter 4 about non-standard work and job screening, it seems that six months may be becoming the *de-facto* screening period when employers decide whether or not to allow a new entrant into the traditional workforce.

Studies also show that people are less happy at work and that perceived job insecurity is an important factor in this increased unhappiness. Yet, once again, these studies show that the majority of workers are content, albeit less content than they were ten years earlier. The Kelley et al. (1998) study is one of the few to clearly establish the link between unstable, non-standard jobs and declines in worker satisfaction but virtually all other studies cited in this chapter are capable of being interpreted in this way.

One possible interpretation is that non-standard employment is playing a major role in dividing the labour market by creating groups of the secure and less secure, the satisfied and less satisfied and the well paid and less well paid. Non-standard work is not the only factor and possibly not the major factor, but it is one of the few consistent factors affecting labour markets across the world. It is increasingly being used as a rite of passage both into and out of the traditional labour market.

NOTES

1   See, Picot et al. (1997, p. 1) for further discussion of this data source.

2   There are a number of reasons, principally related to the incidence of collection, why Canadian data is preferable to US (CPS) data for studying job tenure. See Heisz (1996a, p. 6.)
    p. 6.

3   Only part of the results are reported in Table 5.3. For a full listing see Heisz (1996a, pp. 11-12).

4   Percentage point movements were evaluated at the mean.

5   The SEUP is a longitudinal survey whereby information was collected from a panel of persons living in private dwellings in both urban and rural areas between May 1995 and September 1997.

6   The theory of compensating differentials implies that if workers value job security there will be an implicit trade-off between pay and security. See Kelley et al. (1998, p. 1) for a discussion of the origins of this theory.

7   Kelley, Evans and Dawkins (1998) do not appear to explore the likely simultaneous relationship between union decline and job insecurity. For a discussion of the likely relationship between the two see Mangan and Williams (1999).

8   The *Pay Squared* variable is used to capture the declining marginal utility of pay.

6. Implications for Labour Market Organisations and Economic Performance

6.0   INTRODUCTION

The shift towards non-standard forms of employment has and will continue to impact on those government agencies and labour market organisations that developed their current format and means of operation in the era of traditional employment. Trade unions are a good example of institutions that are struggling to cope with the changing labour market. Not only are trade unions less attractive to non-standard workers than traditional workers but also there has been a long-standing antipathy felt by unions to the concept of non-standard work. As well, some employers of non-standard labour are strongly anti-union and actively attempt to limit union involvement with their workforce. The decline in union coverage has increased fears of further marginalisation among the less-skilled and more contingent groups of the non-standard workers, as well as raising general concerns about equity, training opportunities and workplace health and safety issues. On the other hand, some claim that the new flexibility in the labour force is already showing the rewards of greater productivity and employment growth. This chapter will examine both the relationship between non-standard workers and trade unions and the evidence linking changes in employment relationships to economic performance. Within this whole area of debate government regulators are caught somewhere in the middle, having a responsibility to ensure that minimum acceptable levels of worker protection are maintained in the absence of effective trade union coverage while, at the same time, attempting to encourage labour market flexibility and productivity growth.

6.1   TRADE UNIONS

It is well known that trade unions are facing declining memberships in many countries, both in an absolute and relative sense. For example, average union membership in the USA is currently at 14 per cent, down from a postwar high of 36 per cent in the 1960s. Even in those few countries, such as Canada, where unions have actually improved their relative position over the last decade, they are poorly represented in the growth, particularly information-based, industries (Dagg, 1997). It is not unusual for individual unions, particularly craft unions, to experience problems of declining membership as a result of technical change or changes in consumer tastes that have impacted on employment in particular industries and occupations. In part, they have solved these problems by merging with other unions or recruiting in growth industries. However, the movement to non-standard working arrangements represents a different and possibly more serious problem for trade unions because a large percentage of those entering into non-standard hours are choosing not to remain in or join a trade union of any kind. In addition, there is evidence that some employers of non-standard workers are strongly anti-union and discourage their workers, where possible, from joining a union (Dagg, 1997). Table 6.1 shows ILO data on union membership as a percentage of the total workforce across a range of selected countries.

Table 6.1 Trade union membership as a percentage of wage and salary earners, 1995

Country	Trade unionists as percent of workforce	Country	Trade unionists as percent of workforce
Africa		*Europe*	
Egypt	38.8	Austria	41.2
South Africa	40.9	Denmark	80.1
Americas		Finland	79.3
Argentina	38.7	France	9.1
Brazil	43.5	Germany	28.9
Canada	37.4	Greece	24.3
Cuba	70.2	Hungary	60.0
Mexico	42.8	Iceland	83.3
USA	14.2	Israel	23.0
Venezuela	17.1	Italy	44.1
Asia		Malta	65.1
Indonesia	3.4	Netherlands	25.6
Japan	24.0	Poland	33.8
Republic of Korea	12.7	Portugal	25.6
Malaysia	13.4	Spain	18.6
Philippines	38.2	Switzerland	22.5
Thailand	4.2	UK	32.9
Oceania			
Australia	35.2		
New Zealand	24.3		

Source: ILO (1997b, p. 2).

The ILO reports that in 1995 only 14 of the 92 counties surveyed had trade union membership rates in excess of 50 per cent. By comparison in 1975, union membership rates exceeded 50 per cent of the workforce in over 50 countries 50 (ILO, 1997b). The drop in trade union membership has been sharpest in Europe, caused principally by the demise of the Soviet bloc in Eastern Europe. For example, unionisation rates in Estonia fell by 49 per cent, Poland (-45 per cent), Slovakia (-40 per cent) and Hungary (-38 per cent). Other notable declines occurred in the UK (-20 per cent), Australia and New Zealand (-18 per cent). According to the ILO, the declines in Australia and New Zealand 'resulted partly from the weakening of legislation protecting workers organisations' (ILO, 1997b, p. 2). Losses were also recorded in the USA and Japan. Countries to experience increase in union member ship were Bangladesh (+58 per cent), Spain (+92 per cent) and Canada (+10.7 per cent).

6.2   UNION DECLINE AND NON-STANDARD EMPLOYMENT

The decline in union membership in Australia and New Zealand has been highlighted throughout this book because both these countries have been traditional strongholds of union influence. As well, most of the decline in union membership occurred when both countries were governed by Labour (social-democratic) parties who might have been expected to favour union influence. For union membership to decline so rapidly under these circumstances is an indication of the disruption that labour market transition is causing to traditional labour market institutions. Earlier it was reported that a strong negative relationship existed between union density and the spread of non-standard employment in Australia. This is further evidenced by the data in Tables 6.2 and 6.3.

Table 6.2 Trade union membership, Australia: proportion of employees

Type/Year	1976	1986	1988	1994	1996	Change
Total	51	46	41.6	35.0	31.1	-18.9
Permanent	NA	51	46.6	41.3	37.4	-13.6
Casual	NA	21	19.7	14.7	13.1	-7.9
Private	NA	34	31.5	26.0	24.5	-9.5
Public	NA	71	61.7	63.3	55.4	-15.6
Full-time	NA	47	45.9	39.1	34.5	-12.5
Part-time	NA	40	24.5	22.9	21.6	-18.4
Male	56	50	46.3	37.9	33.5	-16.5
Female	43	39	35.0	31.3	28.1	-14.9

Source: Trade Union Members Australia, ABS (1999b), Catalogue 6325.0.

The data in Table 6.2 indicate that trade union membership as a percentage of all employees in Australia had declined from 51 per cent in 1976 to 31 per cent in 1996. Currently two in every three employees in Australia are not members of a trade union. Even the traditional union stronghold of male full-time work has a union membership of less than 40 per cent. The one bright spot for union membership is in the public sector where 55 per cent of employees are members. However, even here the proportion of employees who are union members has declined from 63 per cent in 1994. Of course the real measure of union influence is union coverage, the numbers of persons whose terms and conditions are covered by pay and work conditions that were negotiated by unions on behalf of their active members. The latest ABS data on award coverage place adult non-managerial coverage at 85.9 per cent of full-time workers and 82.4 per cent of part-time workers. This figure indicates that unions exert an influence beyond their numbers although their impact on managerial employees and 'pseudo employees' (referring to dependent SECs) is believed to be far less. Moreover coverage and membership numbers are not independent. Continued decline in numbers would inevitability mean less overall influence.

Table 6.3 Employees by industry: proportion who were trade union members at August 1994

Industry	Permanent	Casual	Total*
Agriculture, forestry and fishing	16.0	8.4	7.1
Mining	47.2	18.6	44.1
Manufacturing	44.6	15.9	41.7
Electricity, gas and water	67.5	26.9	70.3
Construction	41.3	17.5	32.8
Wholesale trade	16.3	4.4	17.2
Retail trade	25.6	20.5	19.8
Accommodation	22.4	16.7	16.3
Transport and storage	58.4	20.3	52.4
Communication services	69.0	23.3	68.2
Finance and insurance	45.3	3.3	28.4
Property and business	17.4	6.8	13.2
Government administration and defence	58.3	14.2	52.6
Education	63.9	14.6	51.3
Health and community services	44.1	10.6	34.2
Cultural and recreational	29.4	16.8	24.6
Personal and other services	44.9	6.0	41.6
Total	41.3	14.7	33.5

Note:
* Data in total column relates to 1996.

Source: Trade Union Members Australia, ABS 1999(b), Cat. 6325.0.

The causes of the decline in union membership are numerous but revolve around the decline in the relative importance of the traditional union power base, full-time, permanent male employees and the rise of non-standard working arrangements. For example, less than 15 per cent of total casual employees are now trade union members.

The percentage of trade union members who are also employed on a casual basis is greatest in those industries such as electricity, gas and water (26.9 per cent), transport and storage (20.3 per cent) and communication services (23.3 per cent). These industries also have the highest percentage of overall trade union membership. The other industries have mixed results. Wholesale trade has low overall membership and low casual membership. By contrast, retail trade has relatively low permanent membership but among the largest proportion of union membership by casuals. This may reflect the long history of part-time and casual employment in retail which has provided time for the appropriate unions to more effectively organise this workforce than elsewhere. The public service unions show the greatest disparity between permanent and casual trade union membership, for example education (63.9 and 14.6 respectively) and government and defence (59.3. and 14.2). This may suggest a culture of unionism at the work site that either induces casuals to join or retains those former permanent employees that have changed status. A similar pattern exists among part-time workers. Less than 20 per cent of part-time workers are members of unions.

Overall, there appears little doubt that the increase in non-standard working arrangements has helped in the decline of trade union membership although it may be difficult to establish a direct causal effect. For example, it may be that those who have shifted to non-standard employment, particularly those that did so in a voluntary fashion, see no need for union membership, particularly given past union hostility to some forms of non-standard work, such as regular casual work. The relative cost of joining may also be an issue if unions do not provide special part-time rates. For those who were forced into non-standard employment or who are involuntary members of it, union membership may be more attractive but given their weakened bargaining position they may not be able to join unions or make use of union awards if faced with employer opposition. The extent of this form of employer opposition is difficult to measure and so far has only been supplied anecdotally in Australia. However, in Canada, Dagg (1997) and Brault (1997) have found evidence of significant employer resistance to non-standard workers becoming unionised.

The continued decline in union membership in Australia during the 1990s has brought significant pressure on unions to change their ideas on the issue of non-standard employment. Much of the problems unions are now facing may relate to the historical and sometime hostile attitudes unions have shown to non-standard working arrangements. For example, the Women's Charter adopted by the Australian Council of Trade Unions (ACTU) in 1981 adopted the following resolutions:

- Part-time work should not be created at the expense of full-time work. The first priority of trade unions must be the protection and preservation of full-time employment opportunities.
- Part-time work is not and must not be used as a substitute for effective economic policies.

By 1990, in the ACTU guidelines on part-time work, casual work and job-sharing, there had been a softening in the union attitude. The unions were encouraged to enrol part-time workers and remove any barriers to their recruitment. Unions were also requested to negotiate specifically on behalf of part-time workers and to maintain accurate data on the distribution between part-time workers and full-time workers.

However, the ACTU still recommended that part-time work should be negotiated on the basis of permanent part-time work with pro-rata benefits. In respect of casual employment, the ACTU guidelines were opposed to the hiring of 'permanent' casuals. They argued that casuals should not be used in place of permanent workers for protracted periods. The appendix to the ACTU report suggested the use of permanent part-time workers to displace casuals and the use of award provisions to restrict the employment of casuals for a limited period and to a certain number of hours. Researchers such as Dagg (1997) have documented the continuing antagonism felt by many employers of non-standard workers to unions:

> For the vast majority of small enterprise employers, unionisation is highly unwelcome to say the least. Unionisation is resisted because it limits the power of employers in the workplace in key areas such as discipline, hiring and layoffs, scheduling of work and the content of jobs. Employers have significant resources at their disposal to resist unionisation. Almost by definition, short-term and contract workers can be easily dismissed and the hours of part-timers can be changed. Workers in precarious jobs fear employer reprisal or workplace closure if they join a union (Dagg, 1997, p. 51).

Freeman (1996) and others have emphasised the role of unions in combating low wages among workers and fear the income distribution outcomes of the growth of non-standard employment in non-unionised work sites. The changing nature of the workplace is also putting pressure on unions in an organisational way, even for those unions anxious to recruit non-standard workers. Once again, Canadian data provides an indication of the scope of the problem.

Half of all workplaces in Canada today have fewer than 50 employees, but, given overburdened staff and resources, many unions find it very difficult to take on small bargaining units because of the costs of bargaining contracts and other representational functions (Krahn, 1995, p. 14).

The other uncertainty facing unions is the impact of further labour market deregulation. Brosnan and Thornthwaite have argued strongly that the spread of non-standard work has been encouraged by changes in wage-fixing procedures and other workplace regulations by a series of structural efficiency principles. Industrial legislation and many awards now specifically allow for non-standard working arrangements to be made on an individual basis. As well, Romeyn (1992) states that:

In many decisions examined, however, restrictions have been removed from both part-time and casual work, including restrictions on the length of casual employment and, at one extreme, regular, long term casual employment has been provided for in the award.

Brault (1997) argues that the challenge now is for unions to renew themselves. This, he argues, may be achieved by unions also going global and organising labour across national boundaries and across industries. For example, the same information technology that has threatened unionism should be used to unite workers faced with common problems. He argues that unions should become central reference points for otherwise disunited groups of non-standard workers such as teleworkers.

Others would like to see unions work in cooperation with government legislation to protect other groups of home-workers. For example, the 1995 ILO convention on home-work argued for tripartite (government, business and labour) cooperation in the preparation of:

- Legally enforceable standards on homework, covering payments, pension entitlements, workplace health and safety.
- Formal definitions of home-work.
- Laws and regulations prohibiting certain types of work and certain substances in the home.
- A system of inspections and adequate remedies, including penalties for violation of laws and regulations.
- Employers to inform home-workers in writing of their specific conditions of employment and changes when they occur.

- The right to organise and bargain collectively.
- Hours of work to be formalised and rest periods built into agreements.
- Social security recognition and maternity allowances built in.

6.3   IMPLICATIONS OF A DECLINE IN TRADE UNION ORGANISATIONS

Whether organisations that attract less than 20 per cent of private sector employees as members can continue to have a major influence in the labour market is doubtful. As well, the antagonism between some unions and non-union members, who are also employed under non-standard conditions, is unlikely to disappear in the near future. Moreover, the emphasis on individual and plant-level bargaining as the preferred process of wage formation means that unions now have less influence at the sharp end of labour markets than previously. To this point some unions have not fully come to terms with atypical workers. Nor have they understood the forces that are causing so many to take up non-standard positions. The attitude seems to have been that permanent full-time work is the ideal, permanent part-time is tolerable but any other form of atypical work is to be resisted. This is particularly true for home-workers. Brooks argues that:

> This reflects the widely held belief that homework (and for that matter other atypical working arrangements) is inimical to effective trade unionism (Brooks, 1991, p. 6).

National unions have, in the past, demanded the prohibition of home work. The basic problem with this form of strategy is that casual employment and contract employment are the fastest growing areas of the labour market from which, to this point, unions have largely locked themselves out. One short-term tactic for the union movement may be to attempt to organise industries and work sites rather than individuals and by which all employees by virtue of their employment become union members. Unions might also set up advisory services for their members and other workers contemplating a change in working arrangements.

There is now local and international evidence that the trade union movement is starting to address the issue. The UK Trade Union Congress (TUC) has established a separate section to organise and cater to the special needs of home-workers and the TCFUA has adopted a policy 'which has actively encouraged the regulation, protection and representation of home-workers' (Marshall and Ginters, 1995). The 82nd session of the International Labour Conference of June 1995 put forward an international policy to:

Promote equality of treatment between home-workers and other wage earners, taking into account the special characteristics of home-work and where appropriate, conditions appropriate to the same or similar work carried out by an enterprise (ILO, 1995, p. 14).

In the absence of such strategies union influence in the labour market, particularly the private sector, will continue to fall and as a result put in jeopardy award and industry agreements on productivity and training. Historically, unions have effectively formed a barrier against the spread of low-wage employment. Their role in doing this has been highlighted by the OECD:

Higher rates of unionism and collective bargaining coverage reduce the incidence of low wages (OECD, 1997, p. 8).

The converse is also true. Freeman has shown that:

In the 1980s, 15 per cent of the workforce lost the 20-25 % wage advantage associated with union membership, the lower dispersion of wages found in union workplaces and the greater provision of pensions and other benefits under unionism (Freeman, 1996, p. 11).

If these arguments are true then the decline in unionism, concurrent with the spread of non-standard employment, will increase income inequality and place further pressure on the social security net.

6.4 PRODUCTIVITY

A central argument used to justify the movement towards non-standard hours is the belief that labour productivity will be improved and that the benefits of this productivity growth will flow to the participants, through lower costs and higher wages, and to the economy through reduced inflation and ultimately higher growth. The exact mechanisms by which this productivity growth will take place are not often spelt out but there is a widely held belief that this will occur (Hamberger, 1995). For example, a Business Council of Australia survey of members found that a large minority of members supported the proposition that 'truly achieving world class productivity in my company requires individual contracts' (Hamberger, 1995). The link between labour hire practices and work performance is both motivational and cost-based. For example, Cappelli (1999) has suggested that downsizing and other labour changes in US corporations has produced productivity gains but at the expense of labour morale and worker commitment. The last two effects have resulted mainly from greatly increased workloads.

This in turn may introduce a time dimension into the relationship. Whether continued productivity gains can be achieved from a disgruntled and overworked labour force seems doubtful. On the motivational side, proponents of new work relationships argue that only through direct dealings with the individual can that element of trust and commonality of purpose between employer and employee be achieved. Fox identified this point when he argued:

> The greater degree of discretion extended to a person in his work, the more he feels that relevant rules and arrangements embody a high degree of trust (Fox, 1995, p. 27).

In most work situations, the introduction of non-standard work practices has coincided with reductions in the organisational layers. It is for this reason that middle management has suffered from much of the workplace restructuring and downsizing that has taken place.

Irrespective of the role of trust and interpersonal contact, non-standard work arrangements offer employers a good chance to reduce their on-cost commitments and this alone may force down unit labour costs and give the appearance of improved productivity. The productivity gains of approximately 60 per cent cited by Cappelli do appear extraordinarily high. However, it should be remembered that these gains came from labour force restructuring, principally downsizing and not necessarily from the introduction of non-standard employment. More specific evidence on the relationship between productivity and non-standard employment comes from North America. IBM Canada claims that teleworking has cut leasing costs by 55 per cent in some branch plants (Goulet, 1997). Similarly, the New York Telephone and the Control Data Corporation report productivity gains of 43 per cent and 20 per cent, respectively. According to the companies involved these gains were derived from:

- Greater tranquillity.
- Less interruption to work flow.
- The ability to choose hours of work more appropriate to lifestyle.

IBM claims that telework had reduced absenteeism, increased employee retention and enhanced personnel loyalty and overall worker satisfaction (Goulet, 1997).

Under some non-standard arrangements contractors are free to work extended hours, negotiate higher earnings and arrange their tax affairs in a way that minimises the tax loss associated with higher earnings (Fox, 1995). On the basis of perceived gains in productivity, employers are prepared to pay a premium in direct labour costs. Many are also prepared to pay the potentially large transactions costs of individually negotiating with employees or engaging a labour hiring agency to act on their behalf. A central part of modern human resource management (HRM) theory, and its implicit acceptance by management, is the belief that collective bargaining and the acceptance of a pluralist workplace is essentially out of step with efficient work practices (Fernie and Metcalf, 1995). The overall effects are shown in Figure 6.1.

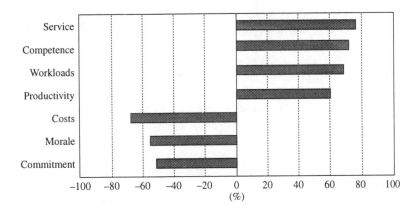

Source: Cappelli (1997, p. 57).

Figure 6.1 Consequences of restructuring

Whether the management rhetoric translates into genuine cost savings and productivity growth is more difficult to predict. One of the few recent empirical studies is by Fernie and Metcalf (1995) for the UK. They found that a work-site where all or most of the workforce were on individual contracts performed better than collective bargaining sites in the same industry in terms of absenteeism, jobs growth, industrial relations climate and productivity performance.

Other, more specific data has been tendered in the submissions by Conzinc Riotinto Australia (CRA) and Hamersley Iron to the Australian Industrial Relations Commission. For example, CRA reported substantial rises for their Bell Bay operations in terms of output to power use ratios from 91 per cent to 92.5 per cent (which translates into a 12 per cent cost saving) since the introduction of staff contacts. Hamersley Iron claims a 33.5 per cent rise in productivity following a 5 per cent contract-inspired pay increase.

These results are selective and the Australian examples are taken from large-scale companies that have substantial scope for savings in on-costs.

There is far less evidence on the impact of non-standard work on smaller companies, with the exception of the negative costs associated with the administration of individual contracts that have been identified in New Zealand (Hamberger, 1995). The other productivity issue concerning the imposition of non-standard working arrangements is their potential for division and industrial relations upheavals where a workforce is divided as to the introduction of changes in labour hiring practices.

A current example of this is the strike at the United Parcel Service in the USA and the 'Justice for Janitors' campaign in Canada. In a country where industrial action is often seen in an unsympathetic light, the strike by the employees of the United Parcel Service received extraordinary support. In brief, the strike was over the continuing non-standardisation of the workforce in which over 50 per cent in 1997 were part-time or casual. There were also substantial differences in wages and benefits between permanents and non-permanents. Union demands for a boost to full-time work 'Struck a chord with many Americans concerned about the insecurity of part-time work' (*The Economist*, 1997b, p. 25). The other significant fact about this (ultimately successful) strike was that the remaining permanent employees were not willing to trade job security for additional income. The victory of the union, resulting in a reversal of hiring practices by the company, is being seen as the most substantial achievement by labour in the USA for several decades (*The Economist*, 1997b).

Similarly the 'Justice for Janitors' campaign in North America organised by the Service Employees International Union has shown it is possible to organise, represent and make gains on behalf of low-paid, non-standard employees in the highly competitive contract cleaning industry. In this case city-wide 'social movement' campaigns were run against owners of buildings that did not recognise the union. The result was negotiation of minimum acceptable wages and conditions. The distinguishing feature about this type of industrial action was that the union avoided the usual route of certification and collective bargaining with individual building cleaning contractors since it was recognised that organising and certifying one contractor would not work because any gains made at that level would be unsustainable.

> The answer lay in organising all of the geographically defined sector in a single campaign (Dagg, 1977, p. 53).

One other consideration is that firms that avoid labour on-costs by forcing employees to become *de-facto* contractors are gaining an unfair cost advantage over firms that do not engage in these activities. This issue has not been given much consideration in Australia but received attention in Canada during the recent inquiry held in that country into the effects of the growth of non-standard employment.

6.5 OTHER INDUSTRIAL RELATIONS ISSUES

Non-standard working arrangements impact upon industrial relations in a number of ways. On the supply-side they have the potential to remove the third parties, particularly unions, from the industrial relations process as workers opt to make arrangements for individualised working conditions or, in the case of casual or marginalised workers, do not feel part of the union process. In either case the likelihood of mass or company-wide industrial action is reduced. From the point of view of companies there is now a widespread belief that collective bargaining and the traditional role of union coverage are incompatible with the principles of modern HRM theory. As Hamberger argues:

> This belief is firmly based on the notion that the interests of employers and employees have more in common than separate them. It sees collective bargaining as unnecessarily adversarial-creating conflict between workers and their employers, rather than simply expressing and regulating that conflict (Hamberger, 1995, p.12).

For this reason employers seem to be the instigators of most moves to change labour hire practices or working arrangements. A survey conducted by McAndrew (1992) in New Zealand found that of those firms that put new individual contracts in place, employers initiated 88 per cent. The survey further reports that where opposition to these changes occurred it was in areas where the workforce was heavily unionised.

Fox used the example of the CRA dispute to show the likelihood of industrial disputation where changes to working arrangements do not have broad worker support. Fox is also critical of the view that collective bargaining and the establishment of high trust relationships are incompatible. This view, he calls unitarianism, because it implies there can be only one source of legitimate authority in the workplace. He argues that such a view loses sight of the realities of modern work sites:

> The high degree of division of labour required by contemporary capitalism means that work must be organised in such a way that gives little discretion to the ordinary worker, breeding a lack of trust between employer and employee. This cannot be overcome simply by talk of common interest and the introduction of some limited form of management controlled participation (Fox, 1995, p. 29).

If Fox is right, he raises a serious dilemma for the proponents of the new work arrangements. Large firms, which stand to gain most in terms of reducing on-costs, are the least suitable organisations to implement such a programme and have most to lose from industrial action. The public policy issues are complex. An assessment of these varying views as a basis for policy making will depend on an understanding of how the labour market and the industrial relations system work together. One way to do this is to use the approach of it being either the unitarist or the pluralist model.

In the unitarist model we have to accept that each enterprise is a single unit which is the subject of the loyalty of the employer and employee(s) and they work together as a team with shared interests. In this situation a union would be an intrusion. The employee would have a strong commitment to the firm and job. The employer building this environment would repay this.

A pluralist approach argues that the parties in the employment relationship are protected by a system of checks and balances normally accepted to be unions or legislation.

In the case of atypical employment it is difficult to see strong general evidence of the unitarist model since the aim of the employer in many cases will be to reduce as far as possible the link between the firm and the employer. Rather the aim is to typify this as a transitory arrangement. Many employees will in fact have more than one job and so the idea of a single mutual attachment would be difficult to sustain.

The case of a DC raises an interesting case since much will depend on whether the relationship is one that has its roots in supply or demand. Where the market power rests with the 'employee' because of the possession of particular skills that are in limited supply then the individual might just be limiting rent-seeking by staying with the firm for a particular reason but it might not be a true mutual commitment. An employee forced into this status is unlikely to feel any true loyalty.

Many cases are therefore more likely to fall into the pluralist net with the employee not seeing themselves as part of the firm and looking to the state for a set of checks and balances. This would be the case for no other reason than the lack of bargaining power and limited access to information. This pluralist approach has been recognised in the current legislative approach adopted in the Australian legislation, which provides for the presence of an Employment Advocate and an Enterprise Commissioner on the Industrial Relations Commission. The legislation is designed to ensure the maintenance of minimum conditions and access to information.

This is particularly important in the context of declining union density and the fact that the agreements do not require the union to be a party. The encouragement of individual contracts allows a greater customising of agreements between individuals and the firm. A continuation of this legislative approach might be one way to contribute to the flexibility of atypical work while protecting against the extremes that would see the development of a true secondary labour market.

The general swing across the world to non-standard work and the almost universality of modern HRM teaching in this area indicate that the experiments with new forms of labour hiring practices will almost certainly spread in the immediate future. The principal challenge for policy makers is to protect marginalised and vulnerable workers at the same time as providing an environment where suitably empowered workers and employers can explore mutually beneficial agreements. A lot will depend on the equity and wage outcomes and their distribution across the economy.

6.6   WAGES AND EQUITY

One of the more frequently mentioned concerns about the growth of non-standard employment is the fear that vulnerable workers will experience unstable working conditions, unsociable working hours, lower wages and increased marginalisation. The issue of gender equity is also raised because casual work, out-work and temporary work (though not unsociable hours) fall disproportionately on women. The exception is in the area of unsociable, particularly night, work, which falls most heavily on men. Detailed research into this area is still difficult to obtain and evaluation of any results is not made easier by the diversity of employment situations grouped together under the term 'non-standard'. A European Industrial Relations Report (EIRR, 1995) found that over 14 per cent of the workforce (15 million) in Europe worked at night with the large majority being males (12 million). The levels of night work are highest in the UK where 28 per cent of men and 13 per cent of women are affected. Social commentators have expressed concern over the effect this has on family relations.

On the core question of wages the evidence seems to be mixed and to have an occupational and industrial distribution. In the USA, the Bureau of Labour Statistics (US Department of Labor) Employment Survey of establishments for June 1996 reported that the gap for average hourly earnings of temporary and permanent production workers was over 20 per cent. Hipple and Stewart (1996a) were among the first to analyse this data when they compared earnings and employer-funded benefits between contingent and non-contingent workers. They used the broadest definition of contingency but excluded the self-employed (both incorporated and unincorporated) and ICs. They found considerable difference between the unadjusted earnings of both groups. Non-contingent workers averaged $416 per week compared to $285 for contingent workers. However, this straight comparison is misleading because of the much higher propensity for contingent workers to work part-time or irregular hours. Nevertheless, among both full-time and part-time workers, contingent workers earn about 20 per cent less than traditional workers. They concluded that the main reasons for this were, even within the part-time category, contingent workers worked 10 per cent less hours and that contingent workers were younger and lower-skilled. This type of evidence seems to suggest that it is the characteristics of contingent work rather than contingency itself that causes the lower earnings. Sullivan and Segal (1997) took up the same theme but more formally introduced control variables into the analysis. They found that the extent of the earnings differential narrowed considerably when factors known to impact upon wage rates such as age, sex and education were used as control variables. The aggregate data also did not adequately reflect variation earnings among temporary workers across occupations. Sullivan and Segal (1997) using CPS wage data were able to show the impact of traditionally important labour market data upon the permanent-temporary wage differential. Their results are summarised in Table 6.4.

Table 6.4 Percentage hourly wage differentials between workers by form of employment

Classification	All	Pink-collar	Blue-collar	White-collar
1. Permanent temporary wage differential	21.8	17.7	29.4	13.4
2. Controlled for age, race, sex, education, census division, region	13.8	16.1	23.8	2.9
3. Controlled for (2) plus union, part-time, one-digit occupation	7.7	12.0	15.6	-2.1*
4. Controlled for union status, part-time status, one-digit occupation and individual fixed effect	3.1	5.7	3.0	2.0

Note:
* not significantly different from zero at the 10 per cent level.

Source: Sullivan and Segal (1997, p. 6).

The results in Table 6.4 show the important role of individual characteristic variables in explaining differences in hourly wage rates between standard and non-standard workers. For example, among white-collar workers, after adjusting for a range of worker and job characteristics, temporary workers appear to be paid 2 per cent per hour more than permanent workers. However, after the same adjustments for blue-collar and pink-collar workers, the wage cost of being employed in a non-standard form seems to be of the order of 15 and 12 per cent, respectively. The results shown above, though interesting, fail to take into account the wage (monetary) value of employer-funded benefits that are not available to temporary workers. Consideration of the present value of these benefits would serve to widen the differentials calculated by Sullivan and Segal.

Yet not all workers in alternative arrangements fared badly in wage comparisons with traditional workers. In her analysis of the 1995 CPS survey of workers in alternative arrangements in the USA, Cohany (1998) found that wages differed widely within this group. However, in most cases these variations were explained by factors such as hours worked, skill level and gender rather than nature of employment, although it was found that any movement towards contingency also tended to decrease earnings. For example, the highest paid group among those in alternative employment were independent contractors. Only 3.5 per cent of this group could be classed as contingent. On average they worked four hours per week (46.3 hour) more and had, on average, 15 per cent higher earnings than traditional workers. There was also evidence of a much higher earnings division by sex among this group than among traditional workers. Among ICs, the average male weekly earnings were $621 while female earnings were 50 per cent lower at $409. The corresponding earnings differential among males and females in traditional employment was 28 per cent. On-call workers, a mixed group which, despite having a significant number of nurses and teachers, tend to have lower average skill levels, were found to earn 15 per cent lower than traditional workers although almost all of this is explainable by their higher propensity to work part-time or irregular hours. Wages were lowest for the most contingent in this group, temporary help agency employees. This group earned, on average, 66 per cent of the earnings of traditional workers. However, once again, job type did not seem to be the major factor in this below average earnings. Cohany argues:

> The low earnings of temporary help agency workers are, in part, a reflection of the fact that the clerical and machine operator jobs they typically hold pay lower-than-average wages (Cohany, 1998, p. 17).

Less positive in their assessment of the wage implications of non-standard employment are Mishel and Bernstein (1995). They argue that the impact of non-standard working arrangements in the USA on the less-skilled has been to increase marginalisation and decrease wages. However much of the American experience seems to be relate to the problem of illegal migrants and their exploitation. For New Zealand, since 1991, the evidence seems to contradict the argument that contract employment has reduced wages:

> The evidence suggests that it is only a relatively small minority of employers who would take advantage of individual contracts to downgrade wages and conditions. Econometric modeling in New Zealand indicates that the reforms have had a neutral wage effect but have been positive for employment and have reduced unit labour costs (Hamberger, 1995, p. 13).

In Australia some smaller firms have reported above-award payments to employees that move to contracts. Still, the process is in its formative stage and has been introduced at a time of relative economic upturn and during which proponents of workplace changes are in competition with the union movement. It is unlikely that at this early stage employers would seek to move against wages. This may not be the case if the economy moved into recession or if the union movement ceased to be an effective countervailing force.

The other big equity question is that concerning differential treatment for different categories of labour. Skilled workers that enter into contracts are likely to prosper by virtue of their skills. However, unskilled workers forced into casual or other forms of marginalised employment are more likely to suffer a reduction in working conditions, particularly in a recession. Traditional safety nets supplied by government may also be put under strain if tax receipts fall as a result of changes in working arrangements. In addition, the macroeconomics of the changes in working conditions is an under-researched aspect. Reduced unit labour costs and increased productivity may feed into reduced inflation and interest rates. On the negative side there may be reduced tax receipts and increased demands on government to provide supplements to marginalised workers and to pick up the slack in employer-funded training and other programmes.

6.7   OTHER MACRO IMPACTS FROM THE INCREASING LEVELS OF ATYPICAL WORK

The macroeconomic impact of the shift to greater atypical work patterns is not certain and these cannot be separated from the equity issues. The trend has to be seen in the context of the benefits that will accrue from a more flexible labour market. The epitome of a flexible labour is often claimed to be that of the USA. The European approach is then seen to be the antithesis.

Freeman (1996) examined the responses of the US labour market in the 1980s and the 1990s to variations in economic conditions. He noted it was viewed by many as the paradise of neoclassical flexibility where wages responded rapidly to changes in demand and supplying local markets with little institutional intervention. Jobs were readily available for those who wanted them; employers were able to hire and fire at will with little or government or union restriction. Spells of unemployment were short and unemployment benefits modest. These responses were accompanied by increased wage inequality and real earnings of the less-skilled fell. This was accompanied by increases in crime, child poverty and an increased and permanent underclass.

These changes cannot be seen in isolation from other economic changes such as technological change, growth of trade, increased immigration, increased supply of women in the labour market and the changed supply of educated workers. The last reduced the pay of college graduates relative to other workers.

The responses that occurred in the USA with a weakened demand for labour relative to supply were numerous:

- Real hourly compensation stagnated from 1977-93 and fell for full-time males.
- The gap in wages between more/less-educated and skilled workers rose greatly. In the context of the monograph this is important since the point that is being made is that it is the low-skilled (less-educated) is the group at risk.
- Earnings distribution widened with significant unequal income distribution.
- The USA was very successful in generating work for those seeking it. There was a high level of mobility.
- The duration of unemployment spells in the USA was shorter than in Europe and so was more widely shared.

Freeman's summary is that:

> The American job market serves well the best firms and the most skilled workers, and generates self-correcting forces, in the form of increased investment by young persons in education and training in response to educational differentials. But it does a poor job in preparing less skilled Americans for the modern world of work and has short changed the children brought up in poverty and surrounded by crime (Freeman, 1996, p. 15).

This is one view of the way that a decentralised and deregulated labour market is likely to work in the context of the economic changes of the kind that are occurring across the world. The changes required for a deregulated labour market could produce the characteristics of the US system, for example, wage rates responding quickly to supply and demand in the local market. The question of observable labour productivity will be complex. If there is a marked decrease in the cost of labour there will be little incentive in many cases to substitute capital for labour, particularly in the service-type industry. The US experience would suggest that increasing flexibility will lead to the growth of employment particularly in a situation where new service-type industries are emerging, for example, temping and parcel delivery. The core issue of course is the nature of these jobs and the data would seem to suggest that as we observe more flexibility it is accompanied by the growth of atypical employment.

Gregory (1996) examined the US data noting the falling real wages and erosion of non-wage conditions. He concluded that:

The US labour market seems far from ideal. Wages and employment conditions are deteriorating on average but the labour market is producing a fast rate of job growth. Furthermore, gross domestic product per head of population has grown at much the same rate as in other countries. The labour market has not produced a faster output growth rate to be distributed among the population. All that seems to have happened is that the United States has created more jobs for less income per job (Gregory, 1996, p. 85).

6.8   TRAINING ISSUES

Any continued decline in union membership will remove one prop from the national system of training and bargaining that has developed over the last decade. However, whether non-standard working arrangements will encourage or hinder training for the workforce as a whole will depend largely upon how the potential conflict between labour force flexibility and skill enhancement for employees is managed and the role that governments are prepared to play.

To this point those that have examined the issue of non-standard work and training have concentrated on employees, either part-time and/or casual workers. Most reports have been pessimistic. This is true even for what most observers regard as the best form of non-standard work, permanent part-time. For example, Winley (1990) claimed:

> Quite often, of course, this sort of work, and the people involved in it, are treated as separate populations of employees, with different jobs, different pay structures, little overlap and no chance of promotion (Winley, 1990, p. 11).

In 1989, the Women's Bureau commissioned a survey of 17 000 part-time employees in the banking industry. Among its findings were:

- The overwhelming majority of these workers are still performing the lowest level of clerical or data processing work with very few occupying above base positions.
- Despite award changes which now permit part-time employees to be in promotional positions and despite identified ambition among part-time employees for promotional opportunities little action is being taken.
- Only limited attention is being given to identifying and developing career paths for them.

Similar results were reported in a survey of part-time employees in the Australian Tax Office.

Romeyn (1992) and a survey of women public servants undertaken in 1991 by the Australian Public Service (APS) bipartite consultative group found that 'training was generally designed for and required full-time participation'.

The most recent survey by the ABS, How Workers get their Training, Australia 1989, found that:

- Part-time (both permanent and casual) employees receive less in-house and external training than full-time employees, and
- Permanent employees receive more in-house and external training than casuals.

Dawkins and Norris (1990) argue that the pool of labour from which many casuals are drawn, school students and mature women, means that 'jobs are not structured to provide training and career progression, since these features are unlikely to be valued by the casual employees taken on'.

Romeyn has identified a number of factors that actively block the human capital development of part-time and casual work. These are:

- Institutional.
- Organisational.
- Attitudinal.
- Structural (particularly the provision and delivery of training).

In an institutional sense, the cultures of most workplaces still see non-standard workers as peripheral and as a result do not fully include them in their training and development plans. In an organisational sense, the concentration of these workers into low-ranking jobs tends to be reinforcing and prevents access to advancement and the training required for advancement. Attitudinal factors relate to management presumptions about the motivations of non-standard workers and their level of commitment to the firm. This in turn encourages a view that these workers are second-class citizens. Canadians are also expressing concern over the decline in training opportunities that seem to be associated with the spread of non-standard work.

> Precarious and contingent work is much more often a trap than an opportunity. Such work usually provides little or no training or access to career ladders. The reality is, at best, movement between unemployment and short-term, low skill, no future jobs (Dagg, 1997, p. 59).

In both Australia and Canada trade unions are seen as not sufficiently protecting the rights of these members in the area of training. Finally access to training and promotion may be constrained by the structure and timing of courses which are organised around a full-time schedule.

If these observations are correct and typical of workplaces throughout the world it appears that the growth of non-standard employment among wage and salary employees is reducing their level of training completed at the workplace and funded by employers. If training levels are to be maintained, responsibility for training provision and funding may need to contain a greater element of self-funding or attract increased government spending.

The recommendations of the recent Canadian inquiry on non-standard employment stressed the need for greater government coordination of training services to atypical workers. For example, suggestions were made for a general training levy to be placed on all employers, discounted by the extent to which a particular company undertook in-house training, and made available money to finance training opportunities for suitable applicants. A variant of this proposal would require SECs to also contribute to a skills enhancement fund for upgrading of skills of those that are now self-employed but who previously benefited from employer training schemes. The fear here is that newly created SECs may be unwilling to fund their future training needs with the result that the national skill base will decline.

There are reasons to believe that an increase in some forms of non-standard work may be indicative of greater self-funding in training and education. Non-standard work, by its nature and from the characteristics of its participants, allows greater emphasis on self-financed training. Many students finance tuition or living expenses from casual and part-time work. The recent imposition by governments of tuition fees has meant that a growing number of students require part-time and casual work to allow them to study on a more or less full-time basis. Even if this is the case, the problem from a national economic point of view is the effect that a shift from private financed to public financed training will have upon the distribution of training by type. For example, it is likely that technical and vocational training that requires on-the-job experience will decline, while formal tertiary and on-campus training will expand.

If job-specific and on-the-job training is restricted to full-time (permanent) employees there may also be some equity issues as casual and part-time workers become less integral to the firm and more removed from the mainstream.

In terms of SECs, the issue is slightly different. In general SECs have above-community average levels of vocational training and it is for this reason that some advantage attaches to their self-employed status. Human capital, however, is prone to depreciation over time; the move towards self-employment brings with it the requirement that SEC retrain at their own expense, although some tax benefits will attach to this training. It may be that

SECs will adopt a short-run attitude to training and not retrain at the required level. The net result would be a diminution of the skill base and a shortage of properly trained SECs in the future.

This need not be the case. A rational skills training approach would:

- In the case of non-standard employees, create provisions in employment contracts with the specific purpose of ensuring a training and career structure. The Canadian scheme described earlier would be another way of inducing employers to contribute to the training of non-standard workers.
- In the case of SECs, government registration and requirements may need to be strengthened to gain professionally accepted standards in a range of activities and occupations. This may be part-funded by users and part-funded by the contractors themselves. Alternatively, government could provide special incentives, for example, tax benefits, to induce independent contractors to regularly update their skills. Similarly Government funding and or tax concessions may be required to induce temporaries, casuals and other non-standard workers to take part in national skills enhancement programmes.

Finally, some labour hire agencies are using training as a means of having a pool of higher standard workers and in this way gaining a competitive edge. The NATSS found that nearly 30 per cent of temps received up to 20 hours training per week in the initiation period. There is less evidence of training occurring in other fields.

6.9 GENDER EQUITY

While the relativities may be changing slightly, women continue to dominate employment in non-standard employment. This is often seen as a positive outcome because women with family and other commitments are able to utilise non-standard work as a means of staying connected with the labour force. This is the view put by:

> It (part-time work) makes it easier to reconcile family responsibilities with employment, with the added advantage of maintaining a link with working life and thus avoiding a total break as is the case with parental leave which can create problems as regards subsequent skills upgrading (Lemaitre et al., 1997, p. 7).

However, especially in places like Europe, the sex segregation of non-standard work is most extreme among prime-aged workers. A report of the European Commission on employment in Europe found that in the EU as a whole only 3 per cent of men of prime working age were in part-time jobs in 1995 (ILO, 1997a). By contrast, 25 per cent of men aged 15-19 and 40 per cent of the over 65s in work were part-time. Therefore, while some men are increasingly likely to be employed part-time, this is not the case for prime-aged males. Almost all part-time workers in Europe in the 24-49 age group are female. As this is the key age bracket for occupational advancement, women are at a distinct disadvantage. Tam (1997) examined the role of women and non-standard work in the context of segmented labour market theory. Her study demonstrates that part-time jobs are inferior to full-time jobs in terms of required skill levels, wage rates and promotion opportunities but not necessarily so in terms of job security, degree of supervision and irregularity of working hours. The degree of disadvantage also seems to be related to the amount of hours worked. The shorter the hours worked, the greater is the degree of disadvantage in comparison to full-time workers. As Tam points out, particularly in the case of women, the status of being part-time appears to accentuate the other negative job characteristics such as low skills. She concludes:

> Part-time work experience carries cumulative disadvantages and has a negative effect on employment prospects. Moreover, because of the low-skill nature of part-time work, it has a channelling effect on women's lifetime employment prospects. While part-time work is not associated with job insecurity and unemployment, it constitutes a trap which lowers lifetime employment prospects and earnings (Tam, 1997, p. 243).

Allied to this is the likelihood that non-standard employment is currently linked to reduced training and promotional opportunities and is inherently unstable. It has been shown that, in such an employment environment, affirmative action legislation and equal employment opportunities (EEO) provisions are likely to be of benefit only to those women who are in permanent and preferably full-time positions. There appears an urgent need to investigate the real impacts of the proliferation of non-standard employment on the labour force aspirations of women and to implement policies that ensure continuity of training opportunities. Sundstrom (1993) has argued for similar policies for Sweden.

6.10   WORKERS' COMPENSATION AND WORKPLACE HEALTH AND SAFETY

For many employees, irrespective of status, workers' compensation and workplace health and safety legislation will still apply at an external work site. The situation facing SECs may be different. Central to the issue is that of duty of care and whether employers are able to transfer duty of care responsibilities to SECs or DSECs. The issue is most problematical for DSECs. These employers are employed at one work site and, or, by one principal employer. As has been pointed out, their conditions of employment are closer to that of employees than self-employed but they may face a reduction in insurance protection as a result of signing an individual contract. There are welfare and equity considerations involved as well as the potential for large additional burdens on social security if injured DSECs are not adequately covered by workplace compensation and safety legislation or have not made proper individual arrangements. There is strong anecdotal evidence to suggest that individuals switching from employee to own-account status may be reluctant or unable to make proper provision for their own work accident insurance.

One means of avoiding such problems may be to require registration of all individual contracts with a publicly funded agency that could ensure that correct provision for either corporate or private compensation provisions are included.

The impact of changes of labour hiring procedures on workplace health and safety has not received much attention and is an issue in serious need of further research. Some results are available from Spain. Spain has the highest percentage of temporary workers and contracted labour in the EC with just over 36 per cent of all workers on contract. A Spanish Labour Ministry study of 1993 showed that 48 per cent of all industrial accidents in Spain involved employees on temporary contacts. The Spanish Trade Union Confederation (CCOO) found that 88 per cent of all fatal accidents involved workers on temporary contracts and 44 per cent of all accidents involved employees with less than one year of service. The union argued that these accidents occurred more frequently with temporary staff because:

It is generally more difficult for employees to become familiar with and trained in labour practices of a particular industry if they are employed on a contract of only a few month's duration (European Industrial Relations Review (EIRR), 1995, p. 29).

Similarly, the Catalan regional government data show that accidents in building and construction (with 50 per cent casual workers) is much higher than in chemicals, which has a predominantly permanent workforce. This showed, they believed:

> a greater level of stability at the workplace would help to reduce the number of accidents at work (EIRR, 1995, p. 30)

On a lesser scale, but still of potential importance, is the workplace health and safety position of at-home workers such as teleworkers. In Canada, this issue arose in relation to the duty of care by the Federal Government towards its home-workers.

> Health and safety is a major concern since few employers are prepared to provide ergonomic offices. We have been told employers such as banks, in the not too distant future, contemplate the back office work for credit cards and electronic banking to be done by home-based workers (Dagg, 1997, p.87).

6.11 LEGAL IMPLICATIONS: WHO CONSTITUTES A WORKER?

Health and safety obligations are just some of the implications that revolve around the legal definition of what constitutes an employee. It has been shown that one potential reason often put forward to explain employer preference for non-standard workers is to avoid labour on-costs often associated with traditional employees. On the other hand it has been shown that some traditional workers are seeking self-employed or contract status as a means of reducing taxation payments. Therefore some on both sides of the employment relationship are attempting to redefine the employment status of themselves or their employees to achieve particular objectives. However, in a legal sense, there are some potentially large costs to doing this because access to employment rights like unfair dismissal legislation depends to a large extent on whether an individual is classed as an employee. Burchell et al. (1999) have recently completed a large study into the ramifications of trends in non-standard employment upon the employment status itself. In other words, who constitutes a worker?

Their research was prompted by a growing number of concerns relating to the growth of non-standard employment and its implications for the interpretation of labour law. For example:

- The basis by which courts and industrial tribunals distinguish between employees and the self-employed.
- The inability of existing job status classifications to properly cover or reflect the growth in casual work, zero-contract hours, fixed-term employment, task employment and freelancing.

The first of these concerns relates to the best means of determining employee status. Deakin and Morris (1998) argue that the legal classifications have been developed through case law and depend upon four tests: control, integration, business reality and mutuality of obligation. Associated with each of these tests are ancillary factors such as payment systems, stability and length of employment relationship, and existence and substance of grievance procedures. The four tests and principal factors which courts take into account when deciding the issue of employment status are shown in Table 6.5.

Table 6.5 The relationship between factors and tests for classifying employment relationships

Control	Duty to orders, discretion on hours of work, supervision of mode of working
Integration	Disciplinary/grievance procedure, inclusion in occupational benefit scheme
Economic reality	Method of payment, freedom to hire others, providing own equipment, investing in own business, method of payment of tax and national insurance, coverage of sick pay and holiday pay
Mutuality of obligation	Duration of employment, regularity of employment, right to refuse work, custom in the trade

Source: Burchell et al. (1999, p. 11).

The control test is the most common form of employee status test and the one with the longest ancestry. An indication of its use is shown from a 1995 Court of Appeal ruling that an individual's status could be determined by showing:

who lays down what is to be done, the way in which it is to be done, the means by which it is to be done and the time when it is to be done (Burchell et al., 1999, p. 5).

Under this principle an independent contractor has much greater control over the work environment than either a traditional employee or a non-standard employee. This is reasonably clear, but the test is less successful in reverse. Are only those subject to close supervision and monitoring to be regarded as employees? This demonstrates that the control test may be inflexible and certainly not suited for an environment of rapidly changing work relations (Brodie, 1998). It has also been shown that as the skill level of the employee rises, to the point where they have a large degree of discretion over the form of the final product, the less significance is the control test in determining status.

A second form of employee status test is the integration test. This places less emphasis on the control of an employee by an employer and more upon work organisation. The central point here is to determine whether the work provided is in fact an internalised procedure of the organisation (the worker is internal to and dependent upon) the company structure or whether they provide services external to the core operations of the firm.

In such a circumstance, the '*de-facto* employee' is clearly integrated to the company whereas the self-employed contractor providing a one-off service is clearly not. The effectiveness of the integration test is less clear in cases of continuing use of subcontract or temp agency staff where the use of these services have become an integral part of daily operations.

The third commonly used test is that of economic reality. This test was used by the US Supreme Court in 1946 and in UK courts since the 1960s. The test requires 'looking to see where the financial risk lies and whether the worker has an opportunity of profiting from sound management in the performance of this task'. In one sense it is a test of economic independence, determining if an individual needs to depend on others in the supply chain before they can derive income from their work.

The fourth and most controversial test is that of mutuality of obligation. For example, its growing use since the 1970s has had the effect of removing casual employees from some legal protections because the mutual obligation to provide work (by the employer) and accept the work offered (the worker) is not clear. Burchell et al. (1999) cite examples where home workers, agency workers, zero-hours contract workers and workers in casualised trades have been held to be outside the protection legislation on the basis of this test.[1] They find that:

> The application of the mutuality test is particularly significant for workers employed in non-standard forms of work, since it may mean that individuals who do not have a business of their own and hence are not genuinely in business on their own account, but who lack a regular and stable employment relationship with a particular employer, are effectively left in a grey zone between employment and self-employment (Burchell et al., 1999, p. 8).

A this stage in the evolution of non-standard employment, the courts are probably best able to decide who is inconsistent with employee status rather than who is an employee. Those factors which are considered inconsistent with employee status include: having contracts that were terminable without notice from both sides; the right to refuse work; lack of obligation on behalf of a company to provide work; custom and practice in the industry; and the belief of the applicants that they were independent contractors (Hartin, 1994).

6.11.1 Redefining the Concept of Worker

The UK National Minimum Wage Act 1998 and the regulations of the Working Time Directive have used a broader term of 'worker' in preference to that of employee in an attempt to circumvent some of the more transparent problems of the current debate over employee status. The idea here is that for major pieces of social and industrial legislation like minimum wages and the coverage of employment protection, the term 'worker' would replace the more restrictive term 'employee'. This would enable the inclusion of those who do not have a contract of employment but who are nonetheless in a 'worker' relationship because they derive a high percentage of their income from one employer or company. This would have the effect of increasing the numbers of persons covered by this type of legislation, but by how much?

An omnibus wave survey conducted in the UK in 1998 provides some estimates of the difference in coverage between the proposed 'worker' definition and the current labour force definition of employee.[2] The survey found that about 80 per cent of those in employment in the UK were clearly either employees or dependent 'workers', 7 per cent were clearly independent self-employed, 1.3 per cent were on government training schemes or were unpaid family workers and approximately 12 per cent had unclear employment status. This 12 per cent undecided category helps set the upper boundary of 92 per cent and a range of 80-92 per cent. The current Labour Force Survey estimates for employees in the UK is 87 per cent. As a result, the use of the alternative 'worker' definition may extend the coverage of worker protection legislation up to a further 5 per cent of the UK workforce. Most of those added would come from non-standard workers whose employment status is currently unclear.

6.12   CONCLUDING REMARKS

This chapter is concerned with the impact of non-standard employment upon labour market institutions such as unions and upon economic performance in general. The two areas are linked because it has long been held by some commentators that freeing up labour markets, principally by reducing the power of labour unions, would result in increased economic performance.

Others, while perhaps agreeing to this claim in a strict sense, add the proviso that this may occur at the cost of wage justice, gender equity and working conditions like training opportunities and health and safety provision. Non-standard employment is the key element in both these scenarios. It has been the principal means of providing numerical flexibility in the workforce and in promoting the growth of an increasing group of workers outside all or some of the traditional legal and institutional protections of the labour market. This has produced genuine cause for concern over wage and equity considerations. Of course, non-standard employment is only one element of the large-scale changes occurring in modern labour markets and cannot be assigned, in a casual sense, to all these events. The decline in trade union membership is a good example of the complex role being played by non-standard employment in labour market changes. In earlier chapters it was shown empirically that non-standard employment spreads most rapidly in industries with low union coverage. It was also shown that the relationship between unionism and non-standard employment was likely to be simultaneous with those industries and workers attracted to non-standard employment also less likely to join a union than traditional workers. In part, this is because of an historical union antipathy towards non-standard employment and a consequent lack of services designed to cater for this group. It is also caused by the reluctance of employers in industries favoured by non-standard workers to encourage union activity and by the irregular nature of the employment itself.

Irrespective of the full causes, the declines in union membership in most countries have coincided with and have been intensified by the growth of non-standard employment. While this trend is of fundamental concern to union organisations, it also has widespread implications for other aspects of working life. Trade unions have tended to operate in a quasi-legalistic way, providing standards on wages, access to workplace training and workplace health and safety that even non-union sites have tended to copy. Declines in the influence of unions places increased responsibility upon individuals to fend for themselves in areas such as training and upon governments to provide minimum levels of protection to all workers. A further complication is the way that the growth in non-standard employment has eroded the value of traditional means of assigning employee status. Research in the UK has shown that up to 5 per cent of the labour force are being denied employee protection rights because they are currently misclassified. This has led to calls to replace the term 'employee' with that of 'worker' to increase the coverage of standard employment rights. The immediate impact of this is to bring back into the fold of legislative protection, those *de-facto* employees and dependent contractors that have artificially ceased to be recognised as employees.

In terms of economic performance, the impact of non-standard employment appears mixed. Some companies report increased productivity and declines in absenteeism. However, it does not appear that non-standard workers are sharing in these gains. Independent contractors are the only component of this group that regularly receive wages above those of traditional workers in their field. The rest of the non-standard workers receive, on US data, about 20 per cent less in earnings than their traditional counterparts although a significant amount of this differential disappears when the data is controlled for age, skill level and gender. The issue of gender equity is also of major importance. The continued domination of non-standard employment by women, the young and older workers appears certain to, at least maintain, and probably intensify labour market inequalities between these groups and prime-aged workers, particularly males. Therefore, non-standard employment has not brought increased earnings or conditions for many. Nor was it necessarily intended to do so. For many, this type of employment was a lifestyle decision that reflected family needs and values and other lifestyle considerations. The impact of non-standard employment on these social issues is discussed in Chapter 7.

NOTES

[1] They cite, for example, *Airfix Footwear Ltd v. Cope* (1978) ICR 1210, *Nethermere (St. Neots) Ltd v. Taverna and Gardiner* (1984) IRLR 240 and *Wickens v. Champion Employment Agency* (1984) ICR 365.

[2] The survey consisted of two parts, a qualitative wave of 4000 surveys of persons in employment and a quantitative wave based on a mix of focus groups, and individual semi-structured interviews.

7. Work and Family Issues

7.0   INTRODUCTION

Stress and the tension between work and the family are increasing (Wolcott, 1990). In repeated polling in the 1990s between 42 and 48 per cent of Canadians fear they will lose their jobs in the next five years. This is reported as having an effect upon marriages, family relations and the quality of life (Canadian Labour Ministry, 1997). Additional research in Canadian work sites argues that downsizing over the past few years has had harmful effects on the motivation and loyalty for both those who leave and those who stay (Brault, 1997). It is unlikely that Canadians are alone in feeling the social impacts of widespread and rapid changes in working arrangements. For example, the ACTU survey on Employment Security and Working Hours (ACTU, 1998) found that over half the respondents placed increased job insecurity (54 per cent) and greater control over working hours (53 per cent), as the major employment issues that are impinging upon family issues and personal well-being. Throughout the world, shifts in working arrangements, irrespective of whether they are predominantly supply- or demand-driven, are placing unique strains on the social, particularly the family, environment.

Foremost among these pressures is that of polarisation in economic and social standing between those who work significantly below 35 hours per week and the growing numbers that work in excess of 50 hours per week. This polarisation is primarily a function of differences in employment opportunities. As a result, for some, work is becoming a reducing part of their activity and social identity, while for others the gap between work and private life is disappearing (Betcherman and Lowe, 1997). Between 1976 and 1995 in Canada, the number of individuals working an average 35-40 hours per week declined by 10 per cent but the average hours worked per employee increased over the same period (Brault, 1997). This is a clear indication that the distribution of work and work opportunities is becoming more skewed. The inevitable result of such a polarisation in employment opportunities is a subsequent polarisation in income distribution. This will in turn threaten one of the basic tenets of democratic societies – ensuring basic economic and social entitlements for all participants – and place increased burden upon the welfare system. The management of many downsizing companies implicitly acknowledges much of this by placing great emphasis on change management as a central part of their human resource effort.

The links between work and social factors are imprecise, but important. For some of the participants, work is the central factor that shapes their identity (Morgan and Millington, 1992). For others it is less important, but for most participants in the workforce, the boundaries between working life and home life have narrowed and become blurred. Many, with varying degrees of willingness, now combine work, home life and education in a manner that overrides traditional demarcation barriers. At the extreme are those whose home is also their workplace. However, early chapters have shown that a substantial minority of the workforce regularly take work home. In many cases even those outside of the workforce, such as retirees and children, are caught up in the new working environments as either providers or recipients of child care.

Arising out of these issues, it becomes clear that the rise of non-standard employment has contributed to the debate between work and family issues in a number of ways. In some respects, the flexible workforce requires the flexible family, living in the flexible society. This chapter examines some of the societal, particularly family-related, consequences of labour market transition associated with non-standard employment. However, it must be remembered that non-standard employment is just one of the many changes in the labour market which are currently impacting upon the non-work environment. The social organisation of the labour market has changed substantially in recent decades. Two groups of major importance now, dual-income families and sole parent families, were far less significant in the past. In this environment of demographic change in the labour force, non-standard employment is both a solution and a problem. Properly organised, it allows the individual to balance both work and family responsibilities in a way that was not possible under traditional employment systems. But these 'good' non-standard jobs may not be the norm for many non-standard workers. In some circumstances, the non-standard workload can be intrusive, unpredictable and destructive of family relations (Burgess and Strachan, 1998). Researchers such as Tilly (1992) believe that most non-standard jobs in the USA fall into this 'bad' job category. If this is the case, it may indicate that the distribution of non-standard jobs is taking a pattern similar to that of traditional jobs. The desirable, socially beneficial non-standard jobs are being distributed on the criteria of human capital and skill to a minority of workers, and the socially less desirable forms of non-standard jobs, which constitute the bulk, are being distributed to the less-skilled or geographically immobile. Having this type of segmentation is potentially more serious among non-standard workers because many of these workers are already removed from the protective net of union membership and labour market legislation that is associated with traditional employment.

7.1 THE DEMOGRAPHICS OF CONTEMPORARY FAMILY LIFE

The USA provides a good example of the pace of demographic change that has simultaneously created a labour supply suited to non-standard work, and increased the potential for work/family conflicts and stress. Researchers on the 'Futurework' project believe that stress among US workers is increasing because major changes in the demographics of the US family structure have not been matched by changes of similar magnitude in workplace practice and policies (US Department of Labor, 1999d). The type of changes in family life they have in mind include the fact that:

- Eighty-five per cent of US workers live with family members and have immediate, day-to-day, family responsibilities.
- Forty-six per cent of wage and salary workers are parents of children under 18 years who live with them at least half the time.
- Nearly one in five employed parents is single; 27 per cent are men.
- More than three out of four married employees have spouses or partners who are also employed - an increase from 66 to 78 per cent since 1977.
- Among full-time employees living in dual-earner households, 75 per cent also have partners who work full-time.
- About one in four workers have non-standard employment. This includes 13 per cent of wage and salary earners who moonlight at secondary jobs.
- Six out of 10 women are in the labour force.
- The proportion of working mothers with children under six years of age rose faster than female participation as a whole during the 1990s.
- Mothers, on average, spend two hours per day less time with the family than they did 30 years ago.
- 70 per cent of both fathers and mothers feel they do not have enough time with their children.
- Many workers care for dependants other than children. About 7.3 million Americans (4 per cent of the population) have disabilities that require external care. Families are the primary source of assistance.

Within this environment can be seen the social basis for the increase in non-standard employment. The extraordinary growth in female labour, particularly those with family responsibilities, initially created the labour force for non-standard jobs. This, combined with the significant but often neglected caring role of families, also provides a demand for flexible jobs and jobs able to be done off-site (Biggs, 1997). The other factor, not explicitly shown in the data, is that of economic need. For example, almost all moonlighters and multiple job-holders indicated that economic need is the main consideration in their work decisions. However, the exact role played by non-standard work in easing or increasing these social tensions is under debate. So too are the exact mechanisms through which employment arrangements interact with the non-work environment and the identification of those forms of employment which are most suited to contemporary family life. An increasing theme within HRM is the need to develop a more rigorous understanding of the links between work, personal well-being and family life (Gonyea and Googins, 1992).

7.2   THE FAMILY-FRIENDLY WORKPLACE

The study of work and family life is relatively new. Early work done in the 1980s took a pessimistic view and essentially argued that 'attempting to balance work and family life under contemporary conditions appears to produce inevitable conflict and stress' (Wolcott, 1990, p. 33). To Wolcott, the causes of this 'inevitable stress' were both long and irregular working hours and the spillover of tensions and work-related problems into the non-work area. These types of argument were not universally accepted, particularly among feminists and others concerned with individual career development (Carmody, 1992). As a result of this social as well as economic agenda, increased research has gone into the feasibility of developing a family-friendly workplace (FFW). The FFW is defined by Burgess and Strachan as:

> a workplace which recognises the non-workplace responsibilities of its employees and develops and implements policies that allow employees to simultaneously fulfil work and family responsibilities (Burgess and Strachan, 1998, p. 251).

They have developed a set of criteria for identifying FFW arrangements at an individual work site. These criteria are shown in Table 7.1.

The information in Table 7.1 provides a useful checklist for identifying those aspects of working conditions that have a family or non-work focus and in this respect is useful for comparing the FFW characteristics of various forms of employment. However, virtually all of these criteria, with the possible exception of split shifts, are employer-funded and represent additional costs to the firm.

Some would also argue that they represent a social agenda and a level of social comfort that is more suited to the era of traditional employment than to the flexible and cost-minimising features of contemporary labour markets. The onus for proponents of FFW policies then becomes to establish a quantitative link between these criteria and job performance. With this in mind, the bulk of recent research has been directed at either how job experiences impact on the home, or how home life affects work performance. Recently, the National Study of the Changing Workforce (1997) in the USA devised a model for understanding the interaction between work, family and personal life. The model was constructed on data relating to the 1997 US labor force and compared with results from the 1977 Quality of Employment Survey and the 1992 National Study of the Changing Workforce. Schematically the links between work, family and personal life are shown in Figure 7.1.

Table 7.1 A classification of family-friendly arrangements

Type of arrangement	Comment
Income security	Achieving at least minimum pay rates; having a regular and predictable income
Employment security	Predictable hours and ongoing employment; ability to take career breaks, ability to undertake financial commitments
Access to care arrangements	Access to standard leave entitlements; ability to switch between different types of leave; access to paid and unpaid maternity, paternity and family leave
Flexible working time arrangements	Ability to vary hours around family commitments, split shifts, flexi-time; job-sharing
Access to training and career path	Generates income and employment security; enhances ability to qualify for benefits
Innovative work arrangements	Study leave; home-work; telecommuting - these can allow for flexible deployment of time

Source: Burgess and Strachan (1998, p. 252).

The central focus of Figure 7.1 is the link between personal well-being and job performance, with personal well-being driving commitment to employer, job performance and job satisfaction. Personal well-being is, in turn, influenced jointly by job and workplace characteristics and the characteristics of life off the job. The model is behavioural and person-specific. No attempts are made to determine the relative importance of each of these factors, but rather to emphasise their mutual dependence. The results find that 'the quality of worker's jobs and the supportiveness of their workplaces are the most powerful predictors of productivity - job satisfaction, commitment to their employers and retention. Job and workplace characteristics are far more important predictors than pay and benefits' (National Study of the Changing Workforce, 1997, p. 1). The study also established a clear link between the characteristics of jobs and workplaces, and the personal lives of workers. For example, the study found:

- Employees with more demanding jobs and less supportive workplaces experience substantially higher levels of negative spillovers from work into their lives off the job - jeopardising their personal and family well-being.
- When workers feel burned-out by their jobs, when they have insufficient time and energy for themselves and their families, when work puts them in a bad mood - these feelings spill back into the workforce, limiting job performance.
- Although more supportive workplaces offer some protection against the hectic and demanding jobs, not even the most supportive workplace can eliminate this problem entirely. To sustain and improve productivity over the long run, employers must not only create supportive workplace environments, but also work with employees to keep job demands in check so they do not endanger personal and family well-being.
- Promoting work life balance appears to be good both for employees and employers.

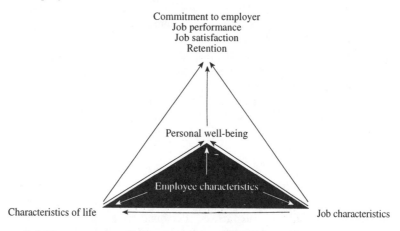

Source: National Study of the Changing Workforce (1997, p. 3).

Figure 7.1 Linking personal well-being and job performance

The study also attempted to rate the performance of the US labour market in addressing the issues of work/family interface. They report good and bad news. The good news indicates that the quality of jobs over the past 20 years has improved and the last five years have seen workplaces, on average, become more supportive through the provision of some of the FFW criteria. However, the study also finds that jobs have become more insecure and more demanding, time consuming and hectic. They conclude that this has made it harder to achieve the balance between work and personal life.

7.3 THE ROLE OF NON-STANDARD EMPLOYMENT IN THE FAMILY-FRIENDLY WORKPLACE

If work has become more hectic and a balanced work/family more difficult to achieve, what part has non-standard work played? As with most aspects of this area of research, the results are mixed and the impacts vary by type of non-standard work. The literature identifies flexibility as the core feature of a workplace that is FFW. Yet, as Dyer (1998) and others have shown, flexibility may be in the eye of the beholder. The term certainly takes on different meanings when translated from either the demand-side or the supply-side of the employment relationship. From the demand-side, labour force flexibility normally applies to three areas: functional flexibility (multi-skilling), numerical flexibility and financial flexibility. However, from the supply-side, particularly in the pursuit of the FFW, the key concept is inter-temporal flexibility. This revolves around both the existence of appropriate working conditions such as split shifts, flexi-time, and career breaks, defined maternity, paternity and other family-related leave provisions, and the length and regularity of working hours. The bulk of the empirical work examined in this book indicates that much non-standard work performs well in comparison to traditional employment in terms of providing less rigid hours of work, less well in terms of regularity of hours and poorly in terms of availability of time-management benefits. In many ways this provides a particularly difficult problem for both those employers and employees who see non-standard employment as a major means of achieving greater work/family harmony.

A considerable amount of space has already been allocated to discussing casual work as it has emerged in Australia and New Zealand. This is because, to a number of commentators (Campbell and Burgess, 1997) it represents the best example within non-standard employment of demand-side dominance, where all the flexibility is coming from the employee. On the basis of their earlier establishment of FFW criteria, Burgess and Strachan (1998) used data from the 1995 Enterprise Bargaining Report to report upon the implementation of FFW on Australian workplaces. Most of their findings, which are summarised in table 7.2, relate to casual workers.

On the basis of this evidence some forms of non-standard employment appear to be making the FFW workplace less, rather than more, attainable. However, it should be remembered that the data was gathered on one of the less desirable forms of non-standard employment. Evidence from other forms of non-standard employment is more supportive of the view that non-standard employment can provide FFW outcomes.

Table 7.2 Impacts of non-standard employment on Australian workplace conditions

Arrangement	Application
Income security	Wage increases averaging 4.5 per cent per annum. Also evidence of exclusion and low pay sector; large dispersion in wage increases
Employment security	Casual employment continues to expand; evidence of removal of barriers to part-time and casual work; some conversion of part-time casual to part-time employment
Care arrangements	Limited; confined to large enterprises - often in conjunction with leave arrangements - limited provision or subsidisation
Leave arrangements	Present in 63 per cent of negotiated arrangements. Child care/family leave in 47 per cent of agreements and in 7 per cent of unregistered agreements. Maternity leave a feature of only 6 per cent of agreements
Working time arrangements	The major item in enterprise agreements - often extending employer discretion over working hours. In general a deregulation of working time - increased spread of normal hours, loss of penalty rates, work at call and unpredictable hours
Innovative work agreements	Very limited - home-based employment and job-sharing in less than 1 per cent of agreements
Career path, training access	Training provisions included in around two thirds of recent enterprise agreements - lower for regional and unregistered agreements

Source: adapted from Burgess and Strachan (1998, p. 259).

7.4   THE IMPACTS OF WORKING FROM HOME

Home-work represents the closest interaction between work and family life. Research reported earlier has stressed the cost-effectiveness and productivity-boosting capacity of this type of employment but it has often been questioned over its potential for isolating workers and transferring work costs into the non-work environment (Moskowitz, 1999; Washington Telework Study, 1999). To resolve some of these issues, Ekos Research Associates conducted a survey of 1139 Canadian workers who had worked (or wanted to work) from home for at least some of the time, concerning the desirability of working from home (Ekos, 1999). There results are shown below in Figure 7.2.

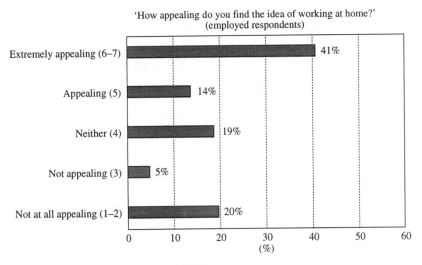

'How appealing do you find the idea of working at home?'
(employed respondents)

Source: Ekos Research Associates Inc. (1998).

Figure 7.2 Desirability of telework

A high minority (41 per cent) of respondents reacted very positively to the concept of working at home for a least part of the week. As well, a majority, 55 per cent, found the idea appealing or very appealing. The results seem to show a high acceptance of teleworking in principle. However, when the question was recast to examine a monetary trade-off between more family-friendly working arrangements and wage increases, the results were less clear cut. Specifically, respondents were asked if they would trade a 5 or 10 per cent pay rise for the right to work, at least part of the time, at home. The responses to the question 'I would prefer my employer allow me to work at least part of the week at home over getting a 5-10 per cent increase in pay' are summarised in Table 7.3.

The highest percentage agreeing to trade a wage increase for some ability to work at home was only 29 per cent, for a trade-off between two days a week at home and a 5 per cent trade-off. When given the option of a complete shift to home-work in lieu of a 10 per cent pay increase, only 14 per cent of respondents were willing to trade. This may indicate that workers are not as serious about off-site work as might have been implied from the results in Figure 7.2 or, alternatively, it may indicate that wages and income are still the major motivation for workers. There is also no clear-cut answer to either the optimum number of hours that persons wish to work or where (on-site or off-site) they wish to work them. The final question in the Ekos survey examined the views of those with actual off-site working experience. The results are shown in Figure 7.2.

Table 7.3 Trading wages for work-site flexibility

Two days per week	No response	Disagree	Neither	Agree
5 per cent increase	4	50	17	29
10 per cent	4	51	18	27
Most of the time at home	-	-	-	-
5 per cent	2	58	6	24
10 per cent	0	55	16	29
Home all of the time	-	-	-	-
5 per cent	0	58	11	28
10 per cent	2	70	13	14

Source: Ekos Research Associates Inc. (1998, (p. 5).

The results in Figure 7.3 indicate a moderate endorsement of working, at least for part of the week, at home. Forty-two per cent felt that their family life had become much better and there was no evidence of any increased working hours as a result of the shift to home-working. As might be expected, the biggest drawback, according to these respondents, was a reduced chance of networking or making workplace contacts. Only 20 per cent felt that the shift in working arrangements had assisted in these areas.

These types of results, which are repeated across a number of the more skilled, individualistic forms of non-standard employment, are another reminder of the potential that non-standard work has to deliver positive social benefits. However, most of the FFW benefits identified to this point, such as paid leave and child care assistance, are currently more associated with traditional employment arrangements. The question then arises as to whether non-standard employment has any potential advantages over traditional employment in the delivery of work/family benefits?

Drolet and Morissette (1997) asked the general question 'Working more? Working less? What do Canadians Prefer?' Unfortunately, in most cases, they found it did not matter what they preferred. Most workers, irrespective of their form of working arrangement, had very little autonomy over what hours they worked. However, of those Canadians who would like a change in working hours, most would prefer more hours to less. The only group actively seeking shorter hours are among professional and skilled workers.

Workers who want a shorter week are professionals, managers, natural and social science workers, have high earnings, high levels of income, have long job tenure, are employed in permanent jobs and already work longer hours (Drolet and Morrissette, 1997, p. 17).

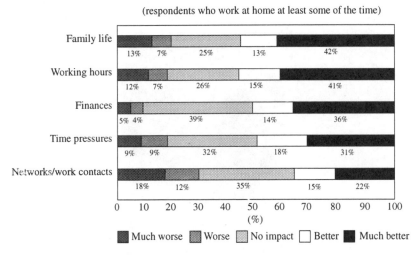

Source: Ekos Research Associates Inc. (1998, p. 6)

Figure 7.3 Impacts of working from home

These workers are part of the current labour market polarisation process that is occurring world-wide. They currently feel they are overworked and they earn enough to cut working hours without significantly affecting their living standards. On the other side of the polarisation process are married women (many of whom would prefer longer hours) and single parents who are seeking more hours to obtain more money. Drolet and Morissette found that 'young workers with very little seniority employed in low-skilled occupations and holding temporary jobs seem to encounter the most severe hours constraints in the Canadian labour market' Drolet and Morissette (1997, p. 17). These three groups make up the core of non-standard workers.

If the Canadian experience is indicative of others, the contemporary labour market process does not seem to be working in a manner that allows inter-temporal flexibility. Those with the traditional jobs and high incomes are paying a price in terms of overwork, while current non-standard arrangements for many workers are not producing the required mix of hours or earnings. Traditional jobs, by their nature, are not particularly flexible in terms of working hours and attempts to make them more so through the increased use of shifts do not appear to be very successful. Shift work has

brought numerical, and perhaps functional flexibility to the workplace but
has done little for family relationships. In four out of every ten dual-earner
couples in Canada, at least one partner regularly works shifts (Human
Resources Development, Canada, 1998).

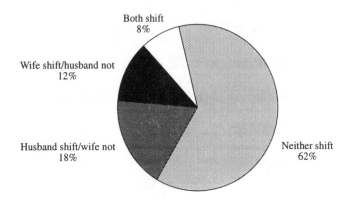

Source: Human Resources Development, Canada (1998, p. 7).

Figure 7.4 Shift work among dual-earner couples

More potentially disruptive of family life is the fact that most of these
couples work conflicting shifts. As high as 30 per cent of dual-income
families regularly work non-compatible shifts. The vast majority of these
workers reported that shift work was a requirement of the job. Most men
reported that they did it for the money but a considerable number of women
were arranging shifts to fit in with child care and other family care. Most
workers reported that the conflicting shifts had a detrimental effect on family
life.

7.4.1 Synopsis: Non-standard Work and the Family

The role of the family life on work performance has taken on a much higher
priority in recent years. Burgess and Strachan (1998) argue that an emphasis
on the family-friendly workplace has superseded the emphasis on equal
opportunity, at least in terms of government rhetoric. They claim this
represents a shift away from gender specificity towards the family. How
deeply this change in emphasis at the official level is impacting in the
workplace is open to debate. Most commentators agree that the push towards
non-standard employment over the last two decades had its genesis in an

available pool of labour, principally married females. This group rejected traditional employment as being incompatible with family responsibilities but at the same time had financial and emotional reasons for wanting to participate in the labour market. The need for flexibility in work arrangements, particularly inter-temporal flexibility, was the main non-monetary need in their work arrangements.

Initially employers appear willing to service this need and throughout most of the 1970s and 1980s surveys of non-standard workers, particularly part-time workers, showed high degrees of acceptance of work arrangements. However a change has come in the 1990s. Spurred on by continuing competitive pressures, employers began to redefine flexibility to stress numerical, functional and financial rather than inter-temporal. As Burgess and Strachan suggest, the notion of flexible work practices 'covers a plethora of conditions' (Burgess and Strachan, 1998, p. 25). They argue that individual choice is declining and that managerial prerogative is increasing. This point is reinforced by Probert:

> Flexible working arrangements often mean working over a longer time span of what constitutes a standard day and a standard week, while at the same time being denied access to penalty rates for working unsociable hours (Probert, 1995, p. 258).

Perversely, the kinds of employer-funded FFW-related benefits that are available to employees tend to be contained within traditional jobs or 'good' non-standard jobs such as permanent part-time. These benefits are increasingly becoming a perk of secure employment rather than a reward for willingness to work short or irregular hours. It is possible to see elements of segmentation in both the provision of FFW and the distribution of non-standard jobs. Certainly there is a gender, age and ethnic bias to the distribution of the less desirable 'contingent' forms of non-standard work (Cohany, 1998). The surveys of alternative working arrangements in the USA show a striking difference between independent contractors who are predominantly male, white, middle-aged, have above-average education, above-average wages and high levels of work satisfaction when compared to temporary-help agency workers who tended to be young, female, frequently black or Hispanic and earn only two-thirds of average earnings. Without necessarily being a carbon copy, the distribution of FFW benefits among non-standard workers is similar to the distribution of other work outcomes. There is a sharp dichotomy between the most and less desired forms. Ironically, the closer the non-standard job is to a traditional job the more likely it is to be compatible with harmonious family life. Why this should be so appears to be a question of bargaining strength. Workers with skills that are in high demand or in heavily unionised or regulated industries are much more likely to achieve FFW benefits than those in non-unionised industries or in unskilled occupations, irrespective of what individual work arrangements are in place.

This is not to suggest that non-standard employment is (potentially) not capable of providing work/family policies and programmes. Bardoel et al. (1999) conducted a cross-sectional analysis using data supplied from a representative sample of human resource professionals in Australian companies and government agencies. The study examined the responsiveness of organisations to employee needs by exploring if 'differences in the implementation of work-family programmes and policies across companies match the demands of key constituent groups' Bardoel et al. (1999, p. 563). Though not specifically targeting non-standard employees, the study concentrated on female-dominated workplaces and, by definition, incorporated large numbers of part-time and casual employees. A number of specific hypotheses were tested:

H1:   There is a positive relationship between the proportion of women in an organisation and the level of responsiveness to institutional pressures for employer provision of work/family programmes.

H2:   There is a positive relationship between the proportion of employees with dependent children in the organisation and the level of responsiveness to institutional pressures for employer provision of work/family programmes.

H3:   There is a positive relationship between the proportion of employees under 35 years of age and the level of responsiveness for employer-funded work/family programmes.

H4:   There is a positive relationship between the proportion of employees with working spouses in the organisation and the level of responsiveness for employer-funded work/family programmes.

H5:   There is a positive relationship between the proportion of employees who are union members and the level of responsiveness for employer-funded work/family programmes.

H6:   There is a positive relationship between the proportion of employees who have been employed in the organisation for over two years and the level of responsiveness for employer-funded work/family programmes.

H7:   There is a positive relationship between the proportion of part-time employees and the level of responsiveness for employer-funded work/family programmes.

H8:   There is a positive relationship between the proportion of city dwellers and the level of responsiveness for employer-funded work/family programmes.

Table 7.4 Output of the regression analyses that related each class of work/family policies to the organisational demographics

	Flexible work options		Leave options		Child dependent care		Career path alternatives		Employee support programmes	
	B	SE	B	SE	B	SE	B	SE	B	SE
Position	-0.113	0.511	0.900**	0.137	-0.020	0.127	-0.331*	0.130	0.095	0.142
Occupational category	-0.050*	0.117	-0.040	0.027	-0.090**	0.025	-0.069**	0.026	-0.083**	0.028
Under 35: over 35	0.029	0.023	0.103	0.075	0.002	0.070	-0.059	0.072	-0.105	0.078
Metropolitan: rural	0.010	0.065	-0.027	0.044	0.025	0.040	0.054	0.041	0.075	0.045
Male: female	0.124**	0.037	-0.100*	0.046	0.074	0.042	0.075	0.043	-0.081	0.047
Non-union union	-0.032	0.039	0.082*	0.041	0.067	0.038	0.045	0.039	0.066	0.042
Part-time: full-time	-0.183**	0.035	-0.083	0.079	-0.090	0.073	0.023	0.076	-0.014	0.083
Under 2 yrs. Over 2 yrs.	-0.036	0.068	0.098	0.075	0.115	0.070	0.232**	0.071	0.125	0.078
Percentage dependent children	-0.131*	0.064	0.113	0.073	-0.134*	0.067	-0.101	0.069	-0.159*	0.075
Percentage working spouses	0.025	0.062	-0.094	0.070	-0.091	0.064	-0.062	0.066	-0.040	0.072
Intercept	2.13**	0.511	2.59	0.596	1.14**	0.551	0.658	0.568	2.25**	0.618
Adjusted R^2	0.362**		0.423**		0.325**		0.316**		0.264**	

Note:

* Indicates significance of the 5 per cent level.
** Indicates significance of the 1 per cent level.

Source: Bardoel et al. (1999, p. 572).

These hypotheses were examined within the confines of a regression analysis that examined the predictors of work/family options including flexible work options, leave, child and other dependent care, career-path alternatives, and employee support programmes.

In interpreting these results, the authors claim support for H2, partial support for H1, H5, H6 and H7 and no support for H3, H4 and H8. Overall they find that:

> certain key demographic factors, particularly employees with dependent family, women, union members and long serving employees are more likely to predispose an organisation to offer family-work benefits (Bardoel et al., 1999, p. 575).

They concluded that employers need to be able to characterise the demographics of their workforce to plan the type of policies and programmes that might be most suitable and contribute to productivity outcomes.

Hypothesis 7 was the only specific test of the impact of the incidence of non-standard work in the provision of work/family programmes. They found that 'none of the other work-family categories (with the exception of flexible hours) were related to the percentage of part-timers'. Therefore, while some employees are responding to the need of a FFW, these are not necessarily those that employ non-standard workers. These kinds of findings have increased calls for legislation to increase the social and family content of non-standard work arrangements.

7.5   RECOMMENDATIONS TO THE CANADIAN GOVERNMENT

It was in the context of the socio-economic implications of the growth of non-standard employment that the Canadian Government convened the 'Collective Reflections on the Changing Workplace'. The conference, under the auspices of the Department of Labour, brought together a range of economists, social scientists, businesspersons and Government officials to examine the extent of non-standard work in Canada, and it implications for individuals and governments. After lengthy deliberation, the Committee came up with seven broad recommendations. These were:

1. The labour regulation framework (that is, labour standards, occupational health and safety and labour relations) does not have to be the same in all sectors, but it does have to set a common base and deliver the same basic human rights to all workers - including those in contingent and precarious employment.

2. Investing in people is the key to Canada's future - unions, firms and governments have to work together to ensure that all workers have access to meaningful training opportunities.
3. Public policy should not create artificial incentives for a longer working week or for creating part-time jobs at the expense of full-time jobs.
4. There should be new provisions for diverse modes of representation in labour relation legislation for workers in the new economy.
5. New models to improve access to, and portability of, social benefits (for example, supplementary medical plans, dental plans, vision plans and pension plans) that are traditionally associated with employment, need to be considered.
6. Government should exercise leadership and provide support for efforts to use the social economy and the voluntary sector to provide training opportunities and work skills development.
7. Government should actively promote and facilitate institution-building for a wider continuing dialogue on issues related to the changing workplace.

These recommendations are wide ranging but are concentrated around a few central issues. The first is polarisation and equity. Are workers in non-standard employment, irrespective of the motivations or financial rewards, being removed from other workers in terms of legal protection and labour relations machinery? (relevant to all non-standard workers); subject to increased social isolation? (for example, teleworkers and other home-workers) or being given full access to training, health and safety and retirement insurance (all non-standard workers); or face increasing economic deprivation? (all those employed in precarious and contingent employment).

The second issue is institutional and societal. Are the existing governmental and labour market institutions flexible enough to cope with systems of employment significantly different from the types of employment that existed at the time of their creation? If not, then the demise of these institutions will have lasting social impacts. For example, distinguished US economist Richard Freeman said of the threat to unions: 'Labour market institutions bring benefits beyond lower inequality' (Freeman, 1996, p. 4).

The central issue is governmental (principally budgetary). Will governments be required to take up the slack in welfare (retirement coverage) and training initiatives left by employers who promote non-standard employment or by those non-standard employees who have deliberately left the legislative protection of permanent wage and salary employment? An additional consideration of government is whether a need exists for legislation covering minimum wages and conditions attached to all forms of employment.

The answers to these questions will become more apparent over time. However, what is clear is that the spread of non-standard work, while potentially beneficial to specific groups in the economy, defined from both the demand-side and the supply-side, has potentially far-reaching and unwelcome implications for many outside those groups, in terms of economic and social stability. As with many complex issues, there is a need for more investigation and for the generation of more information.

7.6   CONCLUDING REMARKS

This chapter examined the social, particularly the family-orientated, implications of the spread of non-standard employment. Many now emphasise the links between work and family, but the specific links between family life and particular forms of employment are less well discussed. Non-standard work, because of its movement away from the time rigidities of traditional employment, holds the promise of greater flexibility in the workplace for its participants. Non-standard employees, in particular, seem interested in flexibility of work location and in inter-temporal flexibility. However, the empirical evidence concerning the ability of non-standard employment to deliver these benefits is mixed.

Without any doubt, the spread of non-standard employment has brought with it flexibility of working hours through split shifts, part-time working, zero-hours working and on-call working. For some workers it has also brought flexibility of work-site location. Whether these changes have increased work/family harmony is hotly debated. The evidence from this chapter shows that some non-standard workers, such as teleworkers, are claiming improved family life following the change in work relationships. Unfortunately these seem to be in the minority. Increasingly, for some non-standard workers, workplace flexibility is being interpreted from the demand-side to mean functional, numerical and financial flexibility rather than inter-temporal. None of these forms of flexibility are compatible with FFW.

It was found that the main employer-funded FFW benefits reside in traditional jobs and stable non-standard jobs rather than with non-standard workers. The best predictors of FFW benefits are, in general, the standard predictors for most forms of job success: occupational type, union membership, seniority, age and gender. This represents something of a paradox in which those individuals that seek non-standard employment for social and family reasons may, on average, be making the wrong choice. This is not to suggest that non-standard employment is inherently incompatible with improved work/family relations. Nor does it suggest that employers of non-standard labour are oblivious to the potential productivity gains from improved work/family harmony. The Bardoel et al. study (1999) has shown that employers will respond to the core needs of their workforce. The problem appears to lie in the mechanisms through which these needs are transmitted. Traditional workers have used unions and the political process to translate their demands in an effective way to employers. Many non-standard employees have no similar collective voice. This led to calls for government intervention in the partial re-regulation of non-standard work agreements.

8. Summary and Conclusions

8.0   INTRODUCTION

While there is considerable controversy about its long-term significance, extent and causes, there is little doubt that across the world, considerable changes in the employment conditions of many workers have been taking place. In particular, there has been a decline in the incidence of the 'traditional model' of employment. Felstead et al. described this model in terms of permanent or life-time employment:

> For many years, the majority of workers in the industrialised west have shared a similar employment life-course... Their job would be full-time and indefinite in length, thereby giving employment protection while also placing a number of obligations on the employer and the state (Felstead et al., 1999, p. 277).

To many, this type of employment system represents a golden age of labour market stability. As a result, non-traditional (non-standard employment), almost by definition, is seen in pejorative terms as an inferior form of employment and one that will give rise to worker exploitation and produce significant social problems. Yet, the traditional model, as it emerged between the 1930s and the 1970s, was clearly an unequal system that favoured white males above virtually everybody else, unionists above non-union members, restricted female participation, retarded female earnings and gave considerable economic and political power to large companies and large unions. The main reason it was so revered was its inherent stability of employment which, in turn, provided stability of income, financial arrangements and life planning. As well, the era of traditional employment led to a considerable narrowing of income differentials, low rates of unemployment (for the most part) and is seen as having been family-friendly.

Cappelli (1999) and others have questioned the sustainability of the traditional model. To them, the era of permanent full-time employment was a one-off and occurred because of the concurrence of a number of favourable circumstances. These include the internalisation of production by large corporations, a sustained period of post-war growth in Western economies and the growth of labour unions that were able to centralise and guarantee supply of labour in exchange for wage concessions and guaranteed employment. The removal or decline in importance of some of these factors has produced the circumstances for the growth in non-standard employment that has been observed over recent decades. In particular, the series of economic recessions that began after the oil shocks of the 1970s increased global competition, particularly in manufactured goods and the removal of protective tariffs, all placed cost pressures upon the traditional system and induced changes in employment policies within the private and public sectors. Working away in the background were new theories of HRM that stressed numerical, functional and financial flexibility and corporate managers who saw labour costs as the quickest and easiest costs to trim. On the supply-side, the traditional system with its rigid hours and location of work, effectively reduced or excluded from the labour force the participation of a number of groups, including females with family commitments, students and retirees from the permanent workforce. Therefore, there were both supply and demand forces lining up in the labour market that were seeking departures from the traditional model. Non-standard employment was a notable response, but one that is difficult to define. The disparate collection of alternative working arrangements that make up non-standard employment are united, principally by the fact that they all represent a departure from traditional employment. This simple fact divides them from 70-75 per cent of the workforce. Their principal form of departure is one of control in the work relationship. The traditional model represented, in some sense, a countervailing model with power shared relatively equally by employers and organised labour within a system of rules set by government. Non-standard work is different. For some, such as independent contractors, the power has shifted to the individual (worker), which has allowed them to manipulate institutional arrangements such as tax concessions to their own advantage. Other non-standard employees, such as casual workers, are defined by their lack of employer-funded benefits and their almost total absence of workplace influence. Three groups make up the main building blocks of non-standard employment: part-time workers, temporary workers and the self-employed. While there is some overlap between these groups themselves, taken collectively, it is possible to locate almost all forms of non-standard employment within one or more of these groups. For this reason, most emphasis in the book was placed on the analysis of these three groups, or one of their sub-components.

In Chapter 1, a number of important questions were raised about the incidence, growth and significance of non-standard employment. These were:

1. How significant is non-standard employment, and what is its relative importance by gender, occupation and industry?

2. What are the similarities and differences in the international distribution of non-standard employment?
3. Have jobs become more or less secure?
4. What are the implications for wages and equity, training and workplace health and safety?
5. What are the implications for trade unions, industrial relations and labour market legislation?
6. What are the work/family and other social implications?

To a large degree, the remainder of the book set out to answer these questions. It was shown that the extent of non-standard employment, in its many facets, and depending upon whether a broad or narrow definition is used, ranges between 10-30 per cent of the workforce for most countries surveyed. The broad definition encompasses the bulk of part-timers, all temporary workers and the 'contingent' element of those in traditional arrangements. This currently seems to be the most favoured definition in the literature and on this basis, there is a remarkable similarity with respect to the relative importance of non-standard employment across different economies. Of the seven economies given special attention in Chapter 2, the highest rates are recorded in Spain, with nearly 60 per cent of employees able to be classified as non-standard under the broad definition. This is almost certainly an aberration caused by specific institutional arrangements in that country. Australia, at 33 per cent, was the second highest of the surveyed countries followed by Sweden (27.3 per cent), the USA (26.1 per cent), Japan and the UK (both 24.9 per cent) and Germany (21.4 per cent). Others have estimated higher rates for the UK (an all-persons' rate of 37 per cent) and provide an estimate for Canada of 33 per cent in 1994 (Felstead et al., 1999). There are differences in the composition of these groups between countries. Part-time workers make up the bulk of non-standard employees in virtually all countries (except Spain, where fixed-term contractors are the majority). Temporary workers are more important in continental Europe (an average of 11 per cent of wage and salary earners) than in the UK or North America. Canada has a higher percentage of self-employed than most, and Australia has by far the largest number of casual employees, albeit that casuals in this part of the world are defined differently than elsewhere. In Japan, part-time and *arubaito* workers are the major form of non-regular worker. Teleworkers are most plentiful in the Netherlands (18 per cent of employees), the USA (12.5 per cent of wage and salary earners) and Finland (10 per cent of employees). This compares to an average for Europe of 4.5 per cent of employees. In the USA, independent contractors make up the bulk of those employed under alternative arrangements.

With the exception of independent contractors, females continue to make up the bulk of non-standard employees. On average, females make up over 70 per cent of all part-time employees and over 60 per cent of temporary employees. Women make up over 90 per cent of out-workers in Germany, Greece, Ireland, Italy and the Netherlands, and over 70 per cent in the UK, France and Spain. They constitute over 70 per cent of casual workers in Australia. There is evidence that things are changing. The last decade has seen an increase in the relative contribution of men to non-standard employment. This growth in the male percentage is seen as evidence of a growing demand-side dominance in the growth of non-standard employment and has been accompanied by a growth in survey data which suggests that most of the increased male participation is involuntary.

There is some truth in this, particularly among prime-aged males, but the other explanation for the increased prominence of males is the increased use of non-standard employment as a means of both entry and exit to the labour market. Employers are increasingly using non-standard employment as a screening device before offering workers more permanent positions. Young males attempting to enter the traditional labour market are increasingly being caught up in this system, with the inevitable effect that their relative contribution to non-standard employment is rising. Whether they then go on to permanent employment is open to debate. The empirical evidence suggests that in the UK, approximately 70 per cent of employers who used temporary workers, have gone on to offer at least one of them a permanent job, and similar results are reported among clerical and secretarial temps in the USA. However, this may not indicate that employers are consciously using non-standard employment as a formal means of screening. It may simply mean that some temporary workers make a good impression on their employers. Survey data from the Upjohn Institute in the USA, found that 21 per cent of employers were making a deliberate policy of offering non-standard jobs as a precursor to permanent employment. Where this is happening, it will disproportionately fall upon the young entrants to the labour market and those attempting re-entry after a prolonged absence.

There is also a wide variation in the occupational and industrial distribution of non-standard workers, although almost all categories of non-standard worker differ in these aspects from traditional workers. For example, in the case of ICs, US data show that they are more likely to hold management, sales or precision production jobs than traditional workers, and less likely than traditional workers to be employed in technical, administrative support, operator, labourer or fabricator positions. ICs are distinct from other non-standard workers because they are older, nearly four out of five US contractors are aged 35 years or over, receive higher incomes than most, have higher formal qualifications and are more likely to be married (70 per cent in the USA) than either other non-standard workers or traditional workers.[1] They are also happy in their work, with job satisfaction levels for ICs being among the highest rates. For example, in the USA, 84 per cent of ICs surveyed in the 1997 CPS indicated that they preferred their current work to traditional employment.

The industrial and occupational distribution of temporary work is more skewed than ICs, and also varies from the pattern of traditional employment. In the UK for example, it was shown that 50 per cent of temporary workers were fixed-term contractors, so it would be expected that they too would exhibit a significant proportion of professional and technical workers (21 per cent of all UK temporaries). However, they also have a high range of manual workers (41 per cent of UK temps) that is well above the distribution of manual workers in both the traditional labour market and for ICs. In general, the age, gender and occupational distribution and degree of job satisfaction of non-standard workers varies with the degree of contingency of the job. The higher echelons of non-standard worker such as ICs, company contract workers and teleworkers are also the only areas with a substantial, and in some cases, dominant, male presence. These jobs are also characterised by above-average income and educational qualifications, and the largest income differential between males and females. On-call workers, which might be regarded as one step down the hierarchy from ICs, certainly in terms of earnings and job satisfaction, still have a high percentage of professionals and para-professionals, mainly teachers and nurses and other medical staff. However, they had a high contingency rate (27 per cent) and more than half of on-call workers in the USA would prefer traditional arrangements. Of all non-standard workers, at least in the North American context, they are the closest in demographic characteristics to traditional workers, although with a slightly higher percentage of women, 51 per cent in 1997, compared to 47 per cent among the traditional workforce, particularly in the child-rearing ages. They were younger than both traditional workers and contractors, with nearly 22 per cent under the age of 25 years of age. A significant proportion of these were attending educational institutions. Surprisingly, on-call workers had, on average, lower educational qualifications than the workforce as a whole. For example, one in seven being an early school leaver and a graduate rate of 26 per cent compared to 34 per cent for ICs, and 30 per cent for the workforce as a whole. However, there was a sharp dichotomy between males and females, in terms of education. At the risk of oversimplification, it seems that many of the teachers and nurses were well-qualified female workers constrained by family concerns and many of the males, particularly the younger ones, were in the low-skilled on-call positions.

The characteristics of temporary workers have already been addressed in the case of Europe, but temporary help agency staff make up a significant sub-component that has some unique characteristics. Once again, the CPS survey from the USA for 1997 provides useful data. They are the fastest growing component of the US workforce with a growth rate over the period 1995-97 of 10 per cent, compared to 2.7 per cent for the workforce as a whole. They are younger than other segments of both the traditional and non-standard labour force with a quarter under 25 years of age. Women are in the clear majority (55-60 per cent) and half of these had dependent children. In contrast to on-call workers, relatively few were attending school or continuing education (16 per cent compared with 43 per cent in traditional jobs). These workers had by far the highest proportion of non-whites, with 21 per cent black and an above-average proportion of Hispanics. Fifty-seven per cent of the temporary hire agency staff were contingent, however, only one-third of these workers preferred a traditional job with many citing flexibility and lifestyle as major considerations in their preference for temp agency work.

Casual employees in Australia were spread over a wide range of industries and occupations as might be expected, comprising such a large proportion of the Australian workforce. They are most prevalent in agriculture (over 50 per cent, retail and wholesale trade and personal and recreation services (both over 30 per cent). They are predominantly female (70 per cent), but most growth is presently among males. This is mainly because casual employment is becoming entrenched in the manufacturing industry.

Almost all surveys of worker attitudes, in recent years, have found evidence of growing feelings of job insecurity. A number of factors have contributed to these feelings including downsizing, and regular periods of recessionary activity since the 1970s. It is also a popular belief in education circles that skills rapidly date with a consequent increase in job redundancy and a need for retraining. The increased use of non-standard employees, as part of a flexible labour force plan, has also played a part. Several questions needed to be resolved on this issue: 'Are the feelings of insecurity linked to the spread of non-standard employment?'; 'Are non-standard employees more likely to have feelings of insecurity than traditional workers?' and finally, 'Are these feelings of insecurity justified?'

The short answers to these questions are 'yes', 'yes' and 'maybe'. In an aggregate sense, both job security and job satisfaction have declined in most countries over the same time period that non-standard work has grown. Therefore, it is likely that these factors are associated, but are they causally related? A number of other factors in the employment relationship have also changed and this creates a problem in establishing clear statistical relationships. By its very nature, any substantial increase in the incidence of non-standard employment will reduce average job tenure (an important indicator of job stability). We know that in most industrial countries, job tenure has declined but not by much. Should we then conclude that the impact of non-standard employment on job stability is minimal? In aggregate, yes, but the labour market has polarised and non-standard employment has played a major part in this polarisation. Canadian data show that once employees pass the six months' barrier of continuous employment their jobs are actually more secure than in previous decades. However, an increasing proportion of workers are failing to reach this six months' cut-off point and the bulk of these are non-standard workers. Some are failing the screening process but many are in jobs that were never designed to go past six months. This is either because employers fear worker protection legislation if they extend the employment period or because the jobs were simply one-off short-term tasks. In either case, the increased instability due to the less than one-year jobs slightly outweighs the increased stability due to jobs that go beyond this period, and causes the modest decline in aggregate job stability. However, almost all of this instability in the early stages is due to the workers being hired under non-standard conditions. The most affected are the young, entry-level workers (also principally young) and retrenched workers over 45 years attempting to re-enter the labour market.

The aggregate decline in job stability has also impacted on job satisfaction levels. While most surveys show a continuing high level of job satisfaction, the current levels are down in comparison with the 1980s and earlier. Part of the reason for this is increased fear of job loss, and non-standard employment clearly plays a role in this. The other major impact is through the discontentment of some non-standard workers with their working conditions. Many casual, on-call workers and temporary workers would rather be employed under traditional arrangements and their dissatisfaction is bringing down the aggregate levels. However, the very large differences in job satisfaction levels between ICs and temporary help agency workers are indicative of the dangers in making broad generalizations about job satisfaction levels, within non-standard employment. As a general rule, the more contingent is the non-standard job, the lower is the degree of job satisfaction, a fact that reinforces the link between job security and job satisfaction.

The shift towards non-standard forms of employment has and will continue to impact on those government agencies and labour market organisations that evolved in the era of permanent full-time employment. Labour market institutions and trade unions have experienced considerable changes in recent years. Trade unions are a good example. They face three distinct challenges from non-standard work. Firstly, evidence suggests that many non-standard workers are reluctant to join a union. Secondly, unions have been slow to devise policies that are specifically tailored to the needs of non-standard workers. Thirdly, some employers of non-standard labour are antagonistic to their workers joining unions. The reluctance of many non-standard workers to join unions stems from a number of reasons. For out-workers and itinerant workers, no effective union structure exists. As well, the unstable nature of many non-standard jobs leads workers to question the need to make regular contributions to an organisation that may only represent them for part of the year. There is also a lingering distrust between traditional unionists in full-time jobs and non-standard workers whose very existence they see as threatening their working conditions. As a result, unions have been slow to devise specific policies to attract non-standard workers. As late as the 1980s, key umbrella unions such as the ACTU in Australia were refusing to recognise casual work agreements as legitimate, and limited their acceptance of non-standard work to permanent part-time, where union-negotiated rights could be apportioned on a pro-rata basis. It was not until 1990 that the ACTU developed policies on a range of non-standard jobs, such as part-time, casual and job-sharing. In 1995, in a watershed agreement, the TUC in the UK organised a separate chapter to cater for the special needs of home-workers. The International Labour Conference followed suit in June 1995, with an international policy on job protection and unionisation of non-standard workers. In some cases, unions have been prevented from recruiting non-standard workers because of opposition from employers, whose very reason for hiring non-standard workers was often linked to their non-union status. How much of this active opposition occurs is difficult to estimate, but Canadian data suggest that it is widespread among smaller firms.

However, Canada is one of the few industrialised countries where union membership rates have actually increased. Elsewhere, union levels, particularly in the private sector, have dropped. The Australian experience is particularly interesting. Here, union rates for the workforce have dropped in aggregate, from 51 per cent in 1976 to 31.1 per cent in 1996. Among permanent workers, the rate for the same period is 37.4, compared to 13.1 for casual workers and 24.6 for part-time workers. Econometric modelling of the determinants of casual employment in Australia has shown that there is a statistically significant and inverse relationship between the rate of growth in the percentage of casual employment and the level of unionisation. This relationship is simultaneous and it is difficult to establish a clear line of causation. However, unions in Australia have protested loudly over shifts in industrial legislation that have both encouraged the growth of non-standard agreements, and the reduction of union influence in the workplace. In an era of declining union membership, it might be expected that unions will increasingly target non-standard workers as potential members and develop specific policies for these workers.

The decline in trade union coverage has a number of implications for the labour market and the economy as a whole, and it is in this area that non-standard employment is having some of its more profound impacts. In a number of countries, unions have played an important role in helping government develop and police training programmes and workplace health and safety legislation. Unions have also played a major role in promoting wage equity and social welfare. In situations where unions have less than 20 per cent of the workforce (currently 14 per cent in the USA), it is difficult to see them being effective in this type of role. The onus then falls upon government to take a more active role in developing training programmes. This is particularly true for non-standard workers. Not only are most of these not in unions but, for some, the unstable nature of their employment interrupts their participation in any formal training programmes of the type developed for permanent workers. Even ICs, operating in a self-regulated environment, may choose to earn maximum rent on their current skills, rather than update their skills through adequate training and retraining packages. What then is the likely impact on training and training quality of increased non-standard employment? This book has argued that several factors will come into play. The decline in the traditional model will almost certainly mean a decline in on-the-job training and formalised accreditation programmes such as apprenticeships. Furthermore, as the onus for training is transferred from employer to employee, the distribution of training will shift from the specific to the general. Non-standard workers have far less identification with one employer than traditional workers. They are less likely to develop firm-specific and process-specific skills. They will also have fewer avenues to do so, even if the incentive were there. Training will shift, in the absence of specific government policies, towards formal educational institutions such as universities and institutes of technology whose training, by definition, is generalist. As a result, again, in the absence of effective government policies, the level of technical and vocational training, or at least its rate of growth, will slow and the rate of growth in generalist educational institutions will grow. This has the potential to harm economic growth and productivity.

This last prediction may seem to be drawing a long bow. Non-standard employment has been a labour market feature for at least the last two decades, and it should now be possible to observe if there appears to be any discernible impact on productivity. Certainly, promises of productivity gains and increased cost effectiveness were key arguments in the development of the flexible firm, and non-standard employment has a central role to play in this development. Cappelli (1999) has cited evidence that downsizing and other changes in hiring policies have created large productivity gains in US corporations but at the expense of worker morale. The New York Telephone and Control Data Corporation report productivity gains of over 40 per cent from the substitution of teleworkers for on-site staff. IBM claim that telework has reduced absenteeism, increased employee retention and enhanced personnel loyalty and worker satisfaction. Fernie and Metcalf (1995) found that workers on sites covered by individual contracts performed better in terms of productivity and industrial relations indicators than similar sites covered by collective agreements. The evidence of productivity gains from switching from traditional to non-standard arrangements becomes less clear cut as the size of the firm decreases. For example, the experience of smaller (less than 50 employees) New Zealand firms with individual contracts were that the cost benefits were minimal or negative when the added costs of individual negotiation were factored in. This has led some to argue that productivity gains achieved in large firms are reflective, not of the merits of non-standard employment, but of the downsizing that occurred simultaneously and which trimmed some of the organisational slack common to most large organisations. If so, the productivity gains may be a one-off and may disappear if they have been instituted in the short run, at the expense of longer-term employee morale.

Of course, worker morale is very much related to wages and perceptions of equity. One of the more frequently expressed concerns about the growth of non-standard employment is the potential it has to produce low-paid workers. The issue of gender equity is also raised because casual work, out-work and temporary work fall disproportionately upon women. On the core question of the relationship between relative wages and non-standard employment, the difficulty lies in separating out the non-standard effect from the normal human capital factors that influence wage distribution. Where this has been done, the evidence suggests that non-standard employees do suffer a relative wage gap in comparison to workers in traditional arrangements, but that the reverse is the case for ICs and the self-employed. Hipple and Stewart (1996b), after making allowances for differences in hours worked, found on average a 20 per cent wage gap favouring traditional workers over non-standard workers employed in similar tasks. Sullivan and Segal (1997) more formally introduced control variables into their analysis of traditional/non-standard wage relativities, and found a wage cost of between 10-15 per cent being experienced by non-standard workers. It could be argued that this is the trade-off paid for the greater flexibility of non-standard employment; however, a more likely explanation could be the large differences in union coverage between traditional and non-standard workers. Once again, the degree of contingency was an influential factor. The least contingent group of non-standard workers, independent contractors, had a 15 per cent advantage over traditional workers although they also, on average, worked four hours per week more. Conversely, in the USA, the most contingent group, temp agency workers, earned on average, 66 per cent of the earnings of traditional workers. In New Zealand and Australia, there is some evidence of small wage gains to workers who moved from traditional arrangements to contracts. These gains however need to be offset by the loss of employer-funded benefits.

The issue of relative wage justice is central to the concept of gender equity. With women still the dominant group in non-standard employment, the wage penalty associated with non-standard employment becomes an important social issue. The ILO (1977b) report into part-time employment was entitled 'Part-time Employment Opportunity or Trap?' The opportunity in the title referred to the way in which part-time employment caters to the needs of special groups, particularly women with dependent children and keeps them in contact with the labour market. The trap aspects refer to the dangers of accepting second-class status in the labour market with regard to wages, training opportunities and promotion. The same report found that the sex segregation of non-standard work was most pronounced in Europe, and in the prime-aged worker bracket. In 1995, only 3 per cent of prime-aged men in employment held non-standard jobs, compared with 25 per cent of women.

Prime-aged workers are so called because it is within these age groups that maximum returns on human capital are gained. Tam (1997) using UK findings concluded that for many women, non-standard work constitutes a trap which lowers lifetime employment prospects and earnings.

The area of training is potentially one of the main areas where non-standard workers may lose out. Part of the reason for this is simply the lack of continuity of non-standard employment. Training, even by osmosis, works best where there is continuity of employment. As well, employers are less likely to invest in the training of non-permanent workers. As a result, non-standard workers may need to engage in more self-funding of training, or risk falling further behind traditional workers. There is some limited evidence that some temp agencies provide training programmes for their workers, but these seem to be in the minority of those companies that employ large numbers of non-standard employers. One implication of a shift to self-funding may be to emphasise general or vocational training. This may not be by choice but by lack of appropriate work-related training sites. An issue closely related to the provision of training is that of workplace health and safety. Under traditional arrangements, employers pay at least part of the cost of workplace health and safety programmes, either directly or through subsidisation of worker compensation insurance (Borooah and Mangan, 1998). Under the variety of non-standard working arrangements, the issue is not so clear. Most employers will still have a duty of care and will need to make workplace health and safety provisions in line with legal requirements. However, where the workers in question are ICs, it is not clear if employers still face the same duty of care. DCs, *de-facto* employees, are caught in the middle. Most genuine ICs will carry their own insurance, this may not be the case for DCs, particularly where they have been forced out of traditional arrangements. Evidence on the impact of non-standard employment on workplace accidents is limited. Data from Spain indicate there is an inverse relationship between traditional arrangements and workplace accidents. A 1993 study in Spain found that 48 per cent of all industrial accidents involved workers on temporary contracts. The CCOO found that 88 per cent of all fatal accidents involved workers with temporary contracts. In Canada, concern has been expressed in relation to the duty of care for home-workers. Trade unionists in that country are advocating that the Federal government assume responsibility of these non-standard workers who seem to be caught in a workplace health and safety grey area. Grey areas are not confined to workplace health and safety issues. Burchell et al. (1999) have recently completed a large study in the UK into the ramifications of trends in non-standard employment upon the employment status itself. In other words, who legally constitutes a worker? In particular, they are interested in deciding the basis by which courts and industrial tribunals distinguish between employees and the self-employed, and in helping to improve the ability of job status classifications to reflect the growth in non-standard employment. They found that four factors are regularly used to determine employment relationships; control, integration, economic reality and mutuality of obligation. As a result of considerations of these types, the 1998 UK National Minimum Wage Act decided to broaden the definition of an employee for coverage under minimum wage legislation. They introduced the concept, 'worker' in preference to employee, to circumvent some of the more transparent problems of the current debate over employee status. Evidence suggests that this simple definitional change may include an additional 5 per cent of the UK workforce within the coverage of minimum wage legislation.

The final chapter in the book examines the work/family implications of the spread of non-standard employment. It was noted that non-standard employment was just one of the many labour market factors now influencing the interaction between work and family. For example, among males, even within traditional employment, shift work and increased unsociable hours was shown to be an element contributing to growing tension between work and family life. As well, many core workers are now working increased hours as part of a general labour market polarisation between those in standard and non-standard employment. However, non-standard employment has a special place in the link between work and family, because it is seen by many as the only practical way for some workers to combine both work and family responsibilities. There is little doubt that the impetus for part-time work in the 1970s was supply-driven by females with dependants, attempting to maintain contact with the labour market. What they were seeking was inter-temporal flexibility, the ability to combine work and family responsibilities in the way that serve best their needs in both areas. Of course, labour force flexibility, as defined from the demand-side, tends to stress other forms of flexibility including functional, numerical and financial flexibility. The way in which these forms of flexibilities are mixed within the non-standard work arrangement will determine its potential to deliver suitable work/family outcomes.

Within 'good' non-standard jobs, workers will have access to certain time-related flexibilities such as holiday, paternity, maternity and compassionate leave. In non-family friendly arrangements, workers will have irregular shifts, split shifts and unsociable hours.

What non-standard work will almost certainly produce is reduced hours. This is its main attraction, but those who are involuntary non-standard workers often cite insufficient hours as their greatest concern over their working arrangements. Recently, governments and others have been stressing the FFW because they, and many HRM experts, see a definite link between family stability, personal well-being and workplace productivity. Burgess and Strachan (1998) developed a set of indicators to determine the level of FFW provisions currently in place on Australian work sites. What they found is similar to other empirical work done elsewhere. The ability of non-standard employment to deliver these FFW benefits is mixed. It was found that the main employer-funded FFW benefits reside in traditional jobs and stable non-standard jobs, rather than with non-standard workers. The best predictors of FFW benefits are, in general, the standard predictors for most forms of job success. These are occupational type, union membership, seniority, age and gender.

This represents something of a paradox because those individuals that seek non-standard employment for social and family reasons may, on average, be making the wrong choice. However, non-standard employment is not inherently incompatible with improved work/family relations. Nor are employers of non-standard labour unaware of the potential productivity gains that may arise from improved work/family harmony among their workforce. The Bardoel et al. study (1999) has shown that employers will respond to the core needs of their workforce. Yet most non-standard workers have no collective voice to push these claims and individual contracts rarely produce standard gains across a group of workers. To many this suggests that for non-standard workers, governments need to cover the gap in employer/employee relations once filled by unions. This, in turn, produces a potential conflict between, on one hand, the government calls for labour market deregulation and the other, to ensure minimum labour market standards are maintained in areas of wages, training and workplace health and safety, as well as allowing genuine work/family compatible solutions to be reached.

Labour markets in transition, away from the traditional model and non-standard employment, are playing a major part. In the 1960s, what we now define as non-standard employment, constituted less than 10 per cent of the workforce. Even then it was heavily divided in terms of skill and income levels of its participants with the bulk of non-standard work being either professional self-employment or itinerant seasonal work. In many countries it is now thought to be between 25-30 per cent of the labour force. Will it go any higher? A number of factors will decide this. It has been shown that the surge in non-standard employment resulted from an unusual combination of demand- and supply-side factors. New sources of labour supply; women with dependent children, students and early retirees seeking non-traditional hours, complementing a management push for reduced fixed labour costs and a more flexible workforce. This resulted in harm to some members of the traditional workforce with blue-collar workers, middle management and males in particular suffering in the adjustment process. Economic conditions also played a part with job stability and job tenure trends in most countries, following a pro-cyclical pathway. However, if economic recessions increased non-standard employment, economic prosperity may reduce it. The experience of the USA is a good example. It is certainly arguable that non-standard employment in the USA has either stabilised or declined in the wake of high levels of economic growth. Comparisons of the 1995 and 1997 estimates of contingent employment show a small decline in the levels of contingency. As well, part-time work as a percentage of the workforce has declined since the late 1980s in the USA. Part of this is because of a tight labour market, but other factors are also influential and provide a guide to future events. There is evidence that women, in particular, are increasingly conscious of the dangers that non-standard employment has to trap them in the secondary job market. In Australia and elsewhere, it is noticeable that men are now entering non-standard employment at a faster rate than women. As a clear consequence, so is the involuntary nature of non-standard employment. There is also an increasing realisation that some forms of labour market flexibility, such as numerical and functional, may in the end become counterproductive as they disrupt family and social harmony. Empirical research cited in this book indicates that there is no overall strategy by employers to replace traditional workers with non-standard employees beyond the needs of flexibility and contingency. The full ramifications of the flexible firm theories, popularised in the 1980s, are unlikely to be fulfilled. Finally, there is a growing social and political backlash against the less socially desirable forms of non-standard employment. Yet, there are factors that may increase the push towards non-standard employment. Apart from a few countries such as Canada, unions continue to decline in membership and significance. At the same time, governments continue their push for labour market deregulation and firms outside of the USA continue to be squeezed by competitive pressures. In a demographic sense, the aging of the population will increase the numbers of persons needing to work beyond the normal retirement ages for traditional workers. This may supply a new source of non-standard workers.

Weighing up these factors, the likely conclusion is that the relative contribution of non-standard employment will remain relatively stable, although the relative contribution of the different components of non-standard employment will change. The relative importance of part-time work may decline with corresponding increases in temp agency employees at one end of the spectrum, and SECs at the other. Spare a thought also for the worker in traditional arrangements. The price of continuing in conditions of relative job stability is likely to be increased (and largely unpaid for) working hours.

NOTES

[1]   Company contract workers are on average more highly paid and also are more likely to receive fringe benefits such as health insurance. There is some overlap between ICs and company contract workers. The chief differences seem to be that company contract workers tend to be higher skilled, particularly in the IT and skilled engineering areas and have a much higher proportion of males aged under 45.

Bibliography

Abell, P., Khalaf, P. and Smeaton, D. (1995), 'An Exploration of Entry and Exit from Self-Employment', *Discussion Paper*, No. 224, London: School of Economics Centre for Economic Performance.

ABS (1986), 'Types and Conditions of Part-time Employment', *ABS Cat. No. 6203.4*, South Australia.

ABS (1989), 'How Workers get their Training', *ABS Cat. No. 8345.0*, Canberra.

ABS (1994), 'Population Survey Monitor', *ABS Cat. No. 4103.0*, Canberra.

ABS (1997), 'Employment and Unemployment Patterns', Chapter 4 - 'Jobseekers' Labour Market Outcomes', *ABS Cat. 6286.0*, 18-28.

ABS (1999a), 'Weekly Earnings of Employees (Distribution)', *ABS Cat. No. 6310.0*, Canberra.

ABS (1999b), 'Trade Union Members', *ABS Cat. No. 6325.0 (unpublished data)*, Canberra.

ABS (1999c), 'Employment and Unemployment Patterns', *ABS Cat. No. 6286.0*, Canberra.

ACIRT (1999), 'Australia at Work', *Just Managing*, Australian Centre for Industrial Relations Research and Training, Sydney: Prentice Hall.

Acs, Z.J., Audretsch, D.B. and Evans, D.S. (1991), 'Why Does the Self-employment Data Vary Across Countries and Time', *Discussion Paper,* No. 871, Ottawa: Centre for Economic Policy Research.

ACTU (1998), Survey on Employment Security and Working Hours, Melbourne.

Adam, P. and Canziani, P. (1998), *Partial De-Regulation: Fixed-term Contracts in Italy and Spain*, London: Centre for Economic Performance.

Airfix Footwear Ltd v. Cope (1978), ICR 1210, Nethermere (St. Neots) Ltd v. Taverna and Gardiner (1984), IRLR 240 and Wickens v. Champion Employment Agency (1984), ICR 365.

Aklerof, G.A. and Main, B.G.M. (1981), 'An Experience Weighted Measure of Employment and Unemployment Duration', *American Economic Review*, **71**, 1003-11.

Appelbaum, E. (1987), 'Restructuring Work, Temporary, Part-time and At-home Employment', in I. Hartman (ed), *Computer Chips and Paper*

Clips: Technology and Women's Employment, Washington DC: National Academy Press, 23-45

Aronson, R. (1991), *Self-Employment: A Labor Market Perspective*, Ithaca, New York: ILR Press.

Atkinson, J. and Court, T. (1998), 'Temps Catch Up With Permanent Workers', *Industrial Relations Services (IRS) Employment Review*, **680**, London.

Atkinson, J. and Meager, N. (1986), 'Is Flexibility Just a Flash in the Pan', *Personnel Management*, **18**, 26-9.

Atkinson, J., Rick, J., Morris, S. and Williams, M. (1996), 'Temporary Work and the Labour Market', *The Institute for Employment*, Report No. 311, 1-32.

Australian Workplace Industrial Relations Survey, (AWIRS, 1991/95), AGPS, Canberra.

Baldwin, J., Diverty, B. and Johnson, J. (1995), 'Success, Innovation, Technology and Human Resource Strategy - An Interactive System', prepared for a conference on *The Effect of Technology and Innovation on Firm Performance and Employment*, Washington DC, May 1-2.

Bardoel, E.A., Moss, M.A., Smyrnios, K. and Tharenou, P. (1999), 'Employee Characteristics Associated with the Provision of Work-Family Policies and Programs', *International Journal of Manpower*, **20** (8), 563-576.

Betcherman, G. and Lowe, G.S. (1997), The Future of Work in Canada: A Synthesis Report, Ottawa: Canadian Policy Research Networks Inc.

Bieback, K. (1992), 'The Protection of Atypical Workers in Australia and West German Labour Law', *Australian Journal of Labour Law*, **6**, 17-37.

Biggs, S. (1997), 'Family-friendly Policies make Business Services', in E. Davies and V. Pratt, (eds), *Making the Link 8*, Sydney, Affirmative Action and Industrial Relations Affirmative Action Agency, 29-32.

Blanchflower, D.G. and Oswald, A.J. (1998), 'What Makes an Entrepreneur', *Journal of Labor Economics*, **16** (1), 26-40.

Blanchflower, D.G. and Oswald, A.J. (1999), 'Well-being, Insecurity and the Decline of American Job Satisfaction', paper presented at a Cornell University Conference, May 3-7.

Blank, R.M. (1991), 'Are Part-time Jobs Bad Jobs?', in G. Burtless (ed.), *A Future of Lousy Jobs*, Washington DC: Brookings Institution, 123-55.

Blau, F.D., Ferber, M.A. and Winkler, A.E. (1998), *The Economics of Women, Men and Work*, 3rd edition, Upper Saddle River, NJ: Prentice Hall Inc.

Boletin Mensual de Estadistica (1996), Madrid Instituto Nacional de Estadistica, http://www.ccs.nent.mx/sinola/Boletin.htm

Borooah, V. and Mangan, J. (1998), 'Why Have Australian Workplaces Become Safer?', *Australian Economic Review*, **31** (3), 224-36.

Brault, S. (1997), 'Collective Reflections on the Changing Workplace', Chapter 4, Ministry of Labour, Canada.

Bray, M. (1991), 'Unions and Owner-drivers in New South Wales Road Transport', *Monograph No. 3*, Centre for Industrial Relations Research and Teaching.

Brodie, D. (1998), 'The Contract of Work', *Scottish Law and Practice Quarterly*, **2**, 138-48.

Brooks, B. (1991), 'Aspects of Casual and Part-time Employment', *Journal of Industrial Relations*, **27** (2), 165-70.

Brosnan, P. and Thornthwaite, L. (1994), 'Atypical Work in Australia: Preliminary Results from a Queensland Study', in R. Callus and M. Schumacher (eds), 'Current Research in Industrial Relations', *Proceedings of the 8th AIRAANZ Conference*, pp. 33-46.

Buchtemann, C.F. (1996) 'International Handbook of Labour Market Policy and Evaluation', *Employment Security and Dismissal Protection*, Cheltenham: and UK, 652-93.

Buchtemann, C. and Quack, J. (1990), 'How Precarious is Non-standard Employment: Evidence from West Germany', *Cambridge Journal of Economics*, September, 315-29.

Burchell, B., Deakin, S. and Honey, S. (1999), *The Employment Status of Individuals in Non-standard Employment*, ESRC Centre for Business Research, and Department of Trade and Industry, 103 pp.

Burgess, J. (1997), 'The Flexible-firm and the Growth of Non-standard Employment', *Labour and Industry*, **7**, 85-102.

Burgess, J. and Strachan, G. (1998), 'The Family Friendly Workplace: Origins, Meaning and Application of Australian Workplace', *International Journal of Manpower*, **19** (4), 250-265.

Cain, G. (1976), 'The Challenge of Segmented Labor Market Theories to Orthodox Theory: A Survey', *Journal of Economic Literature*, **14** (4), 1215-57.

Campbell, I. and Burgess, J. (1997), 'National Patterns of Temporary Employment: The Distinctive Case of Temporary Employment in Australia', *NKCIR Working Paper*, No. 53, Monash University, Melbourne.

Canadian Labour Ministry (1997), *A Reflection on the Changing Workplace*, Ottawa.

Cappelli, P. (1997), *Change at Work*, New York. Oxford University Press.

Cappelli, P. (1999), 'Managing the Market-driven Workforce', *The New Deal At Work*, Boston, MA: Harvard Business School Press.

Carmody, H. (1992), 'Work, Family and Productivity: Business Responses', *Business Council Bulletin*, August, 32-5.

Chandler, A.D. (1977), *The Visible Hand: The Managerial Revolution in American Business*, Cambridge, MA: Harvard University Press.

Christofides, L.N. and McKenna, C.J. (1993), 'Employment Flows and Job Tenure in Canada', *Canadian Public Policy*, **19**, 145-61.

Christofides, L.N. and McKenna, C.J. (1995), *Employment Patterns and Unemployment Insurance*, Human Resources Development Canada, Ottawa.

Clinton, A. (1997), 'Flexible Labor: Restructuring the American Work Force', *Monthly Labor Review*, August, 3-27.

Cohany, S.R. (1998), 'Workers in Alternative Employment Arrangements: A Second Look', *Monthly Labor Review*, November, 3-17.

Copeland, C., Fronstyn, P., Ostuw, P. and Yakoboski, P. (1999), 'Contingent Workers and Workers in Alternative Arrangements', *Employee Benefits Research Institute (EBRI), Issue Brief* **207**, Washington.

Cousins, C. (1999) 'Changing Regulatory Frameworks and Non-Standard Employment: A Comparison of Germany, Spain, Sweden and the UK', in A. Felstead, and N. Jewson, (eds), 'Flexible Labour and Non-Standard Employment: An Agenda of Issues', *Global Trends in Flexible Labour*, London: Macmillan Press Ltd, pp. 100-120.

Dagg, A. (1997), 'Worker Representation and Protection in the New Economy', Chapter 5, in *Collective Reflections on the Changing Workplace*, Ministry of Labour, Ottawa.

Danish Board of Technology (1997), 'Teknologi-Radet', Conclusions from a Conference on Teleworking convened by the Danish Board of Technology, Copenhagen, May 2-5, http://www.tekno.dk/eng/piblicat/telework.htm

Dawkins, P. and Norris, K. (1990), 'Casual Employment in Australia', *Australian Bulletin of Labour*, **15** (2), 156-73.

De Grip, A., Hoevenberg, J. and Williams, E. (1997), 'Atypical Employment in the European Union', *International Labour Review*, **136** (1), 23-49.

Deakin, S. and Morris, G. (1998), *Labour Law*, 2nd Edition, Butterworths, London.

Department of Trade and Industry (DTI) (1998), 'Fairness at Work', Cm 3986, London.

Diebold, F., Neumark, D. and Polsky, D. (1994), 'Job Stability in the United States', National Bureau of Economic Research Working Paper (NBER), No. W4859 (reprinted, *Journal of Labor Economics*, 1977), **15**, 206-233.

Doirion, D.J. (1997), 'The Growth of Part-time Work in the 1980's: A Comparison of Australia and Canada', January, University of Sydney, 1-30.

Doreinger, P. and Piore, M. (1971), *International Labour Markets and Manpower Analysis*, Lexington, MA: D.C. Heath and Co.

Drolet, M. and Morissette, R. (1997), 'Working More? Working Less? What Do Canadian Workers Prefer?', *Statistics Canada, Analytical Branch Research Paper*, No. 104.

Dusseldorp Skills Forum (1998), 'Australia's Youth Reality and Risk', *Executive Summary*, Australian Council for Educational Research.

Dyer, S. (1998), 'Flexibility Models: A Critical Analysis', *International Journal of Manpower*, **19** (4), 223-33.

The Economist (1997a), 21 August.

The Economist (1997b), 28 August.

Ekos Research Associates Inc. (1998), 'Canadians and Telework', *Press Release*, 4 November, Ottawa-Hull, www.ekos.com, 5 pp.

Ekos Research Associates Inc. (1999), 'Teleworking in Canada', Ottawa.

EPI (1999), *Trends in Temporary Employment*, Employment Policy Institute, Report 9, London.

Eurobarometers (1996), *Employment in Europe Survey*, The European Commission, Brussels, May.

European Industrial Relations Review (EIRR) 1995, *Special Survey on Work Conditions in Europe*, **32** (2), 1-45.

Eurostat (1996), *Labour Force Survey*, Luxembourg Office for Official Publications of the European Communities, Luxembourg.

Evans, D.S. and Leighton, L.S. (1989), 'The Determinants of Changes in US Self-Employment', *Small Business Economics*, **1** (2), 111-20.

Faber, H. (1995), 'Are Lifetime Jobs Disappearing? Job Duration in the United States: 1973-1993', Cambridge, MA: *NBER Working Paper*, No. 5014.

Fallick, B.C. (1999), 'Part-time Work and Industry Growth', *Monthly Labor Review*, March, 22-9.

Families and Work Institute (1997), 'Summary of the National Study of the Changing Workplace', www.familiesandwork.org/announcements/workforce.html

Felstead, A. and Jewson, N. (1999), 'Flexible Labour and Non-standard Employment: An Agenda of Issues', in A. Felstead, and N. Jewson (eds), *Global Trends in Flexible Labour*, London: Macmillan Press Ltd, pp. 1-20.

Felstead, A., Krahn, H. and Powell, M. (1999), 'Young and Old at Risk: Comparative Trends in "Non-standard" Patterns of Employment in Canada and the United Kingdom', *International Journal of Manpower*, **20** (5, 6), 277-98.

Ferber, M.A. and Waldfogel, J. (1996), 'Contingent Work: Blessing or Curse', *Radcliffe Public Policy Institute Paper*, February.

Fernie, S. and Metcalf, D. (1995), 'Participation, Contingent Pay, Representation and Workplace Performance: Evidence from Great Britain', *British Journal of Industrial Relations*, September, **33** (3), 379-415.

Fortier, J. (1999), 'Home, Sweet Deductible Home', *Toronto Sun*, 17 February, 3.

Fox, R. (1995), The End of Work: The Decline of the Global Force and the Dawn of the Post-market Era, New York: G.P. Putman.

Freeman, R. (1996), 'Doing it Right: The US Labour Market Responses in the 1980s/1990s', *Discussion Paper*, No. 231, Centre for Economic Performance, London School of Economics.

Gardiner, J. (1995), 'Worker Displacement: A Decade of Change', *Monthly Labor Review*, **118**, 45-57.

Gareis, K. (1997), Telework and the Bottom Line - Costs and Benefits of Telework in German Insurance Companies, Empirica Gesellschaft fur Kommunikations, Bonn, 1-14.

Gonyea, J. and Googins, B. (1992), 'Linking the Worlds of Work and Family: Beyond the Productivity Trap', *Human Resource Management*, **31** (3), 209-26.

Goulet, R. (1997), 'New Technology and Non-standard Employment', Chapter 7, in *Collective Reflections of the Changing Workplace*, Canadian Labour Ministry, Ottawa.

Green, A. and Riddell, C. (1996), 'Job Duration in Canada: Is Long-Term Employment Declining?', University of British Columbia, Centre for Research in Economics and Social Policy, *Discussion Paper DP-40*, Vancouver.

Green, F., Krahn, H. and Sung, J. (1993), 'Non-Standard Work in Canada and the United Kingdom', *International Journal of Manpower*, **14** (15), 70-81.

Gregg, P. and Wadsworth, J. (1995), 'The Short History of Labour Turnover, Job Tenure and Job Security 1975-93', *Oxford Review of Economic Policy*, **11** (1), 73-90.

Gregory, R. (1996), 'Wage Deregulation, Low Paid Workers and Full Employment', in P.J. Sheehan, M. Kumnick and B.S. Grewal (eds), *Dialogues on Australia's Future*, Centre for Strategic Economic Studies, Victoria University, Melbourne, pp. 81-102.

Hagan, P. and Mangan, J. (1996a), 'Labour Force Participation and Earnings in Queensland: A State and Sub-state Analysis', *Australasian Journal of Regional Studies*, **2** (2), 13-34.

Hagan, P. and Mangan, J. (1996b), 'The Employment Performance of the Queensland Labour Market', *Australian Bulletin of Labour*, **22** (2), 126-36.

Hall, R.E. (1982), 'The Importance of Lifetime Jobs in the US Economy', *American Economic Review*, **72**, 716-24.

Hamberger, J. (1995), 'Individual Contracts: Beyond Enterprise Bargaining', *mimeo*, University of Auckland.

Hartin, W. (1994), 'Employment Law', *Corporate Management*, **46** (2), 75-6.

Hasan, A. and de Brouker, P. (1985), *Unemployment, Employment and Non-Participation in Canadian Labour Markets*, Minister of Supply and Services, Ottawa.

Hausman, J.A. (1978), 'Specification Tests in Econometrics', *Econometrica*, **46**, 1251-71.

Hawke, A. and Wooden, M. (1998), 'The Growth in Casual Employment: Evidence from Australian Workplaces', paper presented to the *Australian Labour Market Workshop*, Victoria University of Technology, Melbourne, 19-20 February, 40 pp.

Hecker, D.E. (1992), 'Reconciling Conflicting Data on Jobs for College Graduates', *Monthly Labor Review*, July, 3-12.

Heisz, A. (1996a), 'Changes in Job Tenure in Canada', *Statistics Canada, Canadian Economic Observer*, January, 31-9.

Heisz, A. (1996b), 'Changes in Job Tenure and Job Stability in Canada', *Statistics Canada, Analytical Branch Research Paper*, No. 95.

Herz, D.E. (1995) 'Work After Early Retirement: An Increasing Trend Among Men', *Monthly Labor Review*, April, 13-37.

Highfield, R. and Smiley, R. (1987), 'New Business Starts and Economic Activity', *International Journal of Industrial Organisation*, 5, 51-66.

Hipple, S. (1998), 'Contingent Work', *Monthly Labor Review*, November, 121 (11), 22-35.

Hipple, S. and Stewart, J. (1996a), 'Contingent Workers - Compensation', *Monthly Labor Review*, October, 119 (10), 22-30.

Hipple, S. and Stewart, J. (1996b), 'Earnings and Benefits of Contingent and Noncontingent Workers', *Monthly Labor Review*, October, 119 (10), 22 (9).

Holmes, T.J. and Schmitz, J.A. (1990), 'A Theory of Entrepreneurship and its Application to the Study of Business Transfers', *Journal of Political Economy*, 87, 265-94.

Houseman, S. and Polivka, A.E. (1998), 'The Implications of Flexible Staffing Arrangements for Job Security', paper prepared for a Conference on *Changes in Job Stability and Job Security*, Russell Sage Foundation, 33 pp.

Houseman, S. and Osawa, M. (1995), 'Part-time and Temporary Employment in Japan', *Monthly Labor Review*, October, 118 (10), 10-18.

Human Resources Development, Canada (1998), 'Dual-earner Couples in Canada', Canadian Labour Ministry.

Hunter, L., McGregor, A., MacInnes, J. and Sproull, A. (1993), 'The Flexible Firm: Strategy and Segmentation', *British Journal of Industrial Relations*, 31, 383-407.

International Labour Organisation (ILO) 1995, 'Protecting the Rights of Home-workers', *International Labour Review*, 134 (2), 11-24.

International Social Service Programme (1989), *Survey on Worker Orientations*, Geneva.

ILO (1995), Report of the Committee on Labour Market Regulation, 82nd Session of the International Labour Conference, Geneva.

ILO (1997a), 'ILO Highlights Global Challenge to Employment', *ILO News*, Press Release, November 3, Washington, http://us/ilo.org/news/prsrls/unions.html, 1-5.

ILO (1997b), 'Part-time Work: Solution or Trap?', *International Labour Review*, **136** (4), 1-18.

Jackson, P.J. and van der Weilen, J.M. (eds) (1998), *Teleworking: International Perspectives*, London: Routledge.

Kelley, J., Evans, M.D.R. and Dawkins, P. (1998), 'Job Security in the 1990s: How Much is Job Security Worth to Employees?', *Australian Social Monitor,* **1**, 1-7.

Krahn, H. (1995), 'Non-Standard Work on the Rise', *Prospective on Labour and Income*, 7(4), 35-42.

Kyotani, E. (1999), 'New Managerial Strategies of Japanese Corporations', in A. Felstead and N. Jewson (eds), *Global Trends in Flexible Labour*, London: Macmillan Press Ltd, pp. 181-197.

Larson, T. and Ong, G. (1994), 'Imbalance in Part-time Employment', *Journal of Economic Issues*, **28**, 187-96.

Lemaitre, G., Marianna, P. and van-Bastelar, A. (1997), 'International Comparisons of Part-time Employment', *OECD Economic Studies*, **29**, 139-52.

Lettau, M. and Buchmueller, T.C. (1999), 'Comparing Benefit Costs for Full-time and Part-time Workers, *Monthly Labor Review*, **122** (3), 24-37.

Levenson, A.R. (1997), 'Recent Trends in Part-time Employment', *Contemporary Economic Policy*, **14** (4), 78-81.

Lin, Z., Picot, G. and Yates, J. (1999), 'The Entry and Exit Dynamics of Self-employment in Canada', *Statistics Canada, Analytical Branch Research Paper*, No. 134, Ottawa.

Lin, Z., Yates, J. and Picot, G. (1999), 'Rising Self-employment in the Midst of High Unemployment: An Empirical Analysis of Recent Developments in Canada', *Statistics Canada, Analytical Branch Research Paper*, No. 135, Ottawa.

Luukinen, J. (1998), 'Teleworking in Finland', paper presented to the 8th Conference on *Teleworking*, Tokyo: 23.

Mangan, J. (1998), *Non-Standard Employment in Queensland: An Empirical Analysis*, Department of Training and Industrial Relations, Brisbane, 101 pp.

Mangan, J. (1999), 'Casual Employment in Queensland: Current Situation and Implications for Public Policy', *Queensland Economic Forecasts and Business Review*, **8** (1), 49-61.

Mangan, J. and Williams, C. (1999), 'Casual Employment in Australia: A Further Analysis', *Australian Economic Papers*, **38** (1), 40-50.

Manser, M.E. and Picot, G. (1999), 'The Role of Self-employment in US and Canadian Job Growth', *Monthly Labor Review*, April, 10-25.

Marshall, S. and Ginters, P. (1995), 'Homeworking and the International Economy: A Question of Social Justice', *ILO mimeo,* Geneva, 23 pp.

McAndrew, I. (1992), 'The Structure of Bargaining Under Employment Contracts Act', *New Zealand Journal of Industrial Relations*, **17** (3), 259-82.

Miller, C. (1993), 'Part-time Employment by Married Women: Marginal Effects from a Multinomial Logit Model', *Australian Bulletin of Labour*, **19** (4), 278-97.

Mishel, L. and Bernstein, J. (1995), 'The State of Working America, 1994-95', *Economic Policy Institute*, New York.

Morgan, H. and Millington, F. (1992), 'Keys to Action: Understanding Differences in Organisations Responsiveness to Work and Family Issues', *Human Resource Management*, **31** (3), 227-48.

Moskowitz, R. (1999), 'Common Complaints About Teleworking', www.smallbiz/com, 1-5.

National Study of the Changing Workforce, (1997), 'Executive Summary', Families and Work Institute, Washington DC.

OECD (1997), 'Implementing the OECD Job Strategy Lessons from Member Countries' Experience', *OECD*, http://www.oecd.org.sge.mn.97study/htm, September, 25 pp.

Office for National Statistics (ONS), Employment Department, *UK Labour Force Survey* (1999), www.mimas.ac.uk/surveys/Ifs/Ifs – info.html.

Oi, W. (1961), 'Labor as a Quasi-Fixed Factor', *Journal of Political Economy*, **70** (6), 538-55.

Organisation of Economic Cooperation and Development (OECD) 1996, 'Temporary Jobs in the OECD', *Employment Outlook*, Paris.

Philpott, J. (1999), 'Temporary Employment in the UK', Employment Policy Institute, *Research Paper*, No. 9, London.

Picot, G. and Lin, Z. (1997), 'Are Canadians More Likely to Lose their Jobs in the 1990s?', *Statistics Canada, Analytical Studies Branch, Research Paper Series*, No. 96, Ontario, August, 1-28.

Picot, G., Lemaitre, G. and Kuhn, P. (1994), 'Labour Markets and Layoffs During the Last Two Recessions', *Statistics Canada, Canadian Economic Observer*, March.

Picot, G., Lin, Z. and Pyper, W. (1997), 'Permanent Layoffs in Canada: Overview and Longitudinal Analysis', *Statistics Canada, Analytical Branch Research Paper*, No. 103.

Picot, G., Manser, M. and Lin, Z. (1998), 'The Role of Self-Employment in Job Creation in Canada and the United States', *OECD-CERF-CILN International Conference on Self-employment*, Burlington, Ontario, Canada.

Piore, M. and Sable, C. (1985), *Second Industrial Divide*, New York: Basic Books.

Pollert, A. (1988), 'Dismantling Flexibility', *Capital and Class*, **34**, 42-75.

Pollert, A. (1991), 'The Orthodoxy of Flexibility', in Pollert, A. (ed.), *Farewell to Flexibility*, Basil Blackwell, Oxford.

Probert, B. (1995), 'Part-time Work and Managerial Strategy', Department of Education, Employment and Training, *ACPS*, Canberra.

Rimmer, M. and Zappala, J. (1988), 'Labour Market Flexibility and the Second Tier', *Australian Bulletin of Labour*, **13** (15), 384-99.

Robertson, P. (1989), 'Some Explanations for the Growth of Part-time Employment in Australia', *Australian Bulletin of Labour*, **13** (15), 345-59.

Rogowski, R. and Schoman, K. (1996), 'Legal Regulation and Flexibility of Employment Contracts', in G. Scmid and J. O'Reilly (eds), *International Handbook of Labour Market Policy and evaluation*, Cheltenham: Edward Elgar.

Romeyn, J. (1992), 'Flexible Working Time: Part-time and Casual Employment', *Industrial Relations Research Monograph*, University of New South Wales, No. 1, June.

Rosenberg, S. and Lapidus, J. (1999), 'Contingent and Non-Standard Work in the United States: Towards a More Poorly Compensated, Insecure Workforce', in A. Felstead, and N. Jewson (eds), *Global Trends in Flexible Labour*, London: Macmillan Press Ltd, pp. 62-83.

Rothstein, D. (1996), 'Nonstandard Work Arrangements', *Monthly Labor Review*, October, 76-83.

Rubery, J. (1994), 'The British Production Regime: A Societal-specific System', *Economy and Society*, **23** (3), 335-54.

Rudolph, B. (1998), 'How Six People from AT&T Discovered the New Meaning of Work in a Downsized Corporate America', *Disconnected*, New York: The Free Press.

Sadler, P. and Ungles, P. (1990), 'Part-time Employment Growth in Australia, 1978-1989', *Australian Bulletin of Labour*, **17** (2), 286-96.

Sapsford, D. and Tzannatos, Z. (1993), *The Economics of the Labour Market*, Basingstoke: The MacMillan Press Ltd.

Sato, H. (1994), 'Employment Adjustment of Middle-aged and Older White-collar Workers', *Japanese Labor Bulletin*, February, 5-8.

Schuetze, H. (1998), 'Taxes, Economic Conditions and Recent Public Trends in Male Self-Employment: A Canadian-US Comparison', *Canadian Economic Association Meeting*, University of Ottawa, Ottawa.

Segal, L.M. and Sullivan, D.G. (1997), 'The Growth of Temporary Services Work', *Journal of Economic Perspectives*, **4** (3), 121-34.

Seike, A. (1994), 'Recent Employment Situation and Long-term Structural Change', *Japan Labor Bulletin*, January, 5-8.

Sheehan, P. and Tegart, G. (1998) (eds), *Working for the Future*, Centre for Strategic Economic Studies, Melbourne: Victoria University Press.

Simpson, M. (1994), 'An Analysis of the Characteristics and Growth of Casual Employment in Australia 1984-92', *Western Australian Labour Market Research Centre*, Curtin University of Technology.

Simpson, M., Dawkins, J. and Maddern, G. (1997), 'Casual Employment in Australia: Incidence and Determinants', *Australian Economic Papers*, **36** (2), 194-204.

Sly, F. and Stilwell, D. (1997), 'Temporary Workers in Great Britain', *Labour Market Trends*, Office for National Statistics, London.

Statistics Bureau of the Japanese Government (1992), *The 1992 Employment Status Survey*, www.stat.go.jp/155.htm

Statistics Bureau of the Japanese Government (1999), *The 1999 Special Survey of the Labour Force Survey*, www.stat.go.jp/155.htm

Sullivan, D.G. and Segal, L.M. (1997), 'The Growth of Temporary Services Work', *Journal of Economic Perspectives*, **4** (3), 121-34.

Sundstrom, M. (1993), 'Part-time Employment in Sweden: Trends and Equality Effects', *Journal of Economic Issues*, **25** (1), 167-78.

Swinnerton, K. and Wial, H. (1995), 'Is Job Stability Declining in the US Economy?', *Industrial and Labor Relations Review*, **48**, 293-304.

Tam, M. (1997), Part-time employment: A Bridge or a Trap, Aldershot, Avesbury.

Taylor, M.P. (1996), 'Earnings, Independence or Unemployment: Why Become Self-employed?', *Oxford Bulletin of Economics and Statistics*, **58** (2), 253-66.

Thurman, J. and Trah, J. (1990), 'Part-time Work in the International Perspective', *International Labour Review*, **24**, 23-40.

Tilly, C. (1991), 'Reasons for the Continuing Growth of Part-time Employment', *Monthly Labor Review*, **114**, 34-43.

Tilly, C. (1992), 'Dualism in Part-time Employment', *Industrial Relations*, **31** (2), 330-47.

Tyler, J., Murnane, R.J. and Levy, F. (1995), 'College Graduates in "High School" Jobs', *Monthly Labor Review*, December, 18-27.

Underhill, E. and Kelly, D. (1995), 'Eliminating Traditional Employment: Trouble-shooters Available in the Building and Meat Industries', *Journal of Industrial Relations*, **3** (3), 398-422.

Ureta, M. (1992), 'The Importance of Lifetime Jobs in the US Economy, Revisited', *American Economic Review*, **82**, 322-34.

US Department of Labor (1995), 'New Contingent and Alternative Employment Arrangements', Bureau of Labor Statistics, *News Release No. 95-90*.

US Department of Labor (1996), 'Displaced Workers Summary', *Labor Force Statistics from the Current Population Survey*, Bureau of Labor Statistics, April.

US Department of Labor (1997), 'Contingent and Alternative Employment Arrangements', Bureau of Labor Statistics, *News Release No. 97-422*.

US Department of Labor (1998a), 'Employee Tenure Summary', *Labor Force Statistics from the Current Population Survey*, Washington DC.

US Department of Labor, (1998b), *Issues in Labor Statistics*, Summary 98-5, Bureau of Labor Statistics, May,

US Department of Labor (1999a), 'Workers on Flexible and Shift Schedules in 1998', Labor Force Statistics from the Current Population Survey, Washington DC.

US Department of Labor (1999b), 'Futurework: Trends and Challenges for Work in the 21st Century', May, Washington DC.

US Department of Labor, (1999c), 'Home-based Business: Self-employed Persons by Selected Characteristics', *Labour Force Statistics from the Current Population Survey*, Washington DC.

US Department of Labor, (1999d), Appendix 2 - Glossary, http://www.dol.gov/dol/asp/public/futurework/report/appendix2.main.htm, 12 pp.

VandenHeuval, A. and Wooden, M. (1995), 'Self-employed Contractors', *Journal of Industrial Relations*, **32**, 23-45.

VandenHeuval, A. and Wooden, M. (1999), 'Diversity in Employment Arrangements', in J. Mangan (ed.), *Understanding Unemployment; A National and State Perspective*, Queensland Treasury, Forthcoming 2000.

Washington Telework Study (1999), 'Study Results', www.energy.wsu.euu/telework/suirvey-results.htm, 1-8.

Watson, G. and Fothergill, B. (1993), 'Part-time Employment and Attitudes to Part-time Work', *Employment Gazette*, **101** (5), 213-20.

Whitfield, L. and Wannell, T. (1991), 'Self-employment in Canada: First Choice or Last Chance?', *mimeo*, Business and Labour Market Analysis, Ottawa.

Winley, V. (1990), 'Women, Management and Industrial Relations', paper presented to Graduate School of Management, Macquarie University.

Wolcott, I. (1990), 'The Structure of Work and the Work of Families', *Family Matters*, **26**, 32-8.

Wooden, M. (1995), 'The Australian Labour Market', *Australian Bulletin of Labour*, September, **21** (3), 179-97.

Wooden, M. (1999), 'Changing Bargaining Structures', *CEDA Paper*, No. 4, 1-32.

Wooden, M. and Hawke, A. (1998), 'Factors Associated with Casual Employment: Evidence from AWIRS', *The Economics and Labour Relations Review*, **9** (1), 82-107.

Yeandle, S. (1999), 'Gender Contacts, Welfare Systems on Non-Standard Working: Diversity and Change in Denmark, France, Germany, Italy and the UK', in A. Felstead, and N. Jewson, (eds), *Global Trends in Flexible Labour*, London: Macmillan Press Ltd, 41-165.

Glossary

Non-standard work covers a range of employment forms and definitions vary internationally. Definitions used here are based upon majority usage but important exceptions are detailed. The default definitions are those provided by the Australian Bureau of Statistics (ABS).

Alternative working arrangements: Refers to one of four categories of US worker: independent contractors (ICs), on-call workers, temporary help agency workers and contract company employees. Not all of these are in non-standard employment. In particular, the large majority of independent contractors are in traditional arrangements.

Arubaito: The literal translation is 'side-job worker' and the term refers to irregular and short-term jobs in Japan that are normally taken by students, females or moonlighters.

Atypical employee: Often used an alternative term to non-standard employment in general but more specifically to the more contingent forms of non-standard employment.

Casual employee: A sub-component of temporary worker. In most countries casual employees are among the most irregular and short-term of temporary workers. However in Australia and New Zealand, casual employees are an important part of the workforce and often work full-time hours. In these countries casual workers are defined not by short hours but by lack of employer-funded benefits and security of tenure in a common law sense. In Australasia these workers are further classified as: regular casual; usually works less than 35 hours per week, no paid holidays, is paid for hours worked, has a steady income or irregular casual; usually works less than 35 hours per week, no paid holidays, is paid for hours worked, has an unstable income.

Contingent workers: A term, most used in North America, which refers to workers in a job where the individual does not have an explicit or implicit contract for long-term employment. Increasingly the term is used to illustrate unstable employment. Terms often used synonymously are just-in-time workers and disposable workers.

Contract workers: One of the few definitions of general applicability and refers to workers employed under legally enforceable conditions for a specific time period.

Day workers: Term used in Japan to workers hired on a contract for less than a month.

Dependent contractor (DC): Self-employed contractor (SEC) who is dependent on one employer or firm for the bulk of his or her income.

Despatched workers: Term used in Japan to refer to workers recruited through labour hire companies.

Full-time (permanent) employment: is still the yardstick that defines other labour force categories. Several definitions, depending upon labour force classification are used. These are:

Full-time employees: Permanent, temporary and casual employees who normally work the agreed or award hours of a full-time employee in their occupation and received pay for any part of the reference period. If agreed or award hours do not apply, employees are regarded as full-time if they usually work 35 hours or more per week.

Full-time employees in main job: All employees for which full-time was the response to the question, is your main job full-time or part-time?

Full-time workers: Employed persons who work 35 hours or more in the reference week (in all jobs) and others who although actually working less than 35 hours in the reference week (including those temporarily absent) usually worked 35 hours or more in a normal week.

Home-work: Work carried out for remuneration in the home or other premises chosen by the home-worker other than the workplace of the employer and which results in a product or service as specified by the employer. Alternatively a home-worker may be defined as 'a person who is employed directly by a firm or an intermediary agent to carry out work in his or her home' (Marshall and Ginters, 1995).

Independent contractor (IC): Self-employed contractor (SEC)with a variety of clients and who is not dependent upon one employer or company.

Involuntary part-time workers: Workers who would prefer to make a move to full-time employment. By definition these are a subset of the total numbers of part-time workers who are seeking more hours of work.

Leased worker: Similar to Sukko workers in Japan and refers to workers who are hired out to alternative organisations if there is insufficient work at their original place of employment.

Out-worker: Refers to employees working off-site. However, the term has come to be associated with marginalised workers or workers operating outside of standard labour market protection.

Part-time employees: Permanent, casual or temporary workers who are not classified as full-time workers.

Part- time employees in main job: All employees for whom part-time was the response to the question, is your main job part-time or full-time?

Part-time workers: Employed persons who actually worked 1 to 34 hours in the reference week and who usually did so, or who were temporarily absent and usually worked 1 to 34 hours. In some countries, part-time work is defined, not exclusively on a number of hours but rather on the percentage of normal 'full-time' hours. For example, in France, part-time workers work less than 80 per cent of normal hours and in Spain the ratio is 60 per cent. In Norway, part-time workers may work up to 37 hours per week but in Finland, Canada and New Zealand the cut-off point is 30 hours per week. Other related definitions used by the ABS are:

Permanent part-time workers: 'A permanent part-time worker is one who works less than the normally scheduled weekly or monthly hours or less than a full year and who is entitled to pro-rata holiday and sick pay' (Lewis, 1990, p. 3).

Portfolio worker: Refers to a person who works, simultaneously, in different jobs or aspects of a job. For example, a medical doctor that lectures, writes and makes public appearances as part of his or her overall work profile in addition to the normal activities with patients.

Teleworker: Person employed off-site who maintains contact with employer and clients through phone links, email and other forms of IT.

Temporary worker: Umbrella term for non-permanent employee. A temporary worker may be a fixed-term contractor, an open-ended casual employee or a regular periodic worker such as a seasonal worker.

Voluntary part-time worker: Workers who by choice would not move to full-time employment but may or may not prefer more hours of work up to and including 34 hours per week.

Zero-hours worker: A worker who is contractually bound to an employer but receives no retainer or guaranteed minimum hours of work. These workers are paid only for hours actually worked.

Index